KING GEORGE II
—— AND ——
QUEEN CAROLINE

ALSO BY JOHN VAN DER KISTE

Published by Sutton Publishing unless stated otherwise

Frederick III, German Emperor 1888 (1981)

Queen Victoria's family: a select bibliography (Clover, 1982)

Dearest Affie: Alfred, Duke of Edinburgh, Queen Victoria's second son, 1844–1900
[with Bee Jordaan] (1984, n.e. 1995)

Queen Victoria's children (1986; large print edition, ISIS, 1987)

Windsor and Habsburg: the British and Austrian reigning houses 1848–1922
(1987)

Edward VII's children (1989)

Princess Victoria Melita, Grand Duchess Cyril of Russia, 1876–1936
(1991, n.e. 1994)

George V's children (1991)

George III's children (1992)

Crowns in a changing world: the British and European monarchies 1901–36
(1993)

Kings of the Hellenes: the Greek Kings 1863–1974 (1994)

Childhood at court 1819–1914 (1995)

Northern Crowns: the Kings of modern Scandinavia (1996)

KING GEORGE II
— AND —
QUEEN CAROLINE

JOHN VAN DER KISTE

SUTTON PUBLISHING

First published in 1997 by
Sutton Publishing Limited · Phoenix Mill
Thrupp · Stroud · Gloucestershire · GL5 2BU

British Library Cataloguing in Publication Data
A catalogue record for this book is available from the British Library

ISBN 0 7509 1321 5

ALAN SUTTON™ and SUTTON™ are the trade
marks of Sutton Publishing Limited

Typeset in 10/13pt New Baskerville
Typesetting and origination by
Sutton Publishing Limited.
Printed in Great Britain by
Hartnolls, Bodmin, Cornwall.

Contents

List of Illustrations vi
Preface vii

PART ONE: 1683–1714
1 Prince George Augustus 3
2 Princess Caroline 11
3 'Young Hanover brave' 18
4 'I cling to the hope' 27

PART TWO: 1714–27
5 'He thought his opposers impudent rebels' 35
6 'Not one drop of blood in my veins dat is not English' 44
7 Guardian of the Realm 53
8 'I shall find you out' 62
9 'You English are none of you well bred' 76

PART THREE: 1727–37
10 'The right sow by the ear' 91
11 'You may strut, dapper George' 100
12 'The knowledge of my dear parents' goodness' 109
13 'Something mean and below him' 121
14 'There is baboon enough for you' 129
15 'As great a political coward as ever wore a crown' 137
16 'How is the wind today for the King?' 146
17 'I never yet saw a woman fit to buckle her shoe' 155

PART FOUR: 1738–60
18 'The boldest man I ever saw' 171
19 'Je sens la mort' 184
20 'Now I shall have no more peace' 194
21 'In perfect tranquillity at home' 203

Genealogical Tables 218
Notes 220
Bibliography 223
Index 225

Illustrations

Between pp. 86–7

1 King George I, *c.* 1714
2 Princess Sophie Dorothea
3 George Augustus, Prince of Wales, *c.* 1716
4 Caroline, Princess of Wales
5 Hampton Court Palace
6 Kensington Palace
7 Queen Caroline and William, Duke of Cumberland, *c.* 1730
8 Royal family silver medallion
9 King George II, pottery mug
10 Frederick, Prince of Wales, and Captain Thomas Bloodworth, 1732
11 Sir Robert Walpole
12 Frederick, Prince of Wales, and his sisters, *c.* 1733

Between pp. 150–1

13 Anne, Princess Royal, *c.* 1733
14 Queen Caroline, 1735
15 King George II, *c.* 1744
16 William, Duke of Cumberland
17 Princess Mary of Hesse-Cassel
18 Queen Louisa of Denmark
19 Augusta, Princess of Wales
20 King George II, statue

Preface

If the number of existing biographies is taken as a convenient yardstick, then King George II must be reckoned as the least-known of our monarchs since the Middle Ages. He reigned for thirty-three years and lived to the age of seventy-six, an age unsurpassed by any reigning British monarch until his successor and grandson, King George III, and his grandson's granddaughter, Queen Victoria, both reached their eighties. Yet apart from *George II and his Ministers*, by Reginald Lucas (1910), which as its title suggests is predominantly political in tenor, *A King in Toils*, by J.D. Griffith Davies (1938), which the author calls 'not a biography, but rather a record of "relationships" in the life of George II', and a life by Charles Chevenix Trench (1973), literature has been extremely sparing in its celebration of the second Hanoverian King of Great Britain. He is the only crowned monarch since the Tudor age to be omitted from the Weidenfeld & Nicolson 'Life and Times' series on British Kings and Queens, published in the 1970s and 1980s. For the most part the King, 'the strutting Turkey-cock of Herrenhausen' in Thackeray's elegant phrase, remains an ill-defined caricature known for hating 'boets and bainters', loathing his eldest son and heir even more, and for being the last King of Britain to lead his army on the battlefield – but little more.

Queen Caroline has scarcely fared better. Yet at least she has been vividly portrayed in print by W.H. Wilkins (1901), R.L. Arkell and Peter Quennell (both 1939), all of whom have recognized that she was a remarkable woman and eclipsed the consorts of the other Hanoverian Georges in talent and intellect rather than notoriety. To take a comparatively recent verdict, that of J.H. Plumb and Huw Wheldon in *Royal Heritage* (1977), she was 'by far the ablest of our Queens between the reigns of Elizabeth I and Victoria, and she has been greatly undervalued.'

Contemporaries have left their accounts of the King and Queen to posterity, but the most extensive memoirs, those of Lord Hervey, are the least reliable. Hervey greatly admired the Queen and their third daughter Princess Caroline, but neither liked nor respected the King, or indeed most other people with whom he came into contact. The other great contemporary diarist of the period, Horace Walpole, was a considerably more gifted writer and his court reminiscences have never lost their appeal,

but while he was more even-handed and less reluctant to give praise where it was due, he was not always the most objective of witnesses either. Their thoroughly readable but frequently waspish writings have inevitably formed history in the absence of any other alternative. It is surely no more than mild exaggeration to suggest that Hervey and Walpole were to the King's reign what tabloid journalism has been to the closing decades of the twentieth century. The more kindly if less well-known memoirs of Lords Egmont, Chesterfield and Waldegrave have done something to redress the balance; but with personalities who died over two centuries ago, inevitably, fact and fiction are difficult to separate.

All too often, biographies of one character are written 'at the expense of another'. Wilkins's life of Queen Caroline, for instance, belittles King George II as a small-minded, stupid nonentity with few redeeming qualities, grossly inferior to his father; while most accounts of their eldest son Frederick, Prince of Wales, readily take the side of 'poor Fred' against his allegedly cruel and unsympathetic parents. Where does reality finish and colourful legend – or, to borrow that hideously overworked cliché of modern times and the television age, 'soap opera' – take over? To choose but one example: it is noted by Arkell, much the most fair of those writers mentioned above, that Queen Caroline sent a message of forgiveness to her eldest son while she lay dying, while the vitriolic pen of Hervey would rather have us believe that her last words on Prince Frederick were: 'At least I shall have one comfort in having my eyes eternally closed. I shall never see that monster again.' Under the circumstances, readers might appreciate that from time to time in this book, presented with such a divergence of source material, I have chosen to err on the side of charity.

Continuing on a similar theme, reference must be made to Ragnhild Hatton's biography of King George I (1978). Although it only deals with the early lives of his son and daughter-in-law and not beyond, its exhaustive modern research has gone some way towards correcting the traditional, often inaccurate portrayal of the first two Georges, particularly with regard to their mutual antipathy. I have not sought to hide the fact that such ill-feeling existed, or indeed deny that it played a major part in the history of the dynasty; but I have echoed Hatton's well-supported contention that it has been exaggerated in the interests of making a good story.

One should also consider the brief but excellent, incisive character studies that comprise J.H. Plumb's *The First Four Georges* (1956). With these in mind, the time is ripe for a fuller reappraisal.

The reform of the calendar, as introduced in 1582 by Pope Gregory XIII, was adopted in Hanover by the Elector in 1700, when he decreed that eleven days should be subtracted from the month of February. As from 1 March that year the electorate used the New Style (NS) calendar, which had

already been adopted by most of Europe. England retained the Old Style (OS) until September 1752, when eleven days were removed in order to bring the country into line with the rest of Europe. I have therefore followed Hatton's principle of giving OS dates for Hanoverian events up to 1700 and English events to 1752, but NS dates for other events. Both are given in a few cases where confusion might arise.

In conclusion I would like to acknowledge the efforts of my friends Roman Golicz, Robin Piguet, and Karen Roth, for assistance with or the supply of information; the staff of Kensington and Chelsea Libraries, for regular access to their basement garden of bibliographical delights, in the form of the reserve collection of biographies; my parents, Wing Commander Guy and Kate Van der Kiste, for their encouragement and for reading through the manuscript in draft form; and my editors, Sarah Bragginton and Jaqueline Mitchell, for their hard work in seeing the work through to publication.

PART ONE

1683–1714

Prince George Augustus

Hanover, one of the most northerly German states, took its name from its capital, a town set on the banks of the River Leine. In the late seventeenth century it flourished under the rule of a benevolent despot. Absolute power lay with the Duke of Brunswick–Lüneburg, who was granted the title of Elector* in 1692, though the full electoral dignity was not conferred on him until the state was admitted as the ninth electorate of the Holy Roman Empire in 1699. He appointed and dismissed all ministers; any decisions concerning home or foreign affairs had to be referred to him; he was required to approve any significant expenditure, and to initiate the proceedings of any major criminal prosecution. As Commander-in-Chief of the Hanoverian army, his approval was required before his troops could be sent to fight with or under other European rulers. The state was reasonably prosperous, with a fair share of rich farming land, a flourishing woollen and linen trade, and plentiful mineral resources, including silver mines in the Hartz mountains. Poverty, political dissent, and parliamentary government were almost unknown.

There were three palaces in the town, namely the small Alte Palais; the barrack-like Leine Schloss; and the home of the Court, the far grander Herrenhausen, its foundations and gardens modelled on those of Versailles. A deep-rooted dislike of the French as a people and a nation did not prevent the Germans from copying their architecture and sense of style. The gardens had been planned and laid out by the younger Martin Charbonnier, whose father had been a pupil of one of King Louis XIV's landscape gardeners, and by the end of the seventeenth century Herrenhausen was one of the most splendid of all German courts, boasting acres of parkland and intricate formal gardens containing carefully arranged walks lined with lime trees or neatly trimmed low hedges, dotted with artificial waterfalls, and well-stocked pike ponds. Adding the classical touch were busts of Roman emperors, imported from Paris. The stables,

*The official designation was Elector of Brunswick–Lüneburg, in accordance with the ducal family name. Historical usage has generally preferred the territorial appellation 'Elector of Hanover', cited thus in the following pages.

with room for over six hundred horses, were surrounded by coach houses accommodating an extensive collection of carriages and chaises. An open-air theatre with court players, again brought from Paris, performed for the entertainment of the electoral family. Most impressive of all, especially to foreign visitors, was the Herrenhausen orangery, one of the largest of its kind in Europe. It had its own heating system to help the fruit grow and ripen in the cold northerly Hanoverian climate. According to the much-travelled English church minister and classical scholar John Toland, the Hanoverian Court was 'accounted the best both for Civility and Decorum' in Germany.

All this was a world apart from England, soon to become the kingdom of the Elector of Hanover. To the electoral family, the island territory across the North Sea was merely a nation of 'King-killers and republicans'. After the overthrow and execution of King Charles I in January 1649, an eleven-year republican interlude under Oliver Cromwell and his less capable son Richard as Lord Protectors had come to an end with the restoration of the Stuart monarchy under King Charles II in May 1660. That same year – in fact, almost that same week – Prince George Lewis of Hanover was born.

In 1680 he visited England, the country over which he would reign some three decades hence. The plan was to create an alliance between Hanover and England by marrying Princess Anne, second daughter of the heir apparent James, Duke of York, and third in line of succession to the throne herself. How seriously the match was considered is open to doubt. Apparently George Lewis took a dislike to Anne and she thereafter bore a grudge against the house of Hanover; but the feeling was probably mutual, as it was said that she refused to consider marrying the 'stuffy little German'. Yet such personal differences counted for little in the world of seventeenth-century matrimonial alliances, where political reasons required princes and princesses from different nations to set personal feelings on one side and walk up the aisle together. Another theory suggested that George was snubbed or slighted at court during his visit, and never forgave the British. Yet another, and probably the most plausible, was that a matrimonial alliance was only tentative. At any rate, if the elder generation were contemplating the scheme, he had not been taken fully into his parents' confidence before leaving for England.

A betrothal between the Electoral Prince and his cousin, Princess Sophie Dorothea of Celle, had already been considered. This would be just as advantageous as the Anglo–Hanoverian match, if not more so, for both parties. In the summer of 1682 her parents the Duke and Duchess of Celle visited the court at Herrenhausen to settle the terms of a marriage agreement. A dowry was handed to Prince George Lewis in person, so that his young wife would be completely dependent on him; and on the death of her parents, all their revenues and possessions would become his property.

On 21 November 1682 the Prince and Princess were married. He was aged twenty-two; she was sixteen. The wedding took place in the Princess's apartments with a minimum of ceremony. Ten days later the young couple entered Hanover to the sound of trumpet fanfares attended by a glittering parade of cavalry. Their carriage was at the centre of a triumphant procession consisting of a hundred state coaches, each drawn by eight horses decorated with red velvet trappings and red twisted silk reins, accompanied by footmen dressed in red and blue uniforms with silver buttons.

The marriage was very much a political arrangement in which the private views of bride and groom about each other counted for nothing. The Prince's father Ernest Augustus, Duke of Brunswick–Lüneburg, ruling Duke of Hanover from 1679, intended to strengthen the position of Hanover by assimilating the duchy of Kalenberg, the domain of his brother, the Duke of Celle, on the latter's death. Prince George Lewis was seemingly indifferent towards his young bride, who was still a child. As cousins they had known each other for several years and their mutual dislike was deep-rooted. It was said that when she was told what was in store for her just before the betrothal, Princess Sophie Dorothea swore that she would have to be dragged to the altar, and when presented with a diamond-studded miniature of Prince George, she threw it angrily against the wall. She was half-French; her father George William, Duke of Celle, had morganatically married a Frenchwoman, Eleanor d'Olbreuse. Their daughter had blossomed into an attractive, high-spirited girl, who was more French than German in temperament and sympathies.

Her husband was German through and through. His interests were restricted largely to military matters, hunting and fine horses, good food, and cards for low stakes. While he spoke and wrote French easily, he shared the prevalent Teutonic dislike and distrust of France as a nation. In spite of his naturally cold, somewhat shy manner, he was probably prepared to make a success of the marriage – but on his own terms, not those of his wife. Political considerations had raised her to her position, and her duty was to provide him with an heir. A wedding ring would certainly not keep him from his mistresses.

At sixteen, however, Princess Sophie Dorothea was still too immature and too undisciplined at heart. Any dormant dislike which her husband may have had for his childish young cousin from earlier days soon reasserted itself. He did his princely duty, and by the time he left her for military service under the banner of Emperor Leopold, fighting against the Turks, she was expecting a child. On 30 October (OS)/9 November (NS) 1683 she gave birth to a boy, christened George Augustus. Five years later came a daughter, named after her mother.

By then husband and wife, never close, had grown apart. Perhaps the most to blame was the Elector's conniving mistress, Countess Platen.

Anxious to ensure her future security should the Elector suddenly die, she had encouraged the young, unmarried Prince George Lewis to take mistresses. There is no evidence for the oft-made but unsubstantiated remark that he had enjoyed an incestuous relationship with her daughter by the Elector, the future Baroness von Kielmansegge. Yet the appearance of Princess Sophie Dorothea came as something of a threat to the Countess, who was jealous of the younger, charming and much prettier girl. Sophie Dorothea had always been liked by her father-in-law, but her mother-in-law despised her French blood and parents' morganatic marriage. The more affection the Duke showed the young woman, the more his wife resented her.

Prince George Lewis was away on military service much of the time, and his wife soon became bored. A visit to Venice and Rome with her father-in-law in 1685 provided her with a brief respite, for the social life of both cities provided her with the amusement she never found in Hanover. On her return home she chafed more than ever. Adding to her misery was the discovery that Prince George Lewis, back from the war, had installed a new mistress in another apartment at the palace. Melusine von Schulenburg, seven years younger than him, had entered royal service as a *Hoffraulein* to the Electress of Hanover, and in January 1692 she bore Prince George Lewis the first of three daughters.

Most princesses would have accepted such a situation resignedly. But Sophie Dorothea's boredom soon progressed to tantrums and scenes with her husband. Not particularly maternal by nature, she put up no resistance to the unwritten law that her children's upbringing should be left to governesses. That they always remained loyal to her memory suggests that she must have shown them some tenderness, unless it can be put down simply to detestation of their father. Yet by the time baby Sophie Dorothea was born, her mother was desperate to leave Hanover and return to her parents.

Recklessly she followed her husband's example in looking elsewhere to satisfy the passions which married life could not fulfil. What started out as a casual friendship with Count Philip Christopher von Königsmarck, a Swedish nobleman and Colonel of the Hanoverian army, led to the exchange of secret letters and flirtation, and by 1692 they were lovers. In July 1694 the Count was ambushed while on his way to her apartments and probably murdered. Though it might have been merely the intention to arrest him, some courtiers evidently had execution on their mind, and he was never seen alive again. The Princess's apartments were searched and incriminating letters were found. The Elector of Hanover and the Duke of Celle agreed that the only solution was to arrange a divorce which suppressed the name of Königsmarck altogether, citing the Princess's refusal to cohabit with her husband as the reason. Initially unaware of

Königsmarck's fate, she was more than willing to divorce her uncongenial husband, and refused all attempts by Hanoverian and Celle jurists to arrange a reconciliation. On 28 December 1694 the marriage was dissolved.

As the guilty party Princess Sophie Dorothea was forbidden to remarry, but not her ex-husband. According to one of their granddaughters, Melusine von Schulenburg later became the morganatic wife of Prince George Lewis. Nonetheless Ragnhild Hatton, his most recent biographer, maintains that the then English church law, which precluded marriage while the divorced spouse was alive, deterred King George I, both before and after his accession as King in 1714, from making their union a formal one.[1] The Princess spent her remaining years as a virtual prisoner at Ahlden, in Celle territory. Forbidden access to her children, she was ostracized by her father, who felt that she had let the good name of the family down.

Her imprisonment was not so harsh as has been commonly supposed. She was allowed to live in comfort, and her husband promised her father in writing that the terms of her confinement and financial support would not be made stricter on his death. She had access to financial advisers and was permitted to keep all income from land held by her father after his death in 1705; and her widowed mother was given financial assistance to move from her house in Lüneburg to the castle of Celle to make it easier for her to visit. After a time her husband relaxed the censoring of her correspondence, and made it easier for her to receive visitors. All the same, in her enforced isolation she paid a heavy price for her dalliance.

Prince George Augustus, only son of this disastrous marriage, was eleven years old at the time of his parents' divorce. He probably never saw his mother again. An unsubstantiated story tells of his hunting in the woods nearby as a boy, stealing away from the rest of the party to ride at full speed in the direction of Ahlden, before he was caught by his suite in a wood about four miles from the castle. Another version suggests that he reached Ahlden and waved to his mother at the window, and when the governor of the castle refused him admission he tried to swim across the moat before he was recaptured.

His father took no interest in his children's upbringing. Any mention of their mother, or the mere word 'divorce', would always remain a forbidden subject between them. The dominant figure of their formative years was that of their paternal grandmother, the Electress Sophie. She and the Elector became their legal guardians after their mother's disgrace. Born in Holland in 1630, daughter of the former Princess Elizabeth of England, the 'Winter Queen' of Bohemia, and thus a granddaughter of King James I of England, the Electress Sophie was much more English than German in her tastes and habits. Proud of her Stuart blood, she kept a portrait of Prince

James Edward, the Pretender, son of King James II, in her room, though she was careful to remove it whenever an English envoy called. She spoke English perfectly, and although she never set foot on British soil, throughout her life she took the keenest interest in events in 'her country', as she always called it. 'I care not when I die,' she would say, 'if on my tomb it be written that I was Queen of England.' She liked her friends to call her the Princess of Wales, though she had no official right to the title. Tall, formidable to those who scarcely knew her, her vitality was remarkable. Striding through Herrenhausen gardens she kept the gardeners working hard, examined every plant devotedly, fed her canaries, talking all the time and leaving ladies-in-waiting half her age virtually exhausted. Even at eighty she could still do fine embroidery without needing spectacles.

In January 1698 Elector Ernest Augustus died. From Ahlden Sophie Dorothea wrote to her former husband to condole with him, at the same time begging forgiveness: 'The sincerity of my repentance should move Your Highness to pardon me, and if, to crown your kindness, you would allow me to see you and embrace our dear children, my gratitude for such highly-desired favours would know no bounds.'[2] Her words fell on deaf ears.

From time to time the young Prince and Princess visited their other grandparents at Celle. More than her husband, who accepted that the flighty young girl had brought disgrace on herself and the family, the Duchess of Celle strongly resented her daughter's treatment, and did not hesitate to make her feelings clear to her grandchildren. Therein probably lay the seeds of the antagonism which Prince George Augustus always bore towards his father.

Within the family, the Electress Sophie had readily taken the part of her son against the daughter-in-law whom she had never liked. Nevertheless she was careful not to make it too obvious to young Prince George Augustus, of whom she was always fond. The distance between father and son, a family relationship which would persist throughout the house of Hanover, seems to have had its roots in Prince George Augustus's devotion to the mother whom he was destined never to see again. The Elector was capable of cruelty and would show no mercy towards those whom he thought had crossed him, and perhaps the subsequent insecurity his son felt played its part in widening the breach.

Another cause of the estrangement between King George I and his son was 'the tendency of the Electress Sophie to treat her son with jealous reserve and bestow all her favour and encouragement upon the grandson.'[3] Another biographer suggests that Prince George Augustus's 'small, slender figure, the delicate cut of his features, the lack of self-control demonstrated by blushes and tears' reminded his father of the prisoner at Ahlden whom he wished to forget. Differences of character also played their part, notably the boy's exuberance, garrulity and a habit of putting his father in the wrong.[4]

Prince George Augustus had the customary training and education for German princes of the day. Well grounded in the classics, in addition to his native German he also spoke French, Italian and English, albeit with a heavy accent which he never lost. Maybe the elder generation had some idea of his destiny; maybe they foresaw that Prince George Lewis's inability to speak good English would put him at a disadvantage in the future. His son also had an excellent memory for dates, genealogy, and details of military history. At nineteen, John Toland noted, the Prince had 'a winning countenance, speaks gracefully, for his Years a great Master of History, a generous Disposition and virtuous inclinations'.[5] Methodically minded, he lacked intellectual curiosity. Literature and art meant nothing to him, but he had a passion for anything to do with the army. He was fascinated by weapons, the minutiae of battlefield tactics and the like, and dazzled by the glitter of military uniforms.

The Electress Sophie had once had plans for educating her other grandson, Crown Prince Frederick William of Prussia, at Herrenhausen with his cousin. Once she invited him to stay, but the experiment was unsuccessful. Prince Frederick William was five years younger than Prince George Augustus, but much larger and stronger. His favourite way of settling arguments had more to do with fists than words, and after giving George Augustus a bleeding nose one day he was sent back in disgrace to Berlin. The childhood antipathy between both cousins, later to become monarchs, would endure until porphyria and excessive drinking wore out the younger man in middle age.

Prince George Augustus was nearing the age of maturity when it became evident that his ultimate destiny lay beyond the duchy of Hanover. In 1701 the Act of Settlement was passed by Parliament at Westminster. The heir to the childless widower King William III was his sister-in-law, Princess Anne. Married to Prince George of Denmark, her seventeen pregnancies had only produced one child who survived infancy. The death of this sickly boy, Prince William, Duke of Gloucester, a few days after his eleventh birthday in the summer of 1700, required the nomination of an heir to succeed her on the throne. According to the Bill of Rights passed by Parliament after the abdication of King James II and the 'Glorious Revolution' which had brought his elder daughter Mary and her husband William of Orange to the throne as joint sovereigns, no Roman Catholic could ascend the throne of England.

Of the many surviving Protestant descendants in Europe of King James I, the most eligible was his granddaughter Princess Sophie, Electress and Dowager Duchess of Hanover. The Electress was thirty-five years older than Princess Anne, but although still only aged thirty-six, the latter's long history of miscarriages, still-births and short-lived infants made her chances of producing a healthy heir remote. In fact, nearly twenty pregnancies had

turned her into a virtual invalid, aged beyond her time, and the prospect of another pregnancy was less likely than her premature death.

King William III eagerly endorsed the Hanoverian succession. The electorate had been a devoted standard-bearer of the cause of central Europe against a power-hungry France under the over-mighty King Louis XIV. If the house of Stuart retained the throne after the reign of his sister-in-law Queen Anne, he realized, an alliance with France – such as King Charles II had made – would risk compromising the independence of his beloved Holland. Parliament assented, on several conditions. Firstly, when the Hanoverians ascended the throne, England could not be obliged to go to war in the defence of a foreign country without parliamentary consent, thus ensuring no repeat of the situation when King William had taken England into the war of the League of Augsburg. Secondly, the monarch could not leave England without the approval of Parliament, and no foreigner could sit on the Privy Council or hold office under the crown. These clauses, again, had been drawn up with King William in mind, for he had packed high offices with his Dutch advisers, and left England as frequently as he wanted. Further conditions strengthened the independence of the British judiciary, and limited the individual actions of the monarch and his advisers. The King could no longer dismiss judges, nor protect his favourites from impeachment by the House of Commons or Lords.

Parliament and crown had been almost at war with each other throughout much of the seventeenth century. At the dawn of the eighteenth the Divine Right of Kings, as understood by King James I and his even more headstrong son King Charles I, was effectively about to be consigned to history. A despotic monarch would give way to a despotic Parliament.

Such matters, however, did not concern the electoral family unduly. The Act of Settlement was passed in the same year that Prince George Augustus celebrated his eighteenth birthday. He was third in succession to the throne of England, after his grandmother and mother. It had been little more than half a century since the English Parliament had executed one King, and only thirteen years since they had deposed another. Further parliamentary changes in the succession could be wrought within his lifetime. Meanwhile, there were greater priorities – the ancestral home of Hanover, a career in the army, and perhaps most important of all, the matter of finding a wife.

Princess Caroline

Ansbach was the capital of the small south German state of Brandenburg–Ansbach and the seat of Margrave John Frederick, who ruled from 1667 to 1686. He was a forward-looking if eccentric young man who cared less for military pursuits than for the arts; he wrote romantic novels, and took a keen interest in orchestral music, opera and the theatre. In order to further the state economy he invited foreigners skilled in weaving cloth or making bronzeware to settle in Ansbach, and ordered that his officials were to dress only in uniforms made from locally produced textiles.

The Margrave was twice married. Virtually nothing is known of the first marriage, beyond that it produced two boys and a girl. At the age of twenty-eight he took as his second wife Princess Eleanor, daughter of the Duke of Saxe–Eisenach. Contemporary poets called her 'the most beautiful princess in Germany'.

On 1 March 1683 she gave birth to a daughter, christened Wilhelmina Caroline, but always known by the second name. Two years later a son, William Frederick, joined her in the nursery. The family was now complete, for in 1686 the Margrave died of smallpox. He was succeeded by George Frederick, one of the sons by his first marriage. As he had never shown any affection for his stepmother or her children, she realized that life would be less unpleasant if she took them back to live with her at her old home, Eisenach, on the edge of the Thuringian Forest. Prince William Frederick was heir-presumptive to the margravate, and later returned to Ansbach under the guardianship of the Elector of Brandenburg.

On a subsequent visit to Berlin the Dowager Margravine became betrothed to the Elector of Saxony, John George IV. They married in 1692, but it brought her no happiness. He had never fully recovered from a blow on the head during his youth. A selfish, brutal man, he cared less for her and his stepchildren than for his mistress, Magdalen Sybil von Röohlitz, a woman whose beauty made up for her lack of education. Her ambitious, intriguing mother had had to write her love letters for her, and it was said that the family was in the pay of the Emperor of Austria, while there was a movement afoot in Saxony to establish closer ties with Brandenburg. The Elector had always treated her as though she was his wife, and denied her nothing. At the time Frederick William, Elector of Brandenburg, was trying

to establish an alliance with Saxony, and the Saxon ministers hoped to draw their Elector from the clutches of his mistress and their pro-Austrian leanings.

A betrothal was arranged between the Elector and Eleanor. She was almost destitute, and needed to find a home for herself and her children. As she was largely dependent on the goodwill of the Elector of Brandenburg, whatever her reservations, she had little choice but to comply. But by the time the marriage took place in Leipzig, it was evident that the Elector intended to carry on virtually as though he was married to two women at once, and he made it evident that Magdalen von Röohlitz was his favourite. Soon after Eleanor returned to Dresden with him (or them) as Electress, he promoted his mistress to the rank of Countess, and she declared that she was going to marry him. The rightful Electress soon feared for her life, attempts were made to poison her and the children, and they retreated from the court at Dresden to a dower-house at Pretsch.

Salvation of a kind came in 1694 when the Countess was struck down by smallpox and died. Ignoring all medical precautions, the grief-stricken Elector had stayed by her bedside throughout her illness. Had he been better liked, his ministers and doctors might have persuaded him otherwise for the sake of his health. If they had had a vested interest in the disease carrying him off as well, they did not have long to wait, for he survived her by less than a fortnight. Yet it came too late for the Electress, left widowed for a second time. Her spirits and health were broken by the misery she had endured. The Elector and Electress of Brandenburg realized that they were partly to blame, by encouraging her into this unsuitable second marriage. They promised to look after the young Princess Caroline if anything should happen to her mother.

Perhaps they had foreseen the course of events, for two years later the twice-widowed Electress died. The new Elector of Saxony took no interest in Princess Caroline – he had far too many illegitimate children of his own to bother with her – and she went to Berlin to be brought up by her guardians, the Elector and Electress of Brandenburg. They had only one son, Frederick William, aged eight, and they were glad to treat her as the daughter they never had. The Elector wrote to her, promising that he would 'never fail as your guardian, to espouse your interests, and to care for you as a loving father, and pray your Highness to have me in the same confidence as your mother always had, which I shall perpetually endeavour to deserve.'[1] Soon it was a genuinely royal court, for the Elector and Electress became King and Queen of Prussia in 1701.

Unlike her eldest brother Prince George Lewis, Elector of Hanover, Queen Sophie Charlotte was a woman of considerable personality and lively intellectual interests. Metaphysicians, scientists and free-thinkers would all be assured of a ready welcome at the Palace of Lützenburg, for Sophie

Charlotte relished theological argument and discussion. By the standards of the day, she was politically a liberal, and sometimes jestingly referred to as 'the republican Queen'. Her mentor was Gottfried Wilhelm Leibniz, a philosopher, mathematician and historian, and one of the most scholarly men of the age.

Princess Caroline had inherited her father's love of learning, and as a girl she had adored reading. Through perseverance she had managed to teach herself much from the printed page of which she would otherwise have remained ignorant, for with her unsettled early life, there had been no tutors or governesses to supervise her education. Her handwriting, punctuation and spelling were and always remained poor, although it was a fault by no means uncommon among learned princesses and other women of the time. Before long she fell under the influence of the Queen of Prussia. The kind-hearted elder woman, who though fifteen years older seemed more like a sister than a mother to her, soon made Caroline feel at home. There was no place, let alone friendship, for her at Ansbach under the rule of her stepbrother. She looked up to Queen Sophie Charlotte, and her admiration led to a remarkable likeness between the two in speech and manner. Caroline was always welcome at Lützenburg, to listen to intellectual discussions between philosophers and intellectuals, sharpen her wits, and learn much from the more progressive minds of the day. The Queen always wanted to know 'the why of the why', as others grumbled, and Caroline took after her. She was the Queen's constant companion, and when Caroline left for occasional visits to her brother, the Queen complained that Lützenburg was 'a desert' in her absence.

Even so, it was evident that the elder generation would try to marry her off as soon as they reasonably could. In 1704 she received a proposal of marriage from Archduke Charles of Austria. She turned him down, allegedly as he was a Roman Catholic and she could not change her religion. The Queen of Prussia was loath to part with her, but refrained from expressing an opinion; the Princess must make up her own mind. She would have liked Caroline to marry her son Frederick William, but in her heart of hearts she realized that her uncouth son would hardly suit a girl with such personality and intellect, and if such a marriage turned out badly it would be on her conscience. Although a Protestant himself, the King of Prussia had no sympathy with her religious objections. He pointed out what a splendid match it would be, but in vain. As she was theoretically living on the King's charity, and as he was not used to having his intentions thwarted, least of all by a woman, her refusal indicated no lack of personality on her part.

Her resolve was strengthened by the Queen of Prussia's mother, the Dowager Electress Sophie of Hanover. Much impressed by Princess Caroline, the Electress already decided that she would make a perfect wife

for her grandson, Prince George Augustus; 'we at Hanover shall hardly find any one better'. A Jesuit priest tried to persuade Princess Caroline to change her mind, and she agreed to listen to his arguments, but despite threats on the King's part and tears on hers, her mind was made up. Although poor, orphaned and dependent on the generosity of her guardians, one of whom was strongly in favour of the match, she could not go against the dictates of her conscience, even marrying the Archduke would mean gaining riches and power. Did the young Princess fear more losing her Protestantism or her independence?

By November 1704 her mind was made up. The Electress Sophie wrote with relief to Leibniz: 'Most people here applaud the Princess of Ansbach's decision, and I have told the Duke of Celle that he deserves her for his grandson. I think the Prince [George Augustus] likes the idea also, for in talking with him about her, he said, "I am very glad that you desire her for me."'[2]

Early the following year, while travelling to visit her mother at Hanover, Queen Sophie Charlotte fell ill. Exhausted by her journey, she had to take to her bed on the way, but she soon rallied, insisting that she would go to Herrenhausen. Within a few days of her arrival she suffered a relapse, and the doctors diagnosed a tumour in the throat; they told her that there was no hope. A French chaplain at Hanover offered his services, but she politely declined, on the grounds that she had devoted twenty years of study to religious questions, and he could tell her nothing she did not already know. 'Do not pity me,' she told her lady-in-waiting. 'I am at last going to satisfy my curiosity about the origin of things, which even Leibniz could never explain to me, to understand space, infinity, being and nothingness; and as for the King, my husband – well, I shall afford him the opportunity of giving me a magnificent funeral, and displaying all the pomp he loves so much.'[3] She was only thirty-six and, as she had previously been in good health, her sudden demise gave rise to suspicion. It was rumoured that she had been poisoned with diamond powder by courtiers at Berlin, acting in league with officials who despised her for her liberal views. A post-mortem revealed that 'her stomach was so worn that you could thrust your fingers through it at any place.' Hanover would not readily forget that the court at Berlin had possibly murdered one of her daughters. Nevertheless she was deeply mourned by her husband, who renamed Lützenburg Charlottenburg in her memory.

Princess Caroline was desolate at losing the woman who had been her mother, or even her elder sister, in all but name. 'Heaven, jealous of our happiness, has taken away from us our adored and adorable Queen,' she wrote to Leibniz in March. 'The calamity has overwhelmed me with grief and sickness, and it is only the hope that I may soon follow her that consoles me.'[4]

While she was returning sadly to her brother's palace at Ansbach, the Dowager Electress Sophie was planning for her future. She was increasingly convinced that her grandson, Prince George Augustus, could have no better wife than his young cousin. As the Princess was almost twenty-two years of age, this jewel was certain to be claimed by one or other of the Protestant courts of Europe before long unless Hanover moved in first. The King of Prussia thought that without his wife to strengthen the young woman's resolve, he could easily put pressure on her again to reconsider marriage with the Archduke Charles. Fortunately she found another friend and protector in her brother, now Margrave of Brandenburg–Ansbach. He told his sister that he greatly resented the King's efforts to interfere, and that he fully supported her decision. If she was threatened by her regal guardian in Prussia, she was at liberty to make her home at Ansbach as long as she pleased. As he probably knew, the right marriage would not be long in coming.

Meanwhile the Elector of Hanover decided that his son should visit Ansbach in disguise, under an assumed name, and meet the Princess to see if they were mutually attracted. He knew by bitter experience what misery a state-arranged marriage could bring in its train. Although normally indifferent to the feelings of his family, on this occasion at least he seems to have had the personal interests of his son at heart, in wishing to spare him from the fate he had suffered. There was another reason for secrecy; if the King of Prussia knew what was happening, he would surely try to put a stop to it.

In June 1705, at midnight, three men rode quietly out of Hanover en route for Ansbach. They were Baron von Eltz, a Hanoverian minister and former governor of the Electoral Prince George Augustus, Monsieur de Busch, and his *valet de chambre*. 'Monsieur de Busch' was none other than the Electoral Prince himself. He was travelling incognito as a young Hanoverian nobleman, planning to meet companions at Nuremburg. As they had not arrived, and as he found the city so dull, he told officials, he had decided to come to Ansbach and see the court instead. He and Baron von Eltz presented introductions from the Hanoverian chief minister, Count von Platen, commending them to the Margrave's good offices. At his summer home, Triesdorf, they were treated with all due hospitality by the Margrave and his sister, invited to supper, and spent the rest of the evening listening to music and playing cards.

'Monsieur de Busch' was presented to Princess Caroline, and soon struck up a conversation with her. Later he declared that she had far exceeded all his expectations, and that he fell in love with her at first sight. This brief acquaintance, according to Poley, the British envoy at Hanover, convinced the young suitor that she so completely answered to 'the good character he had of her that he would not think of anybody else after her.'[5] Nevertheless

he behaved himself perfectly and kept up the pantomime, being careful not to reveal his identity. If she had been let into the secret, she too kept her counsel to herself. Having decided that Princess Caroline would evidently make a suitable bride, he and Eltz left Ansbach, ostensibly for Nuremburg, but secretly to return to Hanover. He reported to the Elector that he was genuinely pleased with the Princess. The Elector informed Eltz that Prince George Augustus was 'seized with such an affection and desire for her, that he is most eager to marry her without delay: We therefore should gladly rejoice to see such a union take place, and hope that the Princess may be equally favourably disposed.'[6]

Baron von Eltz was sent back to Ansbach to seek a private interview with the Princess. He explained the mission and their reasons for such secrecy, asked her if she was 'free of all other matrimonial engagements' and in that event whether she was favourably disposed to the Electoral Prince's suit? The Princess 'at first seemed surprised and agitated'. As the negotiations between herself and the King of Spain had been broken off, she was entirely free, but 'she had never flattered herself that any one in Hanover had so much as thought about her.'[7] Though she probably knew no more about the personality of the Prince than he knew about hers, their brief acquaintance must have doubtless made it evident to her that he would be preferable to the boorish Crown Prince of Prussia. Moreover Hanover was one of the more prosperous German states, and the Act of Settlement would undoubtedly ensure her a Queen Consort's crown one day. Once the Margrave had consented to the proposal, a contract of marriage was drawn up.

The news was announced at Herrenhausen just before a Sunday dinner in July. The Elector, Poley reported, 'declared that there was concluded a treaty of marriage between his son the Electoral Prince and the Princess of Ansbach, and the Prince received the compliments of the court upon it, and at dinner there were many healths drunk to his good success. So that the mystery is now at an end which hath hitherto been concealed with so much care.'[8]

The Dowager Electress Sophie expressed her surprise that the matter had been kept secret from her, but she was so pleased that her own wishes were to be realized that she soon forgave them. She probably knew why her son had kept her in the dark, for she was a notorious gossip and her wagging tongue could have put all the plans in jeopardy. Others were quick to offer their congratulations, though a predictably sour note was struck by the King of Prussia. Having received a letter from his mother-in-law expressing her pleasure, he replied coldly that he was angry with the family at Hanover for notifying him of the conclusion of the marriage so late, but he was 'more angry with the Court of Ansbach who are a branch of his family and he a guardian to the Princess'.[9] Making light of it, the Electress suggested

laughingly that the King really wanted to marry Caroline himself since the prospect of her becoming somebody else's wife made him so angry. Significantly, Prince George Augustus's maternal grandfather the Duke of Celle came to Hanover, while the Duchess went to stay with her imprisoned daughter at Ahlden. Her mother's visit was the only notification that Princess Sophie Dorothea had of the news, and she was not even permitted to write in person to her son or future daughter-in-law.

Wedding preparations were well advanced and Princess Caroline, accompanied by the Margrave, were on their way to Hanover, when they were told that the Duke of Celle had died of a chill caught while hunting. The duchy of Kalenberg therefore passed into the hands of the Elector of Hanover. To postpone the wedding would give Berlin a chance to bring pressure on the bride-to-be with a view to preventing the match. In order to forestall them it was agreed that the wedding should take place as soon as she arrived at court, and mourning for the Duke would be observed afterwards.

On 2 September 1705 the Princess of Ansbach and the Margrave arrived at Hanover. The wedding was solemnized that evening in the chapel at Herrenhausen, and the Electress noted that the bridegroom slept throughout the wedding sermon. 'What good news for the bride that he should be well rested,' the Electress's niece Elizabeth Charlotte, Duchess of Orléans, replied to her letter describing the festivities. A court ball was given the following day. With court mourning deferred, there were 'the greatest appearances of entire satisfaction on all sides'. Congratulatory letters arrived from Queen Anne to the bride and groom, his father and his grandmother.

All things considered, Prince George Augustus and Princess Caroline might have seemed an ill-matched couple, perhaps no better suited to each other than the Prince's parents. That they stayed happily married for thirty-two years, until death claimed one of them, was partly a matter of good fortune conspicuously lacking in the marital unions of the other three King Georges of England from the house of Hanover (incompatibility and flagrant infidelity destroying one, severe illness and apparent insanity clouding another, and mutual disgust on first sight damning the last). It was also partly a tribute to the tolerant personality of each.

In the eighteenth century, any quick-witted princess with any claims to being a blue-stocking would be expected to bite her tongue and suppress her personality if her husband wished it. Prince George Augustus of Hanover was a typical German prince, with no pretensions towards intellect, and basically interested in little more than military glory, political power and a wife who would do her duty by providing him with male heirs. A lively-minded wife with a more agile brain than his might put him at a disadvantage; and a wife whose indelicate approach to discussing sex with other men and women might have revolted a less tolerant husband.

'Young Hanover brave'

The Electoral Prince and Princess settled in Leine Schloss, in apartments formerly inhabited by the Prince's mother. If superstitious voices were tempted to suggest that it was a bad omen, the young couple were not disturbed by precedents. For the first few months of their marriage, the Prince could hardly bear to let his wife out of his sight. The Dowager Electress noted approvingly that a happier friendship had never been seen; 'they seem to have been made for each other.' They were obviously extremely happy together, though only one cloud marred the Electoral Princess's happiness – the ill-feeling between her husband and his father. Although he had welcomed the marriage, he resisted all her efforts at friendliness. Charm, tact and apparent submissiveness made her relationships with other male members of the family successful, while good humour with the ladies likewise served her well, but the cold and dour Elector proved immune. At length she had to accept that he did not want to be friends; she probably saw that his jealousy of their happiness was an insuperable barrier. Her father-in-law was to prove the only man whom she could never learn to manage.

Despite their mutual devotion, the Prince soon became restless for the battlefield. Hanoverian contingents were leaving regularly for the theatre of war against France at Flanders or the Upper Rhine. In May 1706 the Elector and his brother went to join the forces. Prince George Augustus was left behind, reviewing troops in Hanover and seething with frustration. He longed to return to a soldier's or commander's life, only to be told that 'the Court is against it and will not give their consent to let him go into the field until he has children.'

By May the Electoral Princess was convinced that she was pregnant, but at length she and her husband realized that their hopes had been premature. Their disappointment was compounded by the behaviour of the Crown Prince of Prussia. Having failed to win the hand of Princess Caroline, he came to the court of Hanover and became betrothed to the Elector's only daughter, 'Sophie Dorothea the younger'. It was another match which met with the Dowager Electress's approval. She hoped that the bullying young Prussian who had behaved so badly towards his elder but smaller cousin had matured and would make a worthy grandson-in-law, although time was to prove that she had been too optimistic by half.

Prince George Augustus was never close to his sister, so the fact that his childhood *bête noire* was to become his brother-in-law did not disturb him unduly. It rankled less than the Crown Prince's victory in the race to the battlefield. He was called to fight in the Netherlands, and returned two months later in high spirits. Meanwhile Prince George Augustus had been left at Herrenhausen, green with envy and beside himself with frustration. When Princess Sophie Dorothea was married by proxy at Hanover and left for Berlin later in the year, their relief at her departure was tempered by the well-founded suspicion that the Elector and his mother had always been much more fond of her than of her brother.

By November there was still no child, and Princess Caroline was coming to the despairing conclusion that she had never been expecting at all. She had evidently been ill-prepared for motherhood, and one suspects that the doctors had simply not bothered to give her a little elementary education. The other possibility is that in her condition she was so irritated by persistent enquiries from both sides of the family, and court officials, that when she discovered she was expecting a child she retired into temporary seclusion, cutting herself off from everyone except her closest relations. Either she miscalculated the expected date of birth of her first child, or the baby was born later than expected. On 20 January (OS)/1 February (NS) 1707 she produced a son, christened Frederick Lewis.

The English envoy at Hanover, Lord Howe, reported four days later:

> This Court having for some time past almost despaired of the Princess Electoral being brought to bed, and most people apprehensive that her bigness, which has continued for so long, was rather an effect of a distemper than that she was with child, her Highness was taken ill last Friday at dinner, and last night, about seven o'clock, the Countess d'Eke, her lady of the bedchamber, sent me word that the Princess was delivered of a son.[1]

This great-grandson of the heiress to the throne of England, it was reported, was a large, strong, healthy baby, much admired by the women of the Hanoverian court. After such a long wait, the Dowager Electress Sophie was less than pleased at not being allowed to have a glimpse of the child until the christening ceremony, held in private in the mother's bedroom. While she wrote with a sense of great-grandmotherly pride to King Frederick of Prussia that the baby 'has merry big eyes, mouth wide open to such and seems to be a lively little fellow,' she told Leibniz, adding a little sourly, 'I hope it will have more sense than his father.'[2]

The secrecy which surrounded Princess Caroline's pregnancy, and her reluctance to let others see him at first, gave rise to suspicions which subsequent actions only served to reinforce. Gossips who recalled the birth

of King James II of England's last child and the warming-pan theory wondered if the Electoral Prince and his wife had resorted to similar subterfuge. Had a healthy baby boy been substituted for a sickly girl, a still-born infant? Were they sure that the Princess had really been *enceinte* and not merely suffering from 'distemper'? That they should produce a son and heir as soon as possible in order to enhance the chances of the Hanoverian succession to the English throne, which was by no means a foregone conclusion at this stage, was important, and people were only too ready to believe that the electoral family were quite prepared to arrange family circumstances to suit themselves if necessary. The Dowager Electress remarked rather ungraciously that if her second surviving son, Duke Maximilian, had as much power as the English Parliament, he would declare his nephew a spurious child, as none of them were present at his birth.

Adding weight to this theory in the eyes of some was Prince Frederick Louis's pronounced lack of Hanoverian characteristics. Unlike his forebears he grew up to be heavy-nosed, thick-lipped, and yellow-skinned. In the family he was nicknamed 'the Griff', a West Indian term for a half-caste. Those outside the family wondered whether his conscience-stricken parents were casting subtle aspersions on his legitimacy, and whether he was the son of one of the Elector's Turkish servants – a ludicrous rumour, coincidentally, later circulated about the possible paternity of Prince George Augustus himself. Of the Prince and Princess's subsequent children, only one son, Prince William, born in 1721, lived to maturity. Physically and temperamentally he was Hanoverian through and through, and the devotion his parents lavished on him added weight to the theories of those who thought that the Prince and Princess cherished hopes of disinheriting 'the interloper' Frederick.

However, now that the succession was apparently secured in the next generation, in England Queen Anne consented with some reluctance to confer titles and honours on Prince George Augustus. She made him Baron Tewkesbury, Viscount Northallerton, Earl of Milford Haven, Marquess and Duke of Cambridge, and accorded him precedence over all other English peers. These place names surely meant little if anything to him, but he graciously sent his humble thanks to Her Majesty through Lord Howe. In March 1707 the patents were brought to the court at Herrenhausen, accompanied by an autograph letter from Queen Anne. Howe maintained that they deserved a formal audience at which they could be presented to the recipient.

At once the Elector, unimpressed by (if not jealous of) the honours granted to his son and heir by a foreign court, declared that he would not permit any grand presentation of the patents of nobility to his son, who was not empowered to grant formal audiences during his lifetime. Instead he

suggested that they could be brought by a footman to Herrenhausen. Already irritated at not having been invited to the young mother's *accouchement* or the child's christening, Lord Howe indignantly refused. Such honours, he felt with good reason, could not be accepted so grudgingly. A fitting ceremonial, he told the Elector, ought to attend the reception of 'the highest gift the Queen had to bestow'. Hanoverian ministers thought perhaps the Elector and Electoral Prince could hold a joint audience. A compromise with the stubborn Elector was reached by which they were conferred at a private ceremony.

Queen Anne was furious at this studied insult. Prince George Augustus, Princess Caroline and 'old Sophy' were alarmed at the effect it could have on their relations with the court at St James's, and the Prince was tactful enough to do what he could in order to atone for his father's churlish actions. Howe reported that he 'made many excuses, and desired me to represent that it was not his fault the receiving of the patent was not performed in the most respectful manner.'[3] To Queen Anne the Prince wrote a gracious letter of thanks, assuring her that he would 'endeavour to make a suitable return' for the honours 'by the most perfect veneration and by the most zealous and respectful sentiments'. Nevertheless she did not fail to advance this disrespect as one of several excuses for not inviting any member of the electoral family to England for the present.

In July 1707 Princess Caroline was stricken with smallpox. At first the doctors told her that her blood was overheated, but when her baby son was kept away from her, and when her husband went about with a worried face, she knew that it was something more serious. He made a bad nurse, fidgeting, scolding and fussing all day, but she knew how deeply devoted he was to her; affection prompted his anxiety. In the evening he went for vigorous rides, intending to keep fit and well himself. After she had passed the critical smallpox stage, she caught a severe chill which turned to pneumonia, and in her weakened state she nearly died. The struggle exhausted her strength, but careful nursing and a strong constitution helped her to recover from a disease which so often proved fatal. As Prince George Augustus insisted on staying by her side for much of the time, for his son to risk his life for such foolishly sentimental reasons was incomprehensible to the Elector, who was jealous of their mutual devotion, and would have been delighted if only the microbe world had relieved him of his own wife.

When the Prince took to his bed with the disease, he received no sympathy from his father, and certainly expected none. The Elector had already been irked by his son's eagerness to ingratiate himself with the Queen of England and her ministers over the honours business; and such touching devotion to his wife drove another wedge between them. For a while the Prince's life was in danger as well. The Princess was deeply touched by his unselfishness, as was the Dowager Electress, and during

their remaining thirty years together she never forgot how he had defied convention and stood devotedly beside her. Though he would prove irascible and unfaithful in time, she always found it in her heart to forgive him.

The increasing likelihood of military action in the near future did nothing to lessen the gulf between father and son. Three of Prince George Augustus's uncles had been killed in battle, his father had already won praise as a brave soldier and commander, and the Electoral Prince chafed at being denied a chance to uphold the reputation of his family.

An opportunity was not long in coming. The Grand Alliance of Britain, most of the states of the Holy Roman Empire and the Netherlands had been engaged for several years in the war of the Spanish succession against France. King Charles II of Spain, a pathetically deformed sovereign whose mere existence bore testimony to the gross folly of generations of inbreeding, not only left no children to succeed him but also no obvious heirs, and on his death in November 1700 he had bequeathed his crown to King Louis XIV of France's grandson Philip, who reigned as King Philip V. The subsequent coordination and combination of military, political and commercial policies of Spain and France upset the traditional power balance of Europe and united most of the continent against an over-mighty France which threatened to annex the Spanish empire by stealth. The alliance strove to prevent Philip from becoming King of Spain, and put Archduke Charles of Austria – the former suitor for the hand of Princess Caroline of Ansbach – on the throne instead.

In the summer of 1708 the Electoral Prince bid an emotional farewell to his wife and infant son at Herrenhausen, promising to write as often as possible. He was to join the combined forces of Prince Eugene of Savoy's army on the Moselle, at the head of twenty squadrons of Hanoverian cavalry, and the English under the Duke of Marlborough as Commander-in-Chief. Suddenly the Elector could take pride in this often unsatisfactory son, who was evidently a chip off the old block. He was proud that the young man should be 'beginning the art of war under so great a captain'.

In July they met the French forces under Marshal Vendôme near Oudenarde. During the battle which followed, Prince George Augustus spared himself nothing. His horse was shot dead under him, and the Colonel who gave him his own was killed while he helped the Prince into the saddle. By the time darkness fell, the French army were completely surrounded. In England, the victory was rightly regarded as Marlborough's; but the role and self-evident courage of the German Prince whom the English expected to succeed to the throne were recognized.

His gallantry was celebrated in a poem by William Congreve, *Jack Frenchman's Lamentation*. The Pretender had been watching the scene of

battle from a safe position in the rear, not out of cowardice so much as in deference to the orders of Vendôme, who did not need or want too many inexperienced princes under his command at once. Nevertheless the contrast was noticed:

> Not so did behave
> Young Hanover brave,
> In this bloody war, I assure ye;
> When his warhorse was shot
> He valued it not,
> But fought it on foot like a fury.
> Full firmly he stood
> As became his high blood
> Which runs in his veins so blue,
> For this gallant young man,
> Being a-kin to Queen Anne,
> Did as, were she a man, she would do.

The poem became popular with those in England who looked forward to the Hanoverian succession, and many a toast would be drunk to their eventual King, 'Young Hanover Brave'.

If the Elector was proud of his son's performance, he kept his feelings to himself. Whereas he might have been expected to confer a regiment or some decoration on him, he did nothing. Marlborough generously wrote to congratulate the Elector on his son who had 'distinguished himself extremely, charging at the head of and animating by his example your Electoral Highness's troops, who played a good part in this happy victory'.[4] Yet his father's jealousy did nothing to lessen Prince George Augustus's sense of triumph. It was one of the happiest days of his long life, and the mere recall of the battle gave him a sense of achievement which the passing years never extinguished.

As England basked in the aftermath of the victory, the Tories suspected that Marlborough and the Whigs planned to send an invitation to Hanover summoning the Electoral Prince or his grandmother to come and visit. Queen Anne questioned him, making her repugnance to any such move beyond question. She insisted that she would invite neither the Prince, his father, nor his grandmother, 'it being a thing I cannot bear to have any successor here though it were but for a week'.[5]

In October the campaign ended and the Electoral Prince returned to his family. Princess Caroline had been more proud of her husband than ever since a courier had brought them news of the battle and the role he had played in the fighting. She noticed that he had gained a new aura of manliness from his baptism of fire, and there were no more tantrums and

sulks, now that he had had the chance to prove himself. There had been family anxieties with the health of little 'Fritzchen', who was small and backward for his age. He spoke only a few words and seemed to make no effort to stand. A case of rickets was diagnosed, and with prompt attention from the doctors the condition was cured.

Early the following year the Princess knew she was expecting another child, and on 22 October (OS)/2 November (NS) 1709 a daughter was born. Her husband was on a hunting expedition in Celle at the time, and promptly wrote a letter mingling tenderness and affection with naïvety: 'I am only a little bit angry that it caused you pain. You should know me well enough my very dear Caroline to believe that everything that concerns you is infinitely precious to me. This new token of your love attaches me the more deeply to you, and I assure you dear heart that I love the baby without having seen it.'[6]

The Elector appeared to show no interest as the child was a girl. More at pains to observe etiquette than his father, Prince George Augustus wrote to Queen Anne in England, asking permission to name the child after her, and inviting her to be a godmother. The Queen sent 'her compliments' through the envoy, and a letter of good wishes followed, together with a small present for her godchild. She nominated the child's maternal great-grandmother, the Duchess of Celle, to act as her proxy. Whether this was done out of courtesy to the elderly Duchess, or out of pure devilry, is not known; but the Dowager Electress hated her, and the Elector can hardly have been pleased by the intrusion into such a family occasion of a reminder of a past which he wanted to forget. At any rate the move did nothing to soothe ruffled feelings across the North Sea.

Two more Princesses were born at Herrenhausen. Amelia Sophie Eleanor, who was always known in the family as Emily, followed on 30 May (OS)/10 June (NS) 1711, and Caroline Elizabeth two years later to the very day. Again, on neither occasion did the Elector show any interest in their arrivals. He doubtless hoped for more grandsons to ensure the succession would be secure. Prince George Augustus was a typical princely father of his time; he did not particularly relish having young children around him, and was too honest to pretend otherwise. Fortunately Princess Caroline was an attentive and kindly mother, though by no means indulgent, and her daughters soon learned to love and respect her.

One consequence of the imminent Hanoverian succession was the arrival of several English families in Hanover, eager to ingratiate themselves with the future King and his family. Among them were Henry Howard and his wife Henrietta. Mr Howard, third son of the Earl of Suffolk, was a spendthrift with a reputation for dissipation, drunkenness and a violent temper. He had married Henrietta Hobart, eldest daughter of a Norfolk baronet, Sir Henry Hobart, mainly for her money. When they found they

could no longer live in England to the style in which they were accustomed, and when Henry Howard found that his unsavoury character was a positive deterrent to any prospective employer, they went to Hanover where the cost of living was considerably less. On their way to Germany they travelled 'in the common wagon', and soon after their arrival, when they wished to make their number known with the ministers by holding a dinner party, Mrs Howard had to sell her long fine brown hair to a periwig-maker in order to settle the account.

Attractive, witty, sensible, and about the same age as Prince George Augustus, she was introduced to him after becoming friendly with the Dowager Electress. Sophie was impressed with this well-born woman from England, finding her pleasant, amiable, well-informed and well-read. A welcome guest in the Electoral departments, she was clever enough to admit to a (possibly diplomatic) interest in the teachings of Leibniz. There was no surer passport to the good graces of Princess Caroline, who appointed her one of her *dames du palais*. Mrs Howard was a considerable improvement on the coarse, ill-read Hanoverian ladies who had previously comprised most of her social circle.

From that it was only a small step to acquaintance with Prince George Augustus who soon fell for her charms. Friendship became intimacy, and she became his *maîtresse en titre*. To accept the theory of prudish souls who regarded their relationship as little more than platonic is to underestimate the conventions, manners and morals of the time. There can be little doubt that she became his mistress in the full sense of the word. Princess Caroline knew better than her ill-fated mother-in-law, and readily accepted the situation. Much as Prince George Augustus loved his wife, and always would, he was too much a man of his time not to baulk at social convention. He was not one to accept or appreciate intellectual friendships between man and woman, and with his wife's desire for reading and learned discussion he was often out of his depth, finding refuge in teasing her for being 'more schoolmistress than princess'. His boasting and strutting, his outbursts of temper and his inability to appreciate or sympathize with the higher side of her nature, meant that Princess Caroline could easily have too much of his company. If Mrs Howard could give her a break from time to time, she would be the last to complain.

As well as following time-honoured custom, perhaps Prince George Augustus was also taking a mistress out of boredom. The aged Electress Sophia, a sharp-tongued old lady but a lively companion, was often better company for the independent-minded Princess Caroline, who spent many a happy hour in her rooms at the Herrenhausen, surrounded by the elderly lady's lovingly acquired collections of porcelain and books, with cosmopolitan guests – the ever-favoured Leibniz, the composer and *kapellmeister* George Frideric Handel, or princes and generals from all

corners of Europe. Moreover the Elector, jealous of his son's success on the field at Oudenarde and his well-deserved reputation for bravery which had made him something of a hero in England, frustrated him by his refusals and petty indignities. He took care to restrict the military activities which the young man so enjoyed. Prince George Augustus chafed at the boredom and constraints placed on him by a cold, distant father. An undemanding mistress who was flattered by his attentions, and who provided the appropriate creature comforts as well as companionship, made an adequate diversion.

As for Mrs Howard, in her financial state she was obviously not slow to take advantage of such a situation, and neither was her husband. The short, dapper, red-faced Prince George Augustus, with his vanity and uncertain temper, was no Prince Charming, and she was certainly not swept off her feet by him. Nevertheless, a prince with a not inconsiderable inheritance in front of him could rightly be regarded as something of a catch. The Dowager Electress Sophia approved wholeheartedly of the situation. It did not surprise her that her grandson wanted to indulge in extra-marital affairs, and if he did then he could hardly have chosen better than a woman who made no attempt to exploit her royal connections outside the court and behaved with discretion. Moreover, as she remarked sagely, *la maîtresse* would undoubtedly improve her grandson's English.

Princess Caroline took advantage of opportunities to improve her linguistic skills as well. She was determined to learn English at the same time. Among her servants was a Hanoverian-born English girl, Miss Brandshagen, who read and talked the language with her every day. Nevertheless Princess Caroline always spoke with a heavy German intonation, which suggests that her young teacher had lost her English accent to some extent after spending much of her life in Hanover. As yet it was by no means certain that the German electorate would not always be home for the Princess and her husband.

'I cling to the hope'

As the second decade of the eighteenth century approached, it began to look as though the Hanoverian succession in England could certainly not be taken for granted. A new Parliament which met in December 1710 was dominated by the Tories, who were more sympathetically inclined towards the Jacobite cause. Many of the ministers preferred not to declare too firmly for one claimant or the other – the Electress Sophie or James Edward Stuart – but found it prudent to prepare for either eventuality. The following year Emperor Joseph died, giving war-weary England a chance to press for the end of armed conflict. Queen Anne addressed a personal letter to the Electress, asking her to use her influence to promote the cause of peace in Europe. Hurt by the Queen's recent behaviour, and angry at her refusal to invite any of the family to England, the Electress replied acidly that it suited Hanoverian interests to continue the war against France, and that England should not complain about sharing the burdens of her allies in the conflict. To underline their point, the Elector broke with his previous principle of abstention from involvement in British affairs by instructing his envoy Hans von Bothmer, who had come over to England with Marlborough, to present a memorial against the peace.

Queen Anne and her ministers were united in anger. Bothmer and the Hanoverians were strongly denounced in England, Marlborough was dismissed from his military command and retired to Antwerp in disgrace, and after protracted negotiations, peace was signed at the treaty of Utrecht in 1713. Though England was relieved to see an end to the fighting Hanover was not satisfied, and her objections did nothing to promote English enthusiasm for the Elector and his family. The Elector alone was unconcerned, but his mother, his son and daughter-in-law were all disturbed at the knowledge that their succession might have been jeopardized by the turn of events.

A letter from Leibniz to Princess Caroline, expressing his 'perpetual devotion' and the hope that 'you may one day enjoy the title of Queen of England so well worn by Queen Elizabeth, which you so highly merit', brought forth a reply (27 December 1713) that

of all the letters which this season has brought me yours has been the most welcome. You do well to send me your good wishes for the throne of

England, which are sorely needed just now, for in spite of all the favourable rumours you mention, affairs there seem to be going from bad to worse. For my part (and I am a woman and like to delude myself) I cling to the hope that, however bad things may be now, they will ultimately turn to the advantage of our House. I accept the comparison which you draw, though all too flattering, between me and Queen Elizabeth as a good omen. Like Elizabeth, the Electress's rights are denied her by a jealous sister with a bad temper [Queen Anne], and she will never be sure of the English crown until her accession to the throne. God be praised that our Princess of Wales [the Electress Sophie] is better than ever, and by her good health confounds all the machinations of her enemies.[1]

The Electoral Princess was not generally given to pessimism, but she could be forgiven for her despondency. She had looked forward to the family ascending the British throne, perhaps even more fervently than her husband, and she realized that it could not be regarded as a foregone conclusion.

Meanwhile Queen Anne's health was deteriorating fast. A fever which reduced her to unconsciousness for several hours resulted in rumours that she was already dead and that the Pretender was about to sail for England with a squadron of French men-of-war. In her last months, she seemed increasingly tortured by guilt at the part she had played in agreeing to her father, King James II, being deposed. She had long felt that her inability to bear at least one healthy heir who lived to maturity was a judgement on her unfilial behaviour, and that the restoration of the crown to her half-brother was the only atonement she could make to the family. Nevertheless as a good Protestant she was ready to maintain that her country must have a Protestant monarch. If her half-brother could be persuaded to change his religion and forswear Roman Catholicism, she would probably assent to the repeal of the Act of Settlement, a measure with which the Tory-dominated Houses of Parliament would concur. An Anglican James Edward Stuart on the throne would be preferable to German Sophie and her equally Teutonic son and grandson.

In this case there would surely be no Hanoverian succession. 'All would be easy,' she told her ministers sadly, 'if he would enter the pale of the Church of England.' However the stubborn attitude of the man who would have been King James III strangled any such ideas at birth. In March 1713 he had declared unequivocally that he would never change his own religion, though if he became King he would undertake not to interfere with the Anglican beliefs of his subjects.

Whether the Church in Britain, and religious freedom, would be equally safe under Queen Sophie and her German Calvinist views, was open to

doubt in the eyes of some, not least the supporters of James. Even the Duchess of Orléans, the Electress's devoted niece and confidante, warned her aunt tactfully in January 1714 that she felt certain Queen Anne's conscience would 'wake her up before her death, and she will do justice to her brother'.

All the same, those who favoured the Hanoverian succession were alarmed by the evident pro-Stuart atmosphere. Their suspicions were strengthened by Queen Anne's last speech from the throne at the opening of Parliament in March 1714, in which she omitted all mention of a Hanoverian succession. To Baron Bothmer, who had remained in London as the Elector's representative, it was a bad omen. Added to that was his feeling – and indeed that of many people in public life in England – that popular opinion appeared to be moving in favour of James as his half-sister's successor. His birthday was still celebrated each year by some as if he was heir to the throne.

The Whig oligarchy intimated that it would be expedient for at least one representative of the house of Hanover to reside in England. Queen Anne had never ceased to make clear her strong opposition to the presence of Sophie and George Lewis in England while she was alive, but the Electoral Prince was a possibility. In the case of his English titles, and in the matter of inviting the Queen to be godmother to his eldest daughter, he had shown himself punctilious in observing etiquette; and as he had been created Duke of Cambridge in addition to his other titles, he had the right to be summoned to Parliament as a Peer of the Realm. This being the case, it would be only right and proper for him to reside in England. Should Anne suddenly die – and it was evident that she would not be much longer for this world – then it would augur better for the stability of the country, as well as counter the Jacobite threat and its champions, for one senior member of the Hanoverian dynasty to be present.

The Elector was not consulted at first; the rest of the family suspected that he would regard it as another intrigue to supplant him in the favour of the English by his son. When he was told, he was angry with his mother and son, but in the interests of family solidarity consented to support their idea. The Electress, her grandson and granddaughter-in-law, on the advice of various Whig emissaries and other friends at Hanover, including Leibniz and Prince Eugene of Savoy, all endorsed the plan. On their behalf an envoy, Salentin von Schütz, was sent to enquire of Lord Harcourt, the Lord Chancellor, whether the Electoral Prince, as Duke of Cambridge, should not have a writ enabling him to take his seat in the House of Lords. To address such a request personally to Queen Anne would be useless. By approaching the Lord Chancellor instead, they hoped, the Whig Lords would support them so vociferously that the Queen would have to agree.

Queen Anne's fury took them by surprise. Her Chancellor of the Exchequer Robert Harley, Earl of Oxford, declared afterwards that he had

never seen her so angry before. Though it was a sensible measure, given her rapidly failing health, it was not a tactful way of reminding her of her mortality. She considered the message 'monstrous', and an insulting breach of etiquette, and told her Cabinet that though she had often expressed her friendship for the house of Hanover, they would not accept it. In her anger she forbade Schütz to return to court, and declared that no member of the Electoral family should be permitted to set foot in her kingdom as long as she lived.

In words probably dictated or suggested by her Foreign Secretary Viscount Bolingbroke, she replied to the Elector:

> . . . as the rumour increases that my cousin the Electoral Prince has resolved to come over to settle in my lifetime, in my dominions, I do not choose to delay a moment to write to you about this . . . I then freely own to you that I cannot imagine that a Prince who possesses the knowledge and penetration of Your Electoral Highness can ever contribute to such an attempt; and that I believe you are too just to allow that any infringement shall be made on my sovereignty which you would not choose should be made on your own . . . I am determined to oppose a project so contrary to my royal authority however fatal the consequences may be.[2]

The Privy Council could find no legal grounds on which they could refuse to issue such a writ, and accordingly did so. Harley announced that his party did not deplore the Prince's coming to England; on the contrary, they welcomed the idea. Leibniz congratulated the Electress on what he saw as a victory for them and for commonsense: 'it is essential to let the nation [Britain] feel that Hanover both has affection for it and care of its interests.'[3]

The Dowager Electress urged her son to let Prince George Augustus go; the Prince pleaded to go; Princess Caroline tried to talk her father-in-law into giving his approval. It all proved a waste of time. The Elector would not countenance anything which might help his son to become the centre of attention. Family solidarity evidently meant less to him than keeping his personal dignity intact. Schütz, he said, had acted without orders in going to England to present the request.

The rest of the family were aghast. In particular Prince George Augustus had at last begun to believe that his life was about to assume some purpose, and it was only natural that he should seize any opportunity of getting away from Hanover and his petty tyrant of a father. He had no seat in the Privy Council at Hanover; despite having a wife and four children, no addition had been made to his income; he had still not been awarded any regimental command, or place in the council of war, and his chances of taking part in

further military action were looking increasingly remote. Unwittingly, Princess Caroline was partly responsible for the problem. The Elector was not too stupid to see the change that marriage had wrought in his son, and decided that he must be too readily influenced by his more intelligent wife. His son, he told his confidantes, 'blabs everything to the women'.

Now the journey to England which had been virtually promised to the Electoral Prince was to be denied him. Princess Caroline, who had been looking forward to the journey as well, stood loyally by her thwarted husband, telling Leibniz that 'he has moved heaven and earth in the matter', and that he was

> now in despair about going to take his seat in the English Parliament, as he had hoped. I do not know how the world will judge of the policy which keeps us still at Hanover. I do not so much regret the loss we personally may suffer, as that we may seem to have abandoned for the moment the cause of our religion, the liberty of Europe and so many of our brave and honest friends in England. I have only the consolation of knowing that everything possible has been done by the Prince to obtain the Queen's permission. The Electress joined him in this, and they now both intend to send the letters they have received from the Queen to their friends in England. I can find no comfort anywhere beyond the belief that Providence orders all things for our good. In fact I may say that never has any annoyance seemed to me so keen and insupportable as this. I fear for the health of the Electoral Prince, and perhaps even for his life.[4]

The Prince may have been irascible, but for the Princess to fear for his health and life was surely overstating matters. The one for whom fears might legitimately have been entertained was his grandmother, the Electress Sophie. Her exchange of correspondence with the Queen, said those around her, had 'cast such a damp upon her spirits'. According to some sources, on receiving Queen Anne's hostile letter, she rose indignantly from her card table and went for a long walk in the Herrenhausen gardens, pacing distractedly to and fro. There may be an element of exaggeration in this; others suggest, rather more realistically, that she was thoroughly depressed, and gave orders for two of Queen Anne's letters to be published, 'so the world might see it was not her fault if her children lost three kingdoms'.[5] It was also said that after her first flush of anger she accepted the situation, albeit grudgingly, and 'quickly mastered her irritation'.[6]

At the grand old age of eighty-four, it was not surprising that her remarkable vitality was beginning to wane anyway. During the previous few months she had defiantly told her family that she would outlive Queen Anne, and that the words 'Queen of England' would be inscribed on her tombstone, even if her health did not permit her to cross the North Sea,

quoting an old Dutch proverb '*Krakende wagens gaan lang*' ('creaking carts last long') to those who pointed out the difference in their ages. Even so, anger probably hastened the end. An associate of the Duke of Marlborough who was in Hanover at the time declared that the shock of Queen Anne's letter had 'broken her heart and brought her in sorrow to the grave'. On 8 (OS)/19 (NS) June she was taking her usual daily walk in the Herrenhausen gardens, accompanied by Princess Caroline and some of her ladies-in-waiting, when a sudden downpour drove them to seek shelter. Waiting under cover for the rain to stop, she felt faint and collapsed in the arms of her companions. They took her back to her apartments, but she had passed away. Her death, it was announced, was caused by 'apoplexy and thwarted ambition'.

In England Queen Anne met the news with indifference. She told her physician, Sir David Hamilton, that 'Princess Sophia was chipping-porridge, it [her death] would neither give more ease nor more uneasiness'.[7] The Electress's death probably came as a relief to her, for she knew that the Elector was far less interested in the succession, and less likely to prove an embarrassment. Moreover she was almost past caring, for she knew that she would soon follow her to the grave. However she commanded court mourning, and with reluctance agreed to the insertion of the Elector's name as heir to the throne in the Book of Common Prayer.

Meanwhile Bothmer was despatched to London with conciliatory letters to the Queen. The Elector, now her heir, assured her in a conciliatory fashion that he and his family had always desired that 'the royal prerogatives might be maintained in all their lustre', and that the presence of any member of that family in England 'could never have any other design than to confirm a good understanding between the two courts, and to render to Your Majesty all possible services'.[8]

On 27 July (OS)/7 August (NS), Hamilton assured Queen Anne that he had it on good authority that, contrary to rumour, the Electoral Prince was not coming over to England. Wearily she answered 'that gave her no uneasiness now', and she was quite prepared to send to Hanover for the Elector, in order that he could be assured of her friendship, and thus inferring that he might come to take the responsibility off her shoulders. She was now too tired to put up any resistance to the once-dreaded idea of one of the Hanoverians coming to England in her lifetime. Her despairing remark that she doubted if she would last much longer was true. The doctors tried every remedy they could to prolong her life, but she was old before her time and had no desire to shoulder her mortal burdens any more. On 31 July (OS)/11 August (NS) she fell into a coma. Her last intelligible words were, reportedly, 'My brother! Oh! my poor brother, what will become of you?'

Early next morning, the seals of the document drawn up by the Elector of Hanover appointing the Council of Regency were broken in the presence of Baron Bothmer. His master, the Elector, was now King George I of Great Britain.

PART TWO

1714–27

'He thought his opposers impudent rebels'

On the morning of 1 (OS)/12 (NS) August, cannons were fired in the City of London to announce the beginning of a new reign. That afternoon the herald proclaimed to crowds outside St James's Palace on behalf of the Lords Spiritual and Temporal of the Realm that 'the High and Mighty Prince George Elector of Brunswick Lüneburg is now by the death of our late sovereign of Happy Memory, become our lawful and rightful liege Lord, George by the Grace of God King of Great Britain, France and Ireland.'[1]

The enactment of the Hanoverian succession was accepted by those in authority almost without question. A group of pro-Jacobite Lords and clerics held a secret meeting that morning, but only Francis Atterbury, Bishop of Rochester, dared to threaten to read the proclamation of King James III. Bolingbroke argued that England would as soon have a Turk as a Roman Catholic for King, warned him that 'all our throats would be cut', and his powers of persuasion won the day. Yet there had been so many upheavals and threats to the royal line of succession within living memory – the triumph of Cromwell, King Charles II's restoration, the Monmouth rebellion and the Glorious Revolution – that the security of the Hanoverian dynasty could not be seen as a foregone conclusion.

The Council of Regency, comprising four Hanoverian Tories and fourteen Whigs, was to govern the country until the new sovereign's arrival. A packet of letters found in the Queen's room was thrown in the fire unopened. As the papers turned to ashes, Bothmer caught sight of handwriting which, he was convinced, was that of Prince James Edward Stuart.

The mission appointed to escort His Majesty King George I of Great Britain to his new domains across the North Sea arrived in Hanover exactly seven days after his reign had begun. At its head was the Earl of Dorset, who asked his sovereign to join them and leave as soon as possible. Fifty-four years old and set in his ways, the King showed no great hurry to come and set foot in, let alone see, his new kingdom. Had Bothmer's despatches been less positive, hinting at any lack of enthusiasm at the public proclamation in

London, or mentioning any stirrings of rebellion, he might have stayed in Hanover. It was and always would be of greater importance in his estimation, and he had to put his affairs in the electorate in order first. The lack of urgency with which the Elector went about his business seemed to confirm opinion that he was 'very indifferent to the succession'. He studied Bothmer's daily reports from London with care, evidently intending to ensure that there was no likelihood of an immediate Jacobite challenge before he put himself to the trouble of departing from his home. For six weeks England was without a monarch in residence. Towards the end of August, with some reluctance, he issued an ordinance delegating authority to the Hanoverian Privy Councillors.

Unlike his father the new heir to the throne, Prince George Augustus, and his wife, were eager to go to England at last. He was aged thirty, she was thirty-one; they were young enough to make a new start in a new home, in a new country. They had prepared themselves for the occasion by learning to speak English, albeit with pronounced accents, and with plenty of French and German expressions, and by finding out what they could about the country from Mrs Howard and the other English visitors who had come their way. However when the news of Queen Anne's death reached them, they were careful to keep their enthusiasm under control. The King was perfectly capable of ignoring everyone's advice and leaving them behind in Hanover to spite them if he chose. Alternatively they would have less chance to intrigue against him if he took them to England. He gave his son instructions to be ready to travel with him, and Princess Caroline was to follow a month later with her daughters.

On 31 August (OS)/11 September (NS) King George and his son, accompanied by a small suite, left Hanover for Holland. They spent a fortnight at The Hague, attending several receptions in the family's honour. On 16 (OS)/27 (NS) September they embarked on the yacht *Peregrine*, specially overhauled for the occasion. Though their journey only took two days, a rough crossing and thick fog delayed their arrival at Greenwich, where they disembarked on 18 (OS)/29 (NS) September. Welcoming dignitaries and peers of the realm jostled unceremoniously with each other as they greeted the King and his heir at a scene illuminated by a picturesque array of candles and torchlight processions. The King replied to the welcoming addresses in fluent French, before going off crossly to bed at Greenwich Palace.

The next day he held his first levée, where he spoke with the Whig Lords and the Duke of Marlborough, but ignored the Tories. A number of people had come to London to catch a glimpse of their new sovereign, and 'His Majesty and the Prince were graciously pleased to expose themselves some time at the windows of their palace to satisfy the impatient curiosity of the King's loving subjects'.[2]

On the following day they made their public entry into London. With his son and heir beside him, the new King travelled in a glass coach, decorated with gold, emblazoned with the royal arms, drawn by eight horses, escorted by the Life Guards and preceded by some two hundred coaches of the gentry and nobility, each with six horses, in reverse order of precedence. At Southwark they were met by the Lord Mayor and civic dignitaries, and drove on through the packed, richly decorated streets. Up to one and a half million people from London and Kent came out to watch the show. Rather than indicating enthusiasm for the new King and his line, it was more an expression of relief that the country had accepted a change of dynasty without the threat of revolution or civil war. Despite the presence of a few Jacobites calling 'Damn King George' or expressions to that effect, the English were ready for a quiet life.

King George I was certainly not a sight to inspire enthusiasm. Short of stature, his face was distinguished only by protruding eyes, a large nose and a surly expression, all framed in a dark periwig. He bowed woodenly to the cheers, placing his hand theatrically on his heart, without the merest flicker of a smile. Sitting beside him was Prince George Augustus, all smiles and affability, yet ordered by his father to sit upright and not bow. The Prince, already renowned as the hero of Oudenarde, was evidently more eager to make a good impression. Behind them came coaches bearing the King's Hanoverian suite, including Madames Schulenburg and Kielmansegge, whose grotesque appearance provoked ribald comments from onlookers.

Despite his impassive demeanour, impartial observers appeared to prefer the King. Lady Mary Wortley Montagu was quick to pronounce her verdict on their sovereign: 'In private life he would have been called an honest blockhead. . . . No man was ever more free from ambition . . . he was more properly dull than lazy, and would have been so well contented to have remained in his little town of Hanover, that if the ambition of those about him had not been greater than his own, we should never have seen him in England; and the natural honesty of his temper, joined with the narrow notions of a low education, made him look upon his acceptance of the crown as an act of usurpation, which was always uneasy to him.'[3]

As for the new heir to the throne, Lady Mary was less charitable:

The fire of his temper appeared in every look and gesture; which, being unhappily under the direction of a small understanding, was every day throwing him upon some indiscretion. He was naturally sincere, and his pride told him that he was placed above constraint; not reflecting that a high rank carries along with it a necessity of a more decent and regular behaviour than is expected from those who are not set in so conspicuous a light. He was so far from being of that opinion that he looked on all the men and women he saw as creatures he might kick or kiss for his

diversion; and, whenever he met with any opposition in those designs, he thought his opposers impudent rebels to the will of God, who created them for his use, and judged of the merit of all people by their ready submission to his orders, or the relation they had to his person.[4]

The procession broke up at St James's Palace at around dusk. Festivities continued into the small hours, with bonfires in the city streets and squares, with ox roasts and barrels of beer opened for the revellers. Not everybody was united in a mood of celebration, however. A Tory member of Parliament, Colonel Aldworth, and a Whig, Colonel Chudleigh, had a drunken argument and Chudleigh taunted Aldworth with being a Jacobite. They challenged each other to a duel, and set off with swords and seconds to Marylebone Fields, where Aldworth was fatally wounded.

The King and Prince spent the night at St James's Palace. Two days later, at a meeting of the Privy Council King George I invested his heir, 'our most dear son, a Prince whose eminent filial piety hath always endeared him to us', with the title of Prince of Wales. The empty formality of such honeyed phrases evidently concealed his true feelings.

Early the following month Princess Caroline, now Princess of Wales, set out from Herrenhausen. Their youngest daughter Caroline, not yet two years old, was ill, and the doctors insisted that she should stay behind until she was better. Princesses Amelia and Anne were sent to The Hague in the care of their English tutor, and their mother followed a few days later. Her brother the Margrave of Ansbach came with her for part of the journey, for he knew it was probably the last chance they would have of seeing each other. The parting with him was almost as emotional for her as that from her son. Mother and daughters crossed the North Sea together on what was to be, for all of them but Princess Anne, their only sea voyage. They landed at Margate in mid-October, to be met by the Prince of Wales. That night was spent at Rochester, prior to their official entry into the capital. As their coach drove over London Bridge salutes were fired from the Tower of London, and again as they arrived at St James's Palace.

Prince Frederick, second in line to the throne, was left behind in Hanover to be looked after by servants and tutors under the supervision of his great-uncle, Prince Ernest Augustus. The decision to leave him there was that of his grandfather, who believed it was important for him to be brought up in the ancestral home and have some knowledge of the electorate – evidently more important than having closer acquaintance with England – and also in order that their Hanoverian subjects would not feel slighted by having no younger representative of the family still among them. The schoolmasters of Hanover who were chosen to educate the young Prince evidently did their work well, for he became fluent in several languages, and more at ease among men of culture than his father or grandfather. That it

was cruelty to separate a child of seven from his parents indefinitely – for they were not to meet for another fourteen years – and place him at the centre of court ceremonial did not trouble King George I in the least. In vain did Princess Caroline plead for him to join them in England. Against the decision of her father-in-law, as she and her husband would find out time and time again, there was no appeal.

The boy lacked companionship from his own class, which might have been regarded as both a help and a hindrance. His playmates were chiefly pages and stableboys, his companions in adolescence footmen and grooms, who were more than ready to initiate him into the customary pleasures of a young man of his time. By the time he was twenty he had already had at least one mistress, and learnt to while away the hours drinking and gambling, not to mention the joy of going around smashing peoples' windows at night. The citizens of Hanover were prepared to turn an indulgent blind eye to such high spirits, although when in time he imported the activity to London he was to meet with some resistance. His acquaintance with people outside the royal circle made him more at ease in general company as an adult than his father; here may be seen the characteristics that made him 'the people's prince', ready to mix with all.

Yet the long separation from his parents and sisters, whom he did not see until he was in his early twenties, undoubtedly stored up trouble for the future. Of his disgraced grandmother, he was probably unaware; if he knew of her existence, it can only have been at second- or third-hand. Apart from the grandfather whom he saw at rare intervals whenever he returned to his beloved electorate, throughout adolescence he was almost an orphan. To the rest of his family, he would always be a stranger.

The reception that greeted Prince George Augustus with his wife and small daughters in London was more enthusiastic than that of King George I. While the modern concept of 'a family on the throne' would not have been recognized in the early eighteenth century, it takes little imagination to compare the unsmiling, elderly Elector, who had divorced and imprisoned his wife, with their son, wife and young children – and to consider the effect which each had on those of their subjects. At the same time there were many who came to see and cheer, more out of curiosity and the desire for some kind of diversion rather than out of any deep-rooted loyalty to the crown.

The difference between the land they had just left and the one in which they were to settle was profound. In 1714 the town of Hanover comprised some 1,800 houses, while Berlin had around 5,000. Eighteenth-century London's 100,000, and her combined living and working population of about 750,000, dwarfed them both. Evidently London and Britain were not the insignificant, second-rate little appendage which the Elector's attitude may have led them to suppose.

The City of London consisted largely of the business centre between St Paul's and the Exchange; of Westminster and the Houses of Parliament; and fashionable life centred on St James's and The Mall. St James's Street was full of coffee, chocolate and 'mug' houses, while St James's Park was the fashionable promenade, lined with avenues of trees, as well as a canal and large duck pond. Piccadilly was a semi-rural road, lined with shady trees and broken by a few large houses with gardens. London south of the River Thames was still in its infancy. In the fashionable world dinner was taken in the middle of the day, or from 2 p.m., with supper the more informal meal. Card parties and supper parties generally went together. Society ladies spent their afternoons visiting houses and drinking tea together, at that time something of a luxury, while men of fashion whiled away their time in coffee and chocolate houses. Streets were badly paved with barely any lighting, and after dark law-abiding citizens stayed indoors to shelter from beggars, drunkards and aristocratic hooligans. As for travel, old and dirty hackney coaches were available for hire at a price. The more fashionable method of getting around was on the river, by boat, wherry or barge, thus avoiding rutted muddy streets and filthy slums. From time to time the King, the Prince and Princess of Wales, and many of the nobility 'took the air on the water'. There was generally entertainment to be had on the Thames; Handel's *Water Music* received its first performance on a river picnic in 1717, and so impressed King George I that he asked for it to be played twice more that same evening.

The population of Britain was estimated at eight and a half million: six million in England and Wales, one million in Scotland (or North Britain, as it was often known), and one and a half million in Ireland. Although inferior in population and area to France and the extensive Habsburg dominions in Europe, Britain's position, colonial possessions and overseas trading posts brought her a profitable commercial position. Norwich was the largest city in England after London, with Manchester and Birmingham close behind and thriving as a result of the boost to manufacturing enterprises from war with France. The small size of Britain made her easier to govern than larger countries, and her taxation system was considered socially fairer than that of many other European countries, by the standards of the day. Land tax was levied on all landowners, noble and commoner alike, with additional income from indirect taxation raised according to the nation's ever-varying economic and political needs.

The country over which the Hanoverians reigned was virtually a one-party state. In 1714, and indeed for almost the next hundred years, all government ministers and all members of the Opposition with similar ambitions were Whigs. The Tory party, said to be 'Jacobite when drunk, and Hanoverian when sober', was represented at Westminster by a small group of country gentlemen, their chief concerns being the extravagance and

corruption of the ministry, and such matters as the burden of a land tax. It took little effort for the chief Secretaries of State at the beginning of King George I's reign to convince him and his son and heir that all Tories were closet Jacobites, with no government potential and no function beyond a negligible nuisance value. Whigs in power and in opposition knew no differences of policy or principle – beyond perhaps the principle of ambition – and opposition Whigs could therefore accept office without any qualms of conscience.

London and the south-east was all the first Hanoverians ever saw of England. Once Princess Caroline had arrived at St James's to make her new home there, she would never travel beyond the city and its semi-rural environs of Kew, Windsor, Kensington and Hampton Court, as well as the large houses in the area to which she would occasionally be invited by the nobility. As for her husband and her father-in-law, they never travelled further in the country than Newmarket races. A brief tour in the south-eastern counties, or a journey to the coast for a return to Hanover, would mark the extent of their English travels. To them Wales, the Midlands and beyond, all seemed to belong to another world.

The Coronation of King George I took place on 20 (OS)/31 (NS) October, an exceptionally fine autumn day, at Westminster Abbey. To Lady Cowper, a future Lady of the Bedchamber, it was 'not a day of joy for the Jacobites; however, they were all there, looking as cheerful as they could, but very peevish with everybody that spoke to them'. The King, who had to have the rites explained to him in hoarse whispers of Latin, was crowned with the crown made for Queen Anne, as the old Stuart one had apparently been taken away by King James II and lost in the Channel crossing. The crown last worn by Queen Mary, consort of King William III, was adapted for Prince George Augustus, as it was the first Coronation for many years that a Prince of Wales had also attended. There was no Queen Consort, so neither the Princess of Wales nor the peeresses walked in the procession, but the Princess watched from her seat in the Abbey. When the crown was placed on the King's head, the peers put on their coronets and acclaimed him with such enthusiasm that his look of boredom momentarily gave way to astonishment.

The Archbishop called out, 'Sirs, I here present to you George, your undoubted King. Wherefore all you who are come this day to do homage, are you willing to do the same?' The Jacobites present would surely have been happy to answer otherwise, but as the elderly Lady Dorchester, once King James II's mistress, commented scornfully to Lady Cowper, 'Does the old fool think anyone will say No to his question, when there are so many drawn swords?' Looking round later she also noticed the Duchess of Portsmouth, a surviving mistress of King Charles II, and Lady Orkney, who

had similarly offered her favours to King William III. 'Who would have thought we three whores would have met together here?' she asked.

Apart from the collapse of a stand in Palace Yard and the death of about ten spectators, the occasion was not marred by any unpleasantness in London. Yet in other parts of the country there were pockets of demonstration and dissent. In Chippenham, Wiltshire, pro-Jacobite riots began on Coronation Day and lasted for a week, while in Bristol bonfires lit by loyal Whigs were put out by local Jacobites who marched through the streets yelling anti-Hanoverian slogans. At Oxford, on the eve of the Coronation an undergraduate decorated one of the college entrances with a large notice declaring, 'The King a Cuckold; The Prince a Bastard'.

On 29 October the royal family attended Lord Mayor's Day, watching from a balcony near Bow Church, with a canopy of crimson velvet above them, the Prince of Wales on the King's right hand, the Princess on his left, and the small Princesses in front. They were delighted with the show, which like the Coronation was far more impressive than any pageantry they had ever seen in Hanover. Afterwards the King offered to knight the owner of the house from whose balcony they had viewed the procession, and he was rather taken aback when the man refused the honour as he was a devout Quaker.

After the procession the royal family were escorted to the Guildhall for luncheon. All went according to plan till the Lady Mayoress, decked in black velvet and a magnificent train, came forward to make obeisance to the Princess of Wales. She was bitterly offended at not being greeted with a kiss. The King and Princess had been told that the 'Lady Mayor' was not actually the Lord Mayor's wife, and had only been borrowed for the day. Lady Cowper was prevailed upon to soothe feelings by assuring the King that she was 'a sort of relation' of the Mayor's first wife. The King remarked wryly that if His Lordship had borrowed a wife, he would surely have chosen someone more beautiful. The season of entertainment ended the following day, the Prince of Wales's birthday, when all the courtiers appeared in new clothes. In the evening a ball was held, at which the Prince and Princess opened the dancing; she 'danced in slippers very well; the Prince better than anybody.'

Shy, obstinate and thoroughly set in his ways, the King remained elusive for much of the time to most but his own select circle, or, as Lady Mary Wortley Montagu called them, 'his German ministers and playfellows male and female'. The ministers included Baron von Bernstorff, who had served him faithfully since he had drawn up the terms of his divorce agreement twenty years previously; Baron Bothmer, who had helped to protect Hanoverian interests since during Queen Anne's reign; and his private secretary Jean de Robethon, a French Huguenot refugee who had held similar positions successively under the Duke of Celle and King William III.

His *maîtresse en titre* was the angular Melusine von der Schulenburg, nicknamed 'the Maypole'. She was created Duchess of Munster in the Irish peerage in 1716, and Duchess of Kendal in the English peerage three years later. His other chief female companion, the excessively fat Sophie Charlotte von Kielmansegge ('the Elephant'), was his half-sister, the daughter of Elector Ernest Augustus by his mistress Countess von Platen. Contrary to popular belief she was not the King's mistress, and there is no evidence to support the rumours of an incestuous relationship between them. She had married Johann von Kielmansegge, a Hanoverian diplomat and courtier, and later the Elector's Vice-Master of the Horse, in 1701. He and his wife accompanied King George to England in 1714, but he died three years later. On her widowhood she became a naturalized British subject, was created Countess of Leinster in the Irish peerage in 1721, and Countess of Darlington in the British peerage a year later. They lived in St James's Palace, and as they hated each other, their suites were well apart, with that of the King between them.

Also part of the King's inner circle were two Turkish servants, Mehemet and Mustapha, whom he had captured as prisoners of war in his campaigns with the imperial forces in Hungary, and taken back to Hanover to be trained as *valets de chambre*. All of them disliked the Prince of Wales, less perhaps from personal differences than a natural desire to serve their master loyally. They constantly spied on the heir to the throne and reported back to his father, so the Prince of Wales could complain with some justification that he never had any privacy. 'The Schulenberg' was particularly fond of stirring up trouble between father and son, especially when it came to the Prince and Princess of Wales's attempts to win the confidence of the British, behaviour which the two Hanoverian ladies deprecated as grossly insulting to the King and to Germany in general. As King George seemed to believe that his son's main purpose was to take advantage of him at every turn, he readily concurred with their views.

His Hanoverian advisers and most trusted English ministers remained his other confidantes. A man of simple pleasures, he had little time for the social life of the court. He preferred living in two rooms at the Palace. Although very fond of the opera, he avoided the royal box. Much as he enjoyed gambling, he did not like to sit down with his court, preferring to go incognito to a friend's house and play with a few of his cronies. He did not dine in state, served by the great officers of the household, but ate privately in his bedchamber. Unable to appreciate that his subjects liked to see their King, with all the pomp of majesty and trappings of splendour, he never undertook any grand tours throughout his kingdom.

'Not one drop of blood in my veins dat is not English'

The Prince and Princess of Wales settled in a wing of the Palace at St James's. Tactfully they only recruited English men and women to their household staff. Their good command of the language placed them on an easy footing with their subjects. She and her husband took care to praise their adopted country and countrymen. While the Prince's assertion that 'I have not one drop of blood in my veins dat is not English' was hardly accurate, it proved his heart was in the right place.

Lady Cowper declared that courtiers were full of praise at all the compliments the Prince had been paying the English – 'that he thought them the best, the handsomest, the best-shaped, the best-natured, the lovingest people in the world, and that if anybody would make their court to him, it must be by telling them he was like an Englishman.'[1] Princess Caroline once declared that she would 'as soon live on a dunghill as return to Hanover'. As the Princess's lady-in-waiting, Lady Cowper could not speak highly enough of her mistress: 'I am so charmed with her good nature and good qualities.' At every meal, she said, she drank the Prince's health, toasting him as 'Young Hanover Brave', in recognition of the title bestowed on him by Congreve. 'I do not wonder I have enjoyed such good health since I came to England, since you took so much part in it,' he declared gallantly. His good manners did much to redress his ignorance. When the poem was first quoted at him he listened with pride, and on being told who the author was, he promptly asked 'And who might Mr Congreve be?'

The courtier Peter Wentworth found 'all backward in speaking to the King, but ready enough to speak to the Prince.' Houses in Pall Mall, the narrow street adjoining St James's Palace, encroached almost up to the palace walls. Yet a lack of privacy when the couple strolled with their children along the Mall and through St James's Park did not bother them. They would incline their heads in gracious acknowledgement to the crowds who acknowledged them every time they appeared. But soon the Princess declared that the Park 'stank of people', and preferred Kensington instead. At that time a semi-rural village, Kensington was separated from the city by Hyde Park and an expanse of open fields. The Palace had been the

favourite residence of King William III, Queen Mary and Queen Anne, and the air was said to be 'very salubrious'. The Princess of Wales took to walking in the Park regularly and it soon became fashionable, although the public were only admitted by ticket.

Court life would have been very dull without the presence of the Prince and Princess of Wales, who both loved the social round. Their morning drawing-rooms and twice-weekly receptions were packed, cheerful affairs, in contrast to the half-empty court of the King. At her first appearance at the English court, Wentworth recorded, the Princess 'came into the drawing-room at seven o'clock and stayed until ten. There was a basset table and ombre tables, but the Princess sitting down to piquet, all the company flocked about to that table and the others were not used.'[2] The stakes were often high. Lady Cowper was reluctant to play as nobody generally sat down to the tables with less than two hundred guineas to spare, while on a particularly lucky streak the statesman Lord Chesterfield won so much that he was afraid to go home without a powerful escort.

Gambling with card games and dice were a regular part of court routine. The Princess of Wales dealt an accomplished hand, and on Twelfth Night, 1715, she and the Duchess of Montagu 'went halves at Hazard' and she won £600. To allow time for cards, supper was served between 9 p.m. and 2 a.m., usually in buffet style, as opposed to the more formal, heavier dinner served at 2 p.m. each day.

The court was less exclusive than in Queen Anne's day, and in the crowded rooms there was much pushing and hustling to catch a glimpse of the royal family. The Venetian ambassadress, Madame Tron, was so unused to the congestion that she kept crying out in alarm, 'Do not touch my face'. Showing a rare touch of humour, the King turned to a courtier and told him that 'she offers you all the rest of her body provided you don't touch her face'. Not everybody was mesmerized by the spell of royalty. Some less easily pleased observers spoke of their excruciating boredom at these receptions, seeing 'nothing but blue noses, pale faces, lying smiles, forced compliments, careful brows and made laughs'.

The Princess of Wales prided herself as a figure of culture, learning and scholarship. Intellectual friendships were the delight of her life. Among the most illustrious men of letters who frequented her gatherings at Leicester House were the statesman turned poet and essayist Joseph Addison and the playwright John Gay, both of whom she had met before coming to England. Addison had accompanied Lord Halifax on a diplomatic mission to Hanover in 1706, and Gay had been Lord Clarendon's secretary. Poetry was never the Princess of Wales's first love, although she and the Prince (whom she persuaded to take his part, albeit reluctantly, towards royal patronage of the arts) subscribed £100 for the publication of Alexander Pope's translation of the *Iliad*.

Philosophy and theology were more to her taste, particularly the writings of Dr Samuel Clarke, a disciple of Sir Isaac Newton, whose views on the divinity of Christ were regarded as suspect. Now elderly, Newton had to be brought across in his chair from his house in St Martin's Street to Leicester House. The Princess of Wales always gave him a special place of honour at her gatherings, listening with reverence to all he had to say. She often saw him in private, and consulted him on the education of her younger children, even if she did not always take his advice. She later appointed Edmond Halley as tutor to her younger son Prince William, even though Newton and Halley were bitter enemies who used to quarrel regularly.

The Prince of Wales made no pretence of thinking himself as anything but a man of action. In his more impatient moods, he might fulminate against her 'dabbling' with things she did not understand, though it would have been more honest of him to admit that he did not understand them himself. As a rule, though, he did not interfere with her 'parties'. Meaning well, he would make himself known in friendly fashion to her guests, and bore them with animated accounts of his experiences on the battlefield at Oudenarde, or his painstaking researches into the genealogies of the German princely families

Among the courtiers were several illegitimate children of the Stuarts. When one of King Charles II's natural sons George, Duke of Northumberland, touched the Prince of Wales by accident at a drawing room, the latter muttered crossly, 'One can't move here for bastards.' 'Sir, my father was as great a King as yours,' was the swift reply, 'and as for our mothers, the less we say about them the better!'[3]

In personality Prince George Augustus was very like his father, a resemblance which would increase with age. The younger man was more affable, though both tended to be moody, short-tempered and above all suspicious of each other. If the Prince had never forgiven his father for his treatment of his mother, the King had been jealous of his son's heroic reputation in battle, although he should have been proud, and saw in him a dangerous rival for the laurels which should have fallen to the elder man. Now, as King, perhaps King George envied him his happy family life, as well as his popularity and winning ways. A popular son and heir in this new kingdom would surely attract opposition and intrigue in political and court circles. Kings who dislike their heirs do not like to be reminded of their mortality, or watch younger ambitious men planning for the future.

King George was rumoured to have asserted in a moment of impatience that the heir was no son of his, but instead the child of his former wife by one of the Turkish servants. Another, more credible reason for what was becomingly referred to by a recent historian as 'the Hanoverian dynasty's recurrent bouts of Oedipal combat' has been advanced.[4] The physical space available to the court was inadequate, and there was no English palace

comparable in size to Versailles or indeed the Hanoverians' own beloved Herrenhausen. Early in the King's reign the Duke of Marlborough, a frequent supper companion, offered to sell the Prince Marlborough House, showing them how easily it could be connected to St James's Palace with a gallery, but the King would not consider the idea. Most of the Tudor and Stuart Kings failed to produce large families of healthy children. The more prolific Hanoverian Kings simply did not find Windsor Castle, Hampton Court or Kensington Palace large enough to keep their heirs apparent and their respective families close by yet still under their surveillance. As a result these heirs tended to purchase their own establishments in London, such as Leicester House and later in the eighteenth-century Carlton House. Such locations invariably created rival centres to the court and potential bases for political opposition. This was undoubtedly a factor in personal differences, often leading to bitter quarrels, between father and son, up to the reign of the last of the four Georges – a George who never provided the country with a legitimate son, and whose only heir was a daughter who predeceased him by dying in childbirth.

With the Princess of Wales, King George I's personal relations were better. Dullard he might have been, but he was not totally immune to the charms or strength of character of the Princess whom many contemporaries admitted was attractive and a lively personality in her own right. With her fine skin, fair hair, bright blue eyes and healthy complexion, with heavy but good features, she was undeniably an improvement on his ugly, elderly mistresses. She was far more intelligent than them, and despite her passion for theological argument she was careful not to show off her superior intellect to those who might feel themselves out of their depth with her. Yet she could always get the better of her husband and father-in-law when she wanted. Initially she developed something of an aversion to the earthy, forthright Lord Townshend and his brother-in-law, Robert Walpole, telling the King that he was an old fool to be led by the nose by them. When she found that he soon gave up attempting to understand the piles of documents passed to him for his signature but signed them as a formality, she told him he had become lazy. Taking it on the chin, he told her that he was busy from morning to night. 'Sir, I tell you they say the Ministry does everything, and you nothing,' she replied. 'This is all the thanks I get for the pains I take,' he muttered, changing the subject.

Loath as he was to admit it, the King gradually acquired a grudging respect for her. In his more amenable moods he would take remarks from her that he would not tolerate from anybody else. The feeling was generally mutual, although the Princess hated her father-in-law's mistresses as much as her husband did.

The Prince of Wales was rigorously excluded from any governmental role in Britain and Hanover, and also denied the military command for which he

had proved himself evidently suited. The only semi-official duty he and the Princess were granted was the empty role of receiving foreign ambassadors and deputations who came to compliment the King on his accession. The heir became bored and frustrated at every turn. With his passion for order, regularity and routine, he developed into a domestic tyrant, taking his frustration out on the most convenient scapegoat – his wife. He criticized and attempted to argue with her, but she was patient and understanding enough to take it in good part, knowing that he merely found fault for its own sake.

The closest the Prince of Wales came to participation in, or rather witnessing, affairs of state during his father's reign, was being granted the privilege of taking his seat in the cabinet and privy council. He was however excluded from the 'closet-interview', at which the King gave audiences to individual ministers, courtiers, private petitioners and foreign diplomats. Yet undue importance should not be attached to his attendance at full cabinet meetings. Several Household officials including the Master of Horse, the Groom of the Stole, and the Master of the Wardrobe, were also generally present. No important discussions ever took place at these meetings; their sole purpose was to act as a rubber stamp, or give formal endorsement to decisions made by the cabinet committee, which had generally sat and formulated policy without the sovereign in attendance.

It is a common misconception that King George I never attended cabinet meetings as he could not understand a word of English. When not in Hanover, he was present at sessions throughout his reign. He had a rudimentary understanding of spoken English, though papers submitted to him were generally translated into French. At a cabinet meeting in October 1714 the Prince of Wales spoke to him in French and English, and the King answered him in French. He also sometimes used English phrases when speaking French, occasionally spoke whole sentences in English in conversation, and once annotated in English a memorandum written in English, but probably with assistance. However, that such matters should have been duly noted by contemporaries is ample evidence that he was never comfortable with the language of his adopted country.

He was equally at odds with the land and its customs in general. The first morning after his arrival at St James's, he complained, he looked out of a window and saw a park with walks and a canal, which the servants told him was his. The next day his ranger, Lord Chetwynd, sent him a brace of carp from the canal, 'and I was told I must give five guineas to Lord Chetwynd's man for bringing my own carp, out of my own canal, in my own park.' Soon afterwards he asked Townshend, his secretary of state, how much it would cost to close St James's Park to the public, plough it up and grow turnips there. The cost, Townshend sagely told him: 'Only three crowns, Sir.'

That French was the language most commonly used at court is not surprising, if perhaps ironic in view of the fact that France had been the

enemy of the Grand Alliance during the wars of the early eighteenth century. French had long been traditionally the polite language of society in Europe, and the one in which King George had been brought up as a child. Like the influence of the palace and gardens of Versailles, *la langue française* held sway throughout western civilization of the day. He had corresponded with his mother in French, and she had written her memoirs in the same language. By no means a poor linguist, he spoke excellent Dutch, which he had learnt at an early age, again thanks to his mother. She had a lifelong attachment to the country which had offered refuge to her parents in exile, and through the historic ties between Hanover and the United Provinces he himself had served as a young man under Prince William of Orange against the French.

The Electress Sophie had ensured that after the Act of Settlement in 1701, all younger members of the family were to take English lessons. At eighteen Prince George Augustus was out of the schoolroom, though he had the benefit of speaking English in Hanover with Mrs Howard. While the Princess of Wales was fluent in spoken English she tended to avoid writing it, and generally employed her daughters as secretaries when the need to write it arose.

She was tactful enough to keep her dislike of the King's mistresses to herself. At pains to make a good impression on those around her, she took a keen interest in gardening, and enjoyed regular walks outside. Ever eager to keep her intellect sharpened, she kept the company of learned divines and clerics, and made a special request for the collected works of Francis Bacon. Unlike her husband she read widely, and had a very retentive memory. Even if her knowledge of theology and metaphysics was superficial, and if she gave the impression of being a dilettante – at least to men who despised or feared cleverness in a woman – she could still draw clever men into intelligent and interesting conversation, and immediately earned their respect as well as their friendship. It troubled her not that certain members of the clergy might be disturbed by her willingness to read books expounding views which verged on the heretical. When the Bishop of London thought himself duty-bound to come and see her with an offer to explain anything which she did not understand about the 'established religion', she took it as impertinence. She told Mrs Howard to send him away; why should he suppose that she, who refused to become an Empress for the sake of the Protestant religion, did not understand it fully?

The Prince and Princess of Wales were regular churchgoers. At divine service they followed the hymns, sermons and prayers with becoming attention. Although the English were not over-religious themselves, the Prince and Princess of Wales understood that their subjects liked them to set a good example. After a while the Prince became rather irregular in his attendance, though the Princess regularly attended morning prayers as well as Sunday services.

For several years the Prince and Princess of Wales had been patrons of Handel, who had come to London during the last years of Queen Anne and been appointed court composer. They were regularly seen at the opera and at river fêtes where his music was performed. His operas waned in popularity after their initial successes and he turned his hand to oratorio, resulting in yet greater triumphs.

The theatre also benefited from their patronage. Although advised by censorious individuals at court that nobody with a good reputation could possibly see a play like Thomas Betterton's comedy *The Wanton Wife*, they took the advice of Lady Cowper and thoroughly enjoyed it, finding it 'not more obscene than all comedies are'. Prudishness had no place in the early eighteenth century, and like the upper classes of their time the Hanoverian royal family enjoyed a healthy dose of comic vulgarity. As the King barely understood English, theatre proprietors ingratiated themselves with him by concentrating more on visual entertainments like pantomime and dance, or 'other things which divert the sense more than the mind.'

The Prince's sociable nature and the Princess's vivacity pleased everybody, as did her kindness to others. During the severe winter of 1715, when the Thames was frozen over from the beginning of December until the third week of January, she contributed to the relief of unemployed watermen from her own funds.

The Prince and Princess of Wales made little effort to conceal their distrust of the King's servants. Monsieur Robethon and Baron Bothmer were 'rogues'. Neither Baron Bernstorff nor his niece, Mlle Schütz, were to be trusted. One day the latter asked to borrow Lady Cowper's diamonds to put in her hair, explaining as she did so that she made 'no scruple in borrowing them from you because you are best in your state of nature, and always worse when you are dressed out, your jewels not becoming you'. 'Commend me to the assurance of their foreigners,' was Lady Cowper's retort. The Countess of Buckenburgh said that English women did not look like women of quality, but made themselves look as pitiful and sneaky as they could; that they always held their heads down and looked in a fright; whereas those that were foreigners held up their heads and breasts, and made themselves look as great and stately as they could, and more nobly and more like quality than the others. Lady Deloraine replied that in England, ladies showed their quality by their birth and titles, 'and not by sticking out our bosoms.'[5]

Lady Cowper thought Schulenburg and Kielmansegge 'no better than they should be'. Mrs Howard particularly disliked Kielmansegge, 'who never stuck a pin into her gown without a design', and the Prince of Wales said that she had lain with every man in Hanover.

The Prince of Wales's court soon had a reputation for 'excelling in feminine attractions'. Henrietta Howard was liked and respected by almost everyone. To combine the roles of mistress or friend to the Prince, dresser

and friend of the Princess, and respected confidante and friend of the lively young maids of honour, was no mean feat. The maids of honour were a chattering, mischievous yet good-hearted group. One of the most high-spirited was Sophia Howe, daughter of a natural daughter of Prince Rupert of the Rhine, brother of the Electress Sophie. This royal descent, albeit on the wrong side of the blanket, facilitated her appointment to the Princess of Wales's service. One day she was scolded by the Duchess of St Albans for giggling in the Chapel Royal. 'You could not do a worse thing!' the Duchess admonished her. 'I beg Your Grace's pardon,' was the less than penitent reply. 'I can do a great many worse things.'

All the maids of honour were notorious for their irreverent behaviour in the Chapel Royal, even in an age not noted for its religious decorum, and in which the King himself regularly slept or discussed politics throughout the service. Attendance rapidly increased, with many of the beaux of London coming to see them. So much tittering and ogling went on, particularly during the sermon, that Bishop Burnet complained to the Princess. She apologized for their behaviour and scolded them, but to no avail. There was nothing to be done but to follow his suggestion that their pew should be boarded up so high that neither they nor their admirers could see each other. This drastic solution found no favours with the maids and those who had come to admire from a distance. One of them, Lord Peterborough, commemorated the occasion in verse:

> Bishop Burnet perceived that the beautiful dames
> Who flocked to the Chapel of hilly St James
> On their lovers alone their kind looks did bestow,
> And smiled not on him while he bellowed below.
> To the Princess he went, with pious intent,
> This dangerous ill to the Church to prevent.
> "Oh, Madam," he said, "our religion is lost
> If the ladies thus ogle the knights of the toast.
> These practices, madam, my preaching disgrace:
> Shall laymen enjoy the first rights of my place?
> Then all may lament my condition so hard,
> Who thrash in the pulpit without a reward
> Then pray condescend such disorders to end,
> And to the ripe vineyard the labourers send
> To build up the seats that the beauties may see
> The face of no bawling pretender but me.'
> The Princess by rude importunity press'd,
> Though she laugh'd at his reasons, allow'd his request,
> And now Britain's nymphs in a Protestant reign
> Are box'd up at Prayers like the virgins of Spain.[6]

One of them, the charming though rather plump Mary Bellenden, was offered the privilege of becoming the Prince of Wales's mistress. He sat with her one evening, discussing the advantages that such a situation would bring her, simultaneously counting out a handful of gold coins as if to give credence to the financial benefits which lay in store. She listened with growing impatience, at length exclaiming wearily: 'Sir, I can bear it no longer. If you count your money once more, I shall leave the room.' Unperturbed, he carried on counting, until she gave the pile of money a swift kick and ran out of the room. When he pressed her later, she excused herself from being considered for such an arrangement as she was in love with Colonel John Campbell, Duke of Argyll, a senior member of his household. He gave her his solemn promise that if she did not marry without his permission, he would treat her husband with favour. A few months later she secretly married the Colonel. Far from being offended, the Prince bore her no ill will, and the Colonel remained in royal service for many more years.

Guardian of the Realm

King George I had been on the throne for less than a year before the Jacobites decided to strike. Shortly after the death of Queen Anne, James Stuart issued a manifesto from his base in Lorraine asserting his right to the throne, dismissing his half-sister's successor with uncomfortable accuracy as 'a foreigner ignorant of the language, laws and customs of England'. There were Jacobite riots in London, Oxford, Bristol, Birmingham, Chippenham and other towns. The French government was prepared to cooperate, and allowed the bags of the French ambassador in London to be used for the transmission of correspondence between the Pretender, James Stuart, and his adherents in Britain. Nevertheless his cause suffered from several disadvantages, not least his persistent refusal to abandon his faith or even to give the Anglicans what they considered adequate guarantees for his toleration of theirs; and the Pretender's uninspiring character (although perhaps no more uninspiring than that of King George I himself).

Even so, he had his supporters in England who were not afraid to display their allegiance. On 28 May people wore mourning to mark King George's birthday, wearing their brightest clothes on the following day to mark the Stuart restoration. Bolingbroke arrived in Paris in July 1715, and accepted 'office' as the Pretender's Secretary of State. However his plans and part in the rebellion were probably betrayed by his mistress, a Parisian prostitute incapable of keeping her mouth shut. Rumours of what was adrift reached the ministers in London, and defences and garrisons in Britain were strengthened accordingly.

In September 1715 the Pretender lost his most powerful ally with the death of the elderly King Louis XIV of France. He was succeeded by his five-year-old great-grandson as King Louis XV, and the Regent of France was unwilling to risk a renewal of war in the Pretender's cause. Uncoordinated and badly led risings north of the border and in the Border Counties fizzled out before the Pretender had landed at Peterhead on the Scottish coast shortly before Christmas. He established his Court at Perth, and issued an extraordinarily self-deprecating message to his followers in which he dwelt on the 'constant series of misfortunes' that had fallen to his lot since the cradle, and 'I am prepared if so it please God to suffer the threat of my enemies and yours'. Such words almost accepted defeat as a *fait accompli*,

but nevertheless plans were made for his Coronation in January 1716. However a message from his supporters that English forces were advancing against him threw him into an agony of indecision. With his army slowly melting away, as much due to his lack of leadership qualities as anything else, he accepted that his cause was lost. In February he returned quietly to France.

An uninspiring claimant had left the field of battle before any clash of arms took place, and an equally uninspiring King was the victor, if only by default. The only really heroic figure of importance, the hero of Oudenarde and popular heir to the throne, was kept in idleness on the sidelines. It could have been argued that the King was reluctant to take risks in letting his son and heir be cut down by an ill-disciplined Jacobite army, although he might secretly have welcomed such a fate for the son whom he so disliked. A more plausible explanation lay in his displeasure at the popularity of Prince George Augustus. Some field command could have been found for him in which he would be placed in no danger. At least he would have something of a chance to prove himself, as well as add some lustre, however small, to the Hanoverian cause. Yet King George I did nothing for him, either out of lack of imagination or jealousy.

All the same, he could afford to be magnanimous. In England several Jacobite peers and officers who had taken an active part in aiding and abetting the rebellion were captured by the government. Some junior officers were court-martialled and executed at once, while the peers were taken to London and tried, a few being sentenced to death. The Princess of Wales was sympathetic to the Jacobites, and understood better than her husband and father-in-law the value of showing clemency. She added her pleas to those of the Archbishop of Canterbury, many Bishops, the Tories and some Whigs, that the condemned Lords should be pardoned. Their intervention met with partial success. Only two, Lords Derwentwater and Kenmure, met their maker at the scaffold on Tower Hill, the others being reprieved or escaping from jail with no serious effort made at recapture. King George attracted some criticism by appearing at the theatre on the evening of the executions; but it did not escape notice either that the Princess of Wales had been at the head of those on the side of mercy.

In July 1716 King George I returned to Hanover for six months. He had been impatient to do so ever since becoming King of Great Britain, and would allow nothing to detain him at London any longer. The government had insisted on his remaining in Britain while the Stuarts were still a threat, but after the previous twelve months' events this no longer seemed a matter of urgency. In addition he had the perfectly reasonable explanation that his Hanoverian affairs needed attention. After the defeat of the Jacobite rebellion the previous year, and partly to please the King, Parliament had

repealed the clause in the Act of Settlement which required its consent to the sovereign leaving his royal dominions. Even so, the ministers begged him to forego his journey for a while. They might have argued that he was displaying a sense of bravado in showing the Jacobites that he felt the Hanoverians were confident enough; he might have shrugged and felt that if his throne was so insecure, then he still had Hanover.

But if he was to stay there for a considerable length of time, as he clearly intended to do, it would be necessary for him to appoint a Regent to act as head of state in his absence. He was loath to leave this position to his son, perhaps for the same reason that Queen Anne had refused to have him (until she was dying) or his mother in England during her lifetime – as a focus for discontented opposition politicians. Antipathy between father and son was becoming more evident. They neither ate nor spoke together, did not visit one another's apartments at St James's, or walk together in the park. Only at full cabinet meetings, in chapel and in the Princess of Wales's evening salons, did they come face to face, and even then without exchanging a word.

So far the Prince of Wales had only attended meetings of the full cabinet, called merely to give formal agreement to decisions taken by the cabinet committee. The King absented himself from meetings of the latter body, partly following precedent set by Queen Anne, and partly because of language difficulties. Nonetheless non-attendance weakened his position as he only heard the final results of their discussions. If he went abroad, a Regent could easily insist on full discussions and important decisions being made not in committee, but in full cabinet, under his chairmanship. He would have more power than the King, and might confide ministerial secrets to his friends in opposition. When ministers pressed for the Prince's appointment, in order for the Hanoverian dynasty to retain the confidence of the people, the King suggested that the Prince's powers should be curbed by setting up a Council of Regency.

Lord Townshend declared that there was no precedent for such a practice. With regard to a regency, 'the constant tenor of ancient practice could not conveniently be receded from.' The King therefore decided to leave his son as a sort of caretaker, with very limited powers and the title 'Guardian and Lieutenant of the Realm', an office unknown in England since the days of the Black Prince almost four centuries earlier. It was much the same arrangement as that which the King made for his deputies in Hanover when he was in England. Minor matters could be settled in London, while affairs of greater importance should be referred to him personally by messenger if they could not await his return.

In view of the mutual dislike between father and son, the King's letter of instructions was quite affectionate in tone. It stressed that 'all imaginable regard' would be promised for his recommendations to posts and places,

and for his advice in general; and assurances were made that His Majesty was 'perfectly persuaded that he might without the least risk confide to his son the full and entire exercise of the powers he has reserved for himself, but for the sake of precedence it has been necessary to set an example lest in the future great inconveniences to our posterity should follow.'[1] The Prince of Wales was empowered to preside over cabinet meetings, which would be useful training for his future as King, but he had no control over important appointments such as those to the cabinet, Privy Council, royal household, Treasury, Board of Admiralty, and colonial governments, and he was not allowed to create peers. He could appoint and promote officers in the army up to the rank of Colonel, and in the Guards to Lieutenant, and was granted powers of suspension for all officers and governors of towns, places and fortresses in the kingdom; he could issue pardons in all cases except for those of high treason, and even in these he was permitted to grant respites. Although he was not allowed to give the royal assent to any parliamentary acts or bills without the King's express consent, or take any decisions regarding foreign policy, he could open a parliamentary session if it was thought necessary.

With this the Prince could have no grounds for complaint. What angered him, and made him in the words of the Princess of Wales to Lady Cowper 'all in flame', was the matter of appointing a new Commander-in-Chief as successor to the elderly Duke of Marlborough, who had just been incapacitated by a stroke. The two obvious candidates were General Cadogan and the Duke of Argyll. It was feared by the ministers, particularly Townshend and Walpole, that Argyll, who was the Prince of Wales's Lord Chamberlain and known to have political ambitions, would intrigue against them once the King was in Hanover, and the Prince would undoubtedly support him.

Cadogan was appointed, and Argyll was deeply offended at being passed over. To add insult to injury the ministers asked the King to insist that the Prince should dismiss Argyll from his household. The Prince was furious, believing that the action had been taken to humiliate him. When he protested, the King threatened to send for his brother Prince Ernest Augustus from Hanover and make him Guardian of the Realm instead. At this the Prince of Wales conceded with a display of graciousness which surely masked his real feelings. With that King George left for Hanover, taking his Secretary of State Lord Stanhope, leaving Bothmer to keep an eye on business while he was away and report back to him on all that happened.

Before he left, he arranged for Walpole and Townshend to be personally responsible for the government in his absence. Once he was away, the intrigues began. Encouraged by the Duke and Duchess of Marlborough, Lord Sunderland followed the King with the intention of maligning certain Ministers by suggesting that they were intriguing with the Prince. He had

gone abroad on the pretext of taking the waters at Aix, telling Townshend that his main intention was to persuade the King to return soon. But at Hanover he joined Stanhope, and between them they played upon the King's hatred of his son to the detriment of their rivals in London. Townshend, he suggested, was in league with the Prince of Wales against the King. This appeared to give credence to reports already received from the mischievous Bothmer, who was however probably telling the King no more than what he wanted (and expected) to be told. As a result the King and Stanhope removed Townshend from his powerful position as Secretary of State, demoting him to the Lord Lieutenancy of Ireland.

Robethon told Lady Cowper that the Prince 'only wanted power to displace everybody the King liked, and dissolve Parliament'. Whether the Prince had any such ambitions is open to doubt, but his powers were severely limited.

Walpole reported to Stanhope in Hanover that the Prince

seems very intent upon holding the Parliament, very inquisitive about the Revenue, and calls daily for papers which may lead to very particular informations; and I am not sure they are not more for other people's perusal than his own. By some things that daily drop from him he seems to be preparing to keep up an interest of his own in Parliament independent of the King's.[2]

Though it was easy enough for politicians who wished to drive a wedge between father and son, such interest in state papers was surely no more than a manifestation of the heir's intention to prove himself a conscientious Guardian of the Realm, even if ministers suspected that his daily request for documents might be 'more for other people's perusal than his own.' He was punctilious in attending cabinet meetings, at which he was seen to pay close attention to subjects under discussion. 'By some things that daily drop from him, he seems to be preparing to keep up an interest of his own in Parliament, independent of the King's,' Walpole wrote to Stanhope. 'We are here chained to the oar, working like slaves, and are looked upon as no other.'[3]

Some might resent the appearance of a new broom sweeping clean, and ministers might fear that he was planning to head the opposition to his father's government, but others appreciated the Prince's ready human touch. The King was barely gone, said Lady Cowper, before the Prince 'took a turn of being kind and civil to everyone, and applied himself to be well with the King's Ministers and to understand the state of the nation'.[4]

Meanwhile Princess Caroline was expecting another child, her first to be born in England, and the doctors advised her to move to the country where the air was better. At the end of July the court went from St James's to

Hampton Court, where the Prince of Wales continued to dine in public and see company every evening. Hampton Court was the perfect country palace, with a profusion of avenues and flowerbeds, and riverside walks along the banks of the Thames leading to bowling greens. The Prince and Princess of Wales lodged in the wing built for King William III by Sir Christopher Wren, where a suite of state apartments overlooked the Great Fountain garden and beyond. They slept in the Queen's Bedroom, newly decorated with Sir James Thornhill's imposing ceiling painting of Aurora rising in her chariot from the sea, surrounded by medallion portraits of the King, Prince and Princess, and the absent Prince Frederick.

A few days after their arrival the second anniversary of the King's accession was celebrated with a vast dinner for well-wishers who had come to bring their congratulations to the heir and his wife. It was the start of a brilliant season in which they played host one way or another to most of the neighbourhood, be it a bailiff of Kingston who had been a diehard Tory and Jacobite, but returned delighted with his princely reception and as devoted an advocate of the Hanoverian as any, or ordinary country folk who came to wander through the palace gardens out of curiosity. Princess Caroline often stopped to talk to people, with the same good grace as she might show towards 'persons of the first distinction'. The Prince organized races for girls in the neighbourhood, with gifts of clothing as prizes for the winners, and consolation prizes of ten shillings and a pair of scarlet stockings for the losers, not to mention free biscuits and wine for everybody at the end.

Most mornings, the Prince and Princess would 'take the air upon the river' in their crimson-decked barge, rowed by watermen attired in royal liveries, accompanied by noblemen and maids of honour. Sometimes the oars would be stilled, and the barge would drift downstream as they listened to the music of the Prince's string band or they would stop under the trees, while the lords and ladies sang to them, or the gentlemen at court would recite lines of poetry they had composed in honour of the Princess and her ladies. They dined in public, and the Princess rested afterwards. In the evening she and her husband walked in the gardens, before going to one of the pavilions by the bowling-green to play cards. Many of those at court who accompanied the Prince and Princess to Hampton Court that summer would ever after look back on it as the most pleasant and carefree time of their lives.

Naturally business had to be combined with pleasure. Tories who came to call and pay their respects to the heir and his wife were pleasantly surprised at the warmth of their reception, with Whigs and Tories treated graciously alike. It would be easy to regard the Prince in a cynical light, and suggest that he was not particular about which political party treated him to free hospitality and dinners; it could equally be suggested that he was trying to be mischievous and irritate his father's inner circle at court by fraternizing

with 'the others'. It would do him less than justice to accept that he and his wife knew that they would one day be King and Queen of the whole country, not of one faction, and that the crown should be above party politics. The Whigs were disgruntled at seeing that they no longer held exclusive sway, Walpole complaining that by Michaelmas 'the company here will be two to one of the King's enemies'. He was not alone in fearing Tory machinations that would surely try to widen the gulf between father and son.

Despite the gaiety of the summer weeks, the Princess of Wales felt a pang at the thought of the King seeing her son again. People who had been to Hanover were regularly invited to come and give her the latest news of him and his progress. The descriptions they gave were inevitably fulsome, but the mother who had never ceased to miss him had no reason to believe that they were not being honest with her. There is little doubt that she would have gone to Hanover to see him herself if it had been possible.

At the end of September the Prince of Wales made his first English progress. He dined at Chichester with the Duke of Richmond, one of his father's Gentlemen of the Bedchamber and a natural son of Charles II, and spent the night in Lord Scarborough's house near Havant. At Portsmouth he was treated to a rousing reception by the civic dignitaries and granted a military review, entertained by the sailors, inspected the shore equipment and fortifications, and boarded a guardship and bomb vessel. On his return to Hampton Court he passed through Farnham, where he was greeted by an escort of mounted dragoons, and Guildford, lavishly decorated in his honour.

The Prince and Princess would have liked the confinement to take place at Hampton Court, but the doctors and court officials decided otherwise; by October, they said, 'the days are getting very short and the roads bad for those who have to come and go'. It was a difficult pregnancy and on at least one occasion she was in danger of miscarrying. Her ladies wished 'she would take a little more care of herself', finding her walks too long and tiring for them, and thinking that she was regularly overtiring herself. By the end of October she was pronounced fit enough to travel, and the court left Hampton Court on their barge, back to St James's. At her own request her own German midwife, who had attended the births of her previous children at Hanover and who spoke no language other than her own, was sent for to attend her.

A week after their return to London she went into labour. Her husband sat up all night with members of the cabinet council, awaiting good news. When there was none by the morning, her ladies urged that her physician Dr David Hamilton, one of the leading British exponents in midwifery, should be allowed to take charge, but the German midwife was outraged at what appeared to be an English act of elbowing her aside. When asked, the Prince said he would only consent if absolutely necessary, while the Princess,

unaccustomed to the idea (already fashionable in France) of a man involving himself in such a feminine matter, would not consider it. It proved a long and difficult confinement, and the council took fright when the Princess had a severe shivering fit. They sent her old friend the Countess of Buckenburgh to the Prince with their request that Hamilton should take full charge. The midwife refused to proceed any further or even touch the expectant mother unless she and the Prince promised to protect her against the English 'frows' and high dames who had threatened to hang her if the Princess miscarried. Furious, the Prince of Wales swore he would throw anybody out of the window who had spoken thus, or who pretended to meddle. The courtiers' mood changed abruptly, and Townshend 'ran and shook and squeezed her [the midwife] by the hand, and made kind faces at her, for she understood no language but German'.[5] At last the Princess produced a stillborn Prince, and for a while she was close to death herself.

The Countess of Buckenburgh was highly indignant at the English doctors' treatment of the King's daughter-in-law. She could not understand why they must use instruments before labour pains had started, against the more sensible German usage, and on this interference blamed the end result of a stillborn son or one that did not live long.

The King's prolonged absence added to complications at home for the Guardian of the Realm and his father's ministers. If the Prince was annoyed by the prorogation of Parliament and his subsequent exclusion from anything more than a ceremonial role, the King was irritated by the government's demands for him to name the date of his return or else to increase the powers of his son. In Hanover Lord Stanhope had negotiated an Anglo-French alliance which he wished to conclude, but Walpole and Townshend failed to agree with him; meanwhile Sunderland, another cabinet colleague, was ingratiating himself at Hanover and intriguing against the brothers-in-law. The Prince of Wales was dissatisfied with the continual atmosphere of petty intrigues, and dreaded the effect it was having on the stability of the country. As Guardian of the Realm he appreciated that he was partly responsible, albeit powerless to control the situation.

At least he could make something of his ceremonial role, such as inspecting army regiments in St James's Park, and nominating the Princess's Regiment of Horse for the honour of guarding the King on his arrival home and progress as far as Greenwich. If his love of military pomp and ceremonial was at odds with the unmilitary British, his devotion to public duty and personal courage did not go unnoticed. When a fire broke out at Spring Gardens early in the morning he was prompt at arriving on the scene and helping to put it out, and he sent £1,000 to those who had suffered from another conflagration at Limehouse. When a madman shot at him and killed a member of his suite one night soon afterwards at Drury

Lane Theatre, he remained unhurt and unruffled. The man was arrested
and sent to Newgate. The Prince of Wales, the people said, was 'truly a
guardian', and his high profile at such incidents did more for the
Hanoverian cause in England than his father's absence.

King George returned from Hanover in January 1717. The Prince of Wales
met him at Blackheath, where the King descended from his coach and
greeted him with open arms. This warm greeting was not a harbinger of
things to come, for it was soon evident that the father's attitude towards the
son had not changed. Leaving his beloved homeland with reluctance for the
kingdom he was beginning to regard as a millstone did nothing to improve
his temper, and he was alarmed at learning of a Jacobite plot for 12,000
Swedish soldiers to invade Scotland in which the Swedish ambassador,
Count Gyllenborg, was heavily implicated. The Count was arrested, his
papers were seized from the Swedish Legation in London, and he was
expelled to Holland.

Reports of his son's popularity irritated him still further. Discontented
Hanoverians at court were only too ready to tell their master how they had
been ignored and insulted in his absence while the Prince and Princess of
Wales gave preference to the rascally English. Their progresses through the
southern counties the previous autumn, and such goings-on as his bravery
at the recent attempt on his life, were all presented to the King as attempts
to curry favour with the English at His Majesty's expense. To a less
jaundiced observer, it was evident that the Prince and Princess of Wales
possessed the common touch, and appreciated the importance of making
the dynasty popular. After all, it was only two years since the Hanoverians
had succeeded the Stuarts, who were still a threat and would remain so for
some years. But King George I was hardly a fair judge of such matters where
his son, if not his rival, was concerned.

One of King George I's first actions on his return was to dismiss
Townshend from the post of Lord Lieutenant of Ireland. Walpole and
several other ministers resigned in protest. They had defended the Prince
of Wales's conduct as 'Guardian of the Realm', and when they formed an
alliance with the Tories in Parliament to try and embarrass the government,
the King was convinced that his son was fomenting rebellion by
encouraging them. The seeds of mutual distrust were sown; and everyone
involved would shortly reap the whirlwind.

'I shall find you out'

Much as the idea revolted him, the King realized that there was something to be said for the principle of showing himself more to his subjects. In the summer of 1717 the family moved out to Hampton Court, where he made a point of dining every day in company. The nobility were pleasantly surprised at being invited to sit down at table with him, 'and by his affable behaviour on those occasions'. Meanwhile the Prince and Princess of Wales kept to their own rooms, and rarely saw him except at chapel on Sunday. The Princess was expecting another child, and after her grim experiences of the autumn, she was determined to take proper care of herself and avoid any scenes between her husband and his father.

Such one-upmanship was only part of the increasing dislike between father and son, and the former became ever more intent on asserting his authority. That autumn events took a turn for the worse, due partly to the King's ministers and their lack of scruple in exploiting the situation to their own advantage – namely, by attempting to break the apparent link between the Prince of Wales and the leaders of the opposition in parliament. If a situation might be contrived whereby the Prince would be disgraced, any opposition leaders and other aspiring politicians who had courted him would surely reconsider their allegiance.

On 20 October (OS) Princess Caroline gave birth to a son. The Prince sent a messenger to provide his father with official confirmation of the birth. When the King called to offer his congratulations, the Prince of Wales 'wasted little ceremony' and declined to come and see him. Nevertheless he asked his father and his uncle, Prince Ernest Augustus, to stand as godfathers. Princess Caroline wanted to call him William, and the King assented until his ministers insisted that, since His Majesty was one of the godfathers, the child's name should be George. As a compromise the King suggested 'George William', and sent his Lord Chamberlain, the Duke of Newcastle, to inform them. The Prince and Princess of Wales had never liked Newcastle, and the message was received coldly.

Further ill feeling arose over the question of the other godfather. Prince Ernest Augustus, recently created Duke of York and Albany and Earl of Ulster, was the ruling Prince Bishop of Osnabrück. He was a bachelor, and it was expected that if invited to be the boy's godparent, he might take an

interest in him as he grew up, and perhaps make him his heir. The British ministers said that it was customary for the Lord Chamberlain to be one of the godfathers, and ever prepared to compromise, the Princess asked that the Duke of Newcastle should stand as proxy for her baby son's absent great-uncle. When the ministers overruled her, she wanted the christening to be postponed, but this likewise fell on deaf ears on the grounds that it would not be respectful to His Majesty. Moreover, as he had been unwell a few months previously, it was vital that the ceremony, as well as a short parliamentary session, should be allowed to take place before he departed for Hanover in the spring of 1718 'to take the cure'.

By the time the christening took place in the Princess's bedchamber at St James's on 28 November (OS), the stage was set for confrontation. The Prince and Princess were angry at having been overruled in one matter after another. When the King was ready to leave afterwards, the Prince escorted him out of the room as etiquette required. On his return he took Newcastle aside, treading on his toes as he did so if rumour is to be believed, accused him of having acted dishonestly when arrangements were made, and shook his fist at him, exclaiming, 'You are a rascal, but I shall find you out!' (I shall get even with you).

In his alarm, Newcastle misunderstood the Prince's guttural accent and thought he had said, 'I shall fight you'. He made haste to tell the King incoherently that he had been challenged to a duel. Next day the King summoned a cabinet council, and asked the advice of everyone present.

In an age when it was normal for sons to fear their fathers, such a relationship was hardly unusual. Even so, filial devotion was singularly lacking in this father and son, as it would be in the next generation. Some historians have ascribed the friction to a German characteristic. Lord Macaulay compared the young heroes of Dickens's stories, Oliver Twist in the workhouse and Smike at Dotheboys Hall, calling them 'petted children' alongside the grim childhood of Frederick the Great.[1] Only a few years hence the latter would be compelled by his father, King Frederick William of Prussia (King George I's nephew), to watch the execution of his best friend and be threatened with a similar fate himself. In the more humane nineteenth and early twentieth centuries, there would be equally irreconcilable if less savagely expressed differences between the three German Emperors and their eldest sons. As for the eighteenth century Peter the Great, Tsar of Russia, did not flinch from what his fellow-sovereign in Prussia considered doing; a few years later he imprisoned and tortured his own son and put him to death. What would the King who had confined his adulterous ex-wife for life not do to his son?

Stanhope allegedly advised the King in writing that, while the Prince of Wales was His Majesty's son, 'the Son of God himself was sacrificed for the good of mankind'. Sunderland suggested that Admiral Berkeley would be

prepared to take him on board ship and convey him to any part of the world where His Majesty would order him, so that he would be heard of no more.

A deputation of ministers was sent to ask the Prince of Wales if the allegations were true. Still in an excitable mood, the Prince denied emphatically that he had challenged Newcastle to a duel, for the distance in rank between them made the idea unthinkable. He admitted that he said he would *find* Newcastle, who had often failed in his respect to him [the Prince], and particularly on this occasion when he insisted on being godfather to the baby Prince when he knew it was against his will. He could very well have made some excuse to avoid doing so. Told that Newcastle merely acted as godfather at the King's command (and the Prince must have understood that the Lord Chamberlain could hardly have refused), he answered that he did not believe a word of it. Yet he expressed his utmost respect for his father, and was astonished at how the issue had escalated.

On 2 December the King ordered his son to leave St James's, a command which the Prince would not obey until he had it in writing. The King ordered him to leave the children 'in the royal care', presumably expecting them to stay with their mother at the Palace, and was disagreeably surprised to be told that she had already gone with her husband. Though they were left in the care of the Countess of Buckenburgh, the mother was granted unhindered access to them. However when their father went to visit them without asking permission or calling on his father first, he was forbidden to do so in future without giving notice. When the Prince of Wales appealed to the courts for them to be returned to his care, he was told that according to English law the royal grandchildren belonged to the crown, and the Prince of Wales was duty bound to leave them and their education in the King's hands if so required.

Mrs Howard was astonished to be prevented from entering the Princess's apartments by two Yeomen of the Guard pointing their halberds at her breast. She declared that it was her duty to attend the Princess, but they informed her firmly that she could not pass.

Knowing that her husband's anger was usually quick to pass, the Princess of Wales was anxious to dissuade him from being too inflexible. On her suggestion he wrote penitently to his father, acknowledging 'with due submission Your Majesty's orders' to remain in his apartment until informed of further wishes. Astonished to find his father so angry, he explained that he was shocked by the Duke of Newcastle's action, and was so indignant that he could not but show it. 'If I have been so unhappy as to offend your Majesty contrary to my intention, I ask your pardon, and beg your Majesty will be persuaded that I am, with the greatest respect, your Majesty's most humble and most dutiful son and servant.'[2]

Nearly everyone in political and court circles felt that the King had overreacted, and that the heir's wife was evidently under arrest made the episode more absurd still. Copies of the Prince's letters to his father were printed and widely circulated, and several ballads and rhymes commemorated the quarrel. It was a gift to the Jacobites, ever ready to condemn 'the German rats' and their unfitness to rule over the British.

Even the King's political allies thought he had gone too far. 'This unhappy difference gives a sensible disturbance to all honest men,' wrote the diarist Sir Gustavus Hume, while some of the ministers tactfully explained to the King the provisions of the Habeas Corpus Act, recommending that it would be politic to release His Royal Highness by an act of paternal clemency rather than a judge's order. At length the King was dissuaded from sending them both to the Tower. As an act of clemency he conceded that the Princess, still recovering from her confinement, might stay with her children as long as she neither saw nor communicated with her husband.

To this she retorted that her children 'were not a grain of sand compared with him'; she would stand by him, taking her ladies into exile with her. It was a brave decision, for she had long been separated from her elder son; to be parted from her little daughters and baby son as well was harder still. She 'went into one faint after another as her weeping little Princesses said goodbye.' Angered at being met by a united front, the King denounced '*Cette diablesse Madame la Princesse*' to his inner circle.

The Prince knew there were limits as to what his father could do. He could not be excluded from succession to the throne; his allowance of £100,000 a year could not be reduced, as it was settled by Parliament; and strictly speaking he could not be placed under arrest. Yet the King drew up a paper to the effect that the Prince and Princess should hand their children over to his guardianship, and cease to hold communication with, or to employ, any person or persons distasteful to the King. When the Prince and Princess refused to sign this document, he forbade them to enter the Chapel Royal, and they attended the parish church of St James's instead.

Turned out of the Palace, they sought their own residence. Initially they stayed at Lord Grantham's house before moving to Savile House in Leicester Fields, and subsequently the adjacent Leicester House. An imposing, two-storeyed residence fronted by a large courtyard with fine gardens at the back, it stood on the north side of Leicester Fields, now Leicester Square. Once it had been the home of Elizabeth, the future Queen of Bohemia, the Prince of Wales's great-great-grandmother. All those who were admitted to the King's court were under strict orders not to visit the Prince or Princess of Wales. Peers and their wives, and Privy Councillors, were all warned formally that if they waited on the Prince, the King would not receive them. Foreign ambassadors were likewise told that they must not

visit the Prince of Wales if they wished to call upon the King. Their sovereigns were all sent a report which accused the Prince of using 'very injurious language' to Lord Newcastle.

Not everybody was alarmed by the threat of royal displeasure. Leicester House became a magnet for disaffected politicians, where Townshend and Walpole, prominent opposition Whigs, gathered with Tories on more or less equal terms. They were tempted by the prospect of fine balls, assemblies and masquerades, which had taken the place of dull, formal visiting days. Young men about town could flirt with the attractive young maids of honour. Leicester House's pre-eminence as a centre of London society was promoted more readily by the King's evident distaste for social functions. To counteract this, he soon found himself forced to forgo the habits of a lifetime and make an effort to appear more in public himself, as well as taking large parties to the opera.

As the King was unable to restrict their social contacts, he felt the next best thing was to gain control of the Prince's household and income. Not without difficulty, the Ministers showed him that the Prince's right to appoint his own household, conferred by letters patent, was inalienable. All the King could do was to suggest that his son should surrender £40,000 of his income of £100,000 for the education of his son Prince Frederick in Hanover. To this the Prince of Wales replied solemnly that nothing would please him better than to arrange for the boy to finish his education in England. If His Majesty could arrange this then he, the father, would be pleased to provide such funds as necessary. This was the end of it; he knew that the King would not want two heirs in the kingdom.

However the King continued to keep the Prince and Princess of Wales away from their children in England, the three small Princesses and the baby Prince who were still at St James's. Missing the children desperately, one evening they visited them without seeking prior approval. When they arrived the Princess fainted with shock, while the Prince sat and cried like a child, and they were both unwell for several days. The Prince had a 'feverish inflammatory distemper, with bumps in his face somewhat like a rash', while the Princess's fainting fits and violent pains in the throat alarmed her doctors. Even so their plight failed to move the King, who commanded Newcastle to inform the Prince of his displeasure. In future, he intimated, he and the Princess must always ask personally to see the children, and permission would be granted once a week.

On one visit the Princess demanded to see her daughters alone. Lady Portland replied with a heavy heart that she had His Majesty's strict orders to forbid such a move. At this the Prince flew into such a rage that he would have literally kicked her out of the room had the Princess not swiftly thrown herself between them.

'We have a good father and a good mother and yet we are like charity

children,' Princess Anne said sadly. Surely the King visited them, she was asked. 'Oh no, he does not love us enough for that,' was the answer. When this came to his attention, the King 'diverted himself above an hour in the nursery', and afterwards took care to call on them regularly. But when he was announced one day while their mother was with them, they fled in terror to the next room.

As the eldest child, Anne took on the role of intermediary between parents and grandfather. She sent a basket of cherries from Kensington to her father, and little notes to her mother assuring her they were well. These were passed secretly to the Princess of Wales through her lady-in-waiting Charlotte Clayton. As she herself was not permitted to see the Princess, they had to resort to subterfuge; a helpful servant in the royal household informed her that the Princess would meet her in a garden house at the end of a terrace so that nobody else would see her. Though few members of the household dared to risk the King's wrath, their sympathies were overwhelmingly with the heir, his wife and their unfortunate children who suffered the most. Once his anger had cooled, by the end of January the King had relented enough to permit the Princess of Wales to see them again unconditionally.

In February the new-born Prince became ill. The smoky winter air was blamed, and despite careful nursing his condition rapidly worsened. With the King's permission the Countess of Buckenburgh took him to Kensington Palace, where his parents were told they could visit him as often as they pleased. It was only just in time. The day after he was moved they came to see him together, and stayed with him until he breathed his last in the evening. In the official words of the *Gazette*, 'His illness began with an oppression upon his breast, accompanied with a cough, which increasing, a fever succeeded with convulsions, which put an end to this precious life.' An inquiry was set up to prove that his death had been due to natural causes not connected with the separation from his mother, and a post-mortem established that he had been born with a polyp on his heart. He was buried privately by night in Henry VII's Chapel, Westminster Abbey.

It was scant consolation to the mother to be told that he was too sickly to have had any chance of survival. Public sympathy went out to her, not only in England but also throughout the courts of Europe.

'The poor Princess is greatly to be pitied,' the Duchess of Orléans wrote a few days after the baby's death. 'There must be something else at the bottom of all this, when everything is given a double meaning. They say that the King is himself in love with the Princess. I do not believe this, for I consider that the King has in no ways a lover-like nature; he only loves himself. He is a bad man, he never had any consideration for the mother who loved him so tenderly, yet without her he would never have become King of England.'[3]

A trusted old friend of the Prince and Princess of Wales, Baroness von Gemmingen, had stayed on at St James's as governess to the Princesses. To their mother's dismay the Baroness was dismissed by the King, and Dowager Lady Portland was appointed in her place. However her programme for the girls reassured the Princess of Wales. With her enquiring mind and appetite for learning, she was anxious for her children to be kept similarly occupied. They did not attend school, but had their own tutors. Every minute was carefully accounted for, and a timetable was devised for the children to rise at 7 a.m., say their prayers, wash, dress and have breakfast by 8 a.m. The next hour was spent walking, followed by an hour's reading in silence and another hour of reading aloud. A session of learning by heart followed, then a further hour at prayer before lunch, which also lasted an hour. Diet was plain and simple, with 'few dishes and low-quality roasts served very simply with no spices or dressings'. In the afternoon they went for a walk or a talk about 'sensible things' if the weather was bad, followed by dancing, riding or music lessons, or games of shuttlecock. Before bed the Princesses generally took their needlework and spent an hour with their mother, or occasionally their father.

With the royal palaces of Windsor, Hampton Court and Kensington temporarily forbidden them, the Prince and Princess of Wales had to seek a summer residence elsewhere. They chose Richmond Lodge, formerly home of the Duke of Ormonde, a leading Jacobite who had fled to France and forfeited his estates to the crown, and the Prince of Wales purchased it for £6,000 from the Commissioners of the Confiscated Estates Court, despite the King's efforts to prevent him. Regarded as 'a perfect Trianon' from an architectural point of view, it was small enough to be described as 'a pleasant residence for a country gentleman', and provided a welcome haven from the appalling stench given off by London's garbage-strewn streets in the warmer months. When the Prince and Princess of Wales first went there in May 1718 they found the house overrun by rats, a problem speedily resolved by John Humphries, a well-known 'rat physician' from Dorset. He allegedly collected five hundred rats from the house and brought them alive to Leicester House 'as a proof of his art in that way'. The Pied Piper of Hamelin's skills were evidently not unique.

As the Princess of Wales was expecting another child, she looked forward to this new addition to the family which would help to console her for the last few unhappy months. However she underestimated the effect of the strain on her health, and the excitement of moving house exhausted her further. Three weeks after their arrival at Richmond, a thunderstorm one night brought a large elm tree crashing down outside her window, and a miscarriage was the result.

Like Leicester House for the rest of the year, Richmond Lodge became a

social and sporting centre in summer with which the King could never hope to compete. Large numbers of the nobility came down by road in their coaches, or on the river by barge. Horse racing and picnics on the water took place during the day, while in the evenings there were music, games, and visits to the theatre. Sometimes the Prince and Princess went hunting, going out early in the morning and returning late in the afternoon, after riding hard over rough country. The maids of honour rode to hounds, though without much enthusiasm. Alexander Pope saw something of the trials and tribulations of their existence after dinner and conversation with Mrs Howard and others:

> We all agreed that the life of a maid of honour was of all things the most miserable, and wished that every woman who envied it had a specimen of it. To eat Westphalia ham in a morning, ride over hedges and ditches on borrowed hacks, come home in the heat of the day with a fever, and (what is worse a hundred times), with a red mark on the forehead from an uneasy hat; all this may qualify them to make excellent wives for fox-hunters, and bear abundance of ruddy complexioned children. As soon as they can wipe off the sweat of the day, they must simper an hour, and catch cold in the Princess's apartment; from thence (as Shakespeare has it), to dinner with what appetite they may, and after that, till midnight, walk, work or think, which they please.[4]

The Prince and Princess became very fond of Richmond, and the Princess gave generously to village charities and schools. In later years she often returned there, regarding it more as home than any of her other dwellings.

With the open breach between monarch and heir, Walpole, Townshend and other politicians including Lord Argyll, the Earl of Chesterfield, Lord Peterborough, and Sir Spencer Compton, saw that while the road to office might be through the King's favour, he was an elderly man and the future lay with his heir and the heir's wife. Leicester House and Richmond Lodge became their main centre, with the King and his court a frequent butt of their jokes. Chesterfield declared that the sovereign's mistresses were 'two considerable specimens of the King's bad taste and strong stomach'. As for Kielmansegge, the Princess of Wales said that with her painted face 'she looks young, if one may judge from her complexion, not more than eighteen or twenty.' 'Aye, madam,' Chesterfield answered, 'eighteen or twenty stone.' Less well received was the news that Chesterfield regularly mimicked the Princess behind her back. She warned him that, while he might have more wit than her, 'I have a bitter tongue, and I always repay my debts with exorbitant interest'.[5]

Sometimes the Prince feared that moves might be made to exclude him from the succession. In fact he misunderstood the motives of the King and

his ministers, who intended to separate the crowns of England and Hanover. In 1716 King George had drawn up a will by which both kingdoms would pass undivided to Prince George Augustus, and then to his son Prince Frederick. On the latter's death his elder son would inherit England, and the second son Hanover. This would avoid the electoral dominions becoming a 'perpetual annex' of the crown which, the King believed, would 'be very disadvantageous to the interests of Hanover'.

English ministers foresaw problems in implementing this by Act of Parliament. It would be difficult for the Parliament of Great Britain to legislate for the succession to Hanover. One possibility was to make the succession to the throne of England conditional on the renunciation of that of Hanover. But if the renunciation took place on the King's death before the succession of the new King, there would be an interregnum, albeit brief. The new King could secure the repeal of the Act of Parliament; and any disputes would only play into the hands of the Jacobites.

Although the scheme was quickly dropped on ministerial advice, that the matter was discussed at all only added to the suspicions of the Prince of Wales. He was steadily becoming more popular than his father, and remained a focus for opposition politicians who adhered willingly to a King-in-waiting in the position of being able to promise without having to deliver.

The Prince of Wales might be regarded as the leader or figurehead of the opposition, but the Princess was regarded as its real inspiration. Robert Walpole was its principal mouthpiece in the House of Commons. Despite her initial aversion to him Princess Caroline soon formed a close friendship with Walpole. Temperamentally they had much in common; they were earthy, worldly, and cynical in outlook. They loved the realities and prospect of power, and were content to allow the Prince – whom everybody knew was intellectually and mentally less sharp-witted than them – to enjoy its appearances and remain the figurehead.

The Caroline-Walpole relationship was undoubtedly platonic. Although the Princess of Wales was no prude, even she found the bawdy-spoken Member of Parliament exceptionally coarse, and with his huge stomach, physically repulsive. Lady Cowper alleged that in his efforts to gain influence with the heir to the throne, he 'let the Prince lie with his wife which both he and the Princess knew'. It would not have been impossible, for Walpole was not really in love with his promiscuous, unstable wife. There was much to be gained from both the wife's and the cuckolded husband's point of view in having an affair with one of the most important and potentially powerful men in the kingdom. Princess Caroline knew her husband's ways and weaknesses. Like an oft-cuckolded Princess of Wales in the next century, she always knew that her husband 'always loved me the best'.

In May 1719 King George I went back to Hanover. Before leaving, he had relented sufficiently towards his daughter-in-law to let her spend summer at

Hampton Court with her children. She replied respectfully that she would not go unless her husband was allowed to accompany her. A Council of Regency was established, with no reference whatsoever to any role for the Prince. The Prince and Princess were not even allowed to hold levées or drawing rooms during the King's absence; the King ordered that they were to be held by his small grandchildren. In their disgust at being ignored, they left town at once for Richmond. When the King returned in November the Princess, ever prepared to keep up appearances, magnanimously waited upon him to congratulate him on his safe return, and he gave her an audience, but her husband was not present.

To the government it boded ill for the state to have a King and heir at loggerheads, and ministers were anxious for a reconciliation. More than the Prince of Wales, the Princess appreciated the harm that it was doing the dynasty. Once tempers had cooled she made a point of attending the King's drawing rooms, and by addressing him in public, she forced him to answer her questions, innocuous as they may have been. The Pretender and his court at Rome were encouraged to believe that the English were weary of the Hanoverians and impatient for a Stuart restoration, in which first Sweden and then Spain might be prepared to assist. Though Swedish offers of help receded with the death of King Charles XII, Cardinal Alberoni, the ruler of Spain proved more accommodating, at least until a naval engagement between British and Spanish forces (resulting in the latter's defeat) and a visit to Madrid on which James Stuart proved to be an unpromising ally.

Even so, a united family on the throne was essential in helping to keep the Stuart threat at bay. In the spring of 1718 a youth of eighteen, James Shepherd, had shot at the King on a visit to the theatre. The bullet missed its target by a wide margin, and Shepherd was sentenced to be hanged. Although the Princess of Wales had interceded for mercy on account of his youth, no pardon was forthcoming and he went to the gallows, declaring James Stuart to be his only King.

Ministers did not know that they were witnessing what would become a regular pattern throughout the eighteenth century. In what was virtually a one-party state, ambitious politicians with no immediate prospect of government office under the King had no alternative but to court the Prince of Wales, with an eye to the future. As this opposition increased in size and posed an ever-growing threat to the Ministry, the latter found itself forced to defuse the threat by taking some of the more able, potentially powerful or clever members into the government. At the same time, a *rapprochement* between King and heir would strengthen national stability.

By the winter of 1719 Walpole was a regular guest at Leicester House. Widely recognized as one of the most able members of the House of Commons, he was quick to realize the extent of the Princess of Wales's

influence over her husband, and the importance of gaining her goodwill. Over the last three years she had changed her opinion of him for the better, and admired his political ability. Lady Cowper complained that he had 'engrossed and monopolised the Princess to a Degree of making her deaf to Everything that did not come from him.' When she received the King's compliments on her birthday for the first time for two years, he suggested that she should induce the Prince to write a submissive letter to His Majesty. Blustering, the Prince retorted that nothing would induce him to make any overtures to the King, and he insisted that he should have the Regency again, the right to enter all the royal palaces, his guards, mounted escorts and salutes, as well as the custody of their children.

King George I cared little for the idea of having his son back in St James's, unless he was 'bound hand and foot'. At length the Ministers persuaded the King that if a reconciliation took place, Walpole – and Walpole alone – could persuade the House of Commons to vote sufficient funds to clear the royal debts, by now over £600,000 in excess of the Civil List. As the King spent so little in England, most of it was evidently going to Hanover, or to his Hanoverian mistresses. Ministers argued that a reconciliation would help to restore public credit as well as the popularity of the royal family.

The Prince of Wales was more amenable, particularly as his purchase of Leicester House had left him with debts of around £100,000. He was not too proud to write his father a letter of apology, but to have to live under his father's roof again was too much. At length a compromise was reached by which he would put in an occasional appearance at St James's, a measure which pleased the irascible King as well. If this plan was not cooperated with, the ministers would be prepared to bring in the still mildly pro-Jacobite Tories to government.

Although keen for them to make their peace, the Princess was determined to have custody of her daughters once more. Ever the loyal wife, she was deeply incensed by her father-in-law's behaviour, but she would do almost anything to have them back. 'This will be no jesting matter to me,' she informed Walpole; 'you will hear of this, and my complaints, every day and hour, and in every place, if I have not my children again.'[6] Lord and Lady Cowper, whose opinions she particularly valued, advised her to hold out for the children; if she did not regain them, 'she would never have a faithful friend again nor be thought a good mother'. Walpole suggested that she should approach the Duchess of Kendal, who had more influence with the King than anyone else; 'she was in effect as much Queen of England as any one was.'* The Princess followed his advice, but to no avail;

*Though the comment was made in jest, it was later taken by some to confirm suspicions that Schulenburg was the King's morganatic wife.

the King refused to agree. He had grown attached to his granddaughters, and he seemed to take a perverse delight in wounding the feelings of his daughter-in-law. Driven into a corner, Walpole declared that the King was 'inexorable'; but if she left everything in his hands, all would be well. She wept that she had been betrayed, and the Prince bribed, but to no effect. 'I can say since the hour I was born, I have not lived a day without suffering.'[7]

Nevertheless a letter of contrition from the Prince was drafted with the aid of his friends and advisers. The Prince insisted that it must contain the bare minimum of apology necessary, and give no guarantees as to his future conduct. He would write nothing to the King, he declared, that would tie his hands.

What advantages would the Prince gain from this arrangement, the Opposition Whig Lord Pulteney asked Walpole. 'Why, he is to go to court again', came the answer, 'and he will have his drums and guards and fine things.' Would the Prince be left as Regent in the event of future visits by the King to Hanover, Pulteney wanted to know. 'Certainly not, he does not deserve it, we have done more than enough for him; and if it were to be done again, we should not do so much.'[8] Disgruntled at being excluded from government office despite a recent change in the ministry, Pulteney repeated the conversation to the Prince of Wales, who held it against Walpole for some time to come. He was already having second thoughts, suspecting that Walpole had engineered the reconciliation for the benefit of his own career rather than out of any desire to bring the family together properly again. Lady Cowper shared his view, maintaining that 'they only made the Prince their cat's foot to compass their own ends, since he is thus betrayed into this most infamous way of making peace, without any real benefit for himself and the kingdom.'[9] The King was likewise less than satisfied, feeling that the Ministers had merely pushed him into the reconciliation. 'Did you not always promise to bring me the Prince bound hand and foot, and don't you bring him back without my having power to put any one servant in or out about his person?'[10] he grumbled.

Any further catalyst for making peace, if any was needed, was the illness of Princess Anne. She had smallpox, and for a few days the doctors feared for her life. The shock of their baby brother's death had brought the three sisters closer together, and though King George could vindicate his conduct in the knowledge that his grandson would not have lived anyway, the possibility that a second grandchild might die while under his care horrified him. At once he allowed the Princess of Wales to visit her, though she was forbidden to bring her own doctor or any medicines.

At last, on 23 April 1720, St George's Day, the reconciliation took place. The Prince of Wales's letter was delivered to the King and a message was brought back that the King would see the Prince, who took his chair and was carried to St James's Palace where he was received by the King in his

private closet. The Prince addressed his father with a set speech, expressing the grief he had felt at being so long under his father's displeasure, declared how infinitely obliged he was to His Majesty for this permission of waiting on him, and hoped that for the rest of his life the King would never have good reason to complain of him.

The King was pale, and seemed nervous. According to the Prince of Wales, whose account of their meeting to his wife afterwards was the only record ever made of it, the only thing the elder man said, over and over again, was '*Votre conduite, votre conduite*'. After the interview – if such a one-sided exchange could be termed thus – the Prince bowed and took his leave. The traditional view of matters is that King George I was still cross, irritated, and reluctant to have any part in the reconciliation. To be equally fair to both previously warring factions, the more likely explanation is that he was moved, the Prince was unsure of himself, and perhaps pride made both reluctant to be the first to offer the olive branch. In fact, as the King wrote a few weeks later to his daughter Sophie Dorothea, Queen of Prussia, 'my son's submission . . . would have been better for coming sooner and without the persuasion of the party'.[11] He was convinced that his son had been brought to St James's by Walpole and Townshend, very much against his will, to make peace.

At Leicester House the Princess of Wales could hear a distant hubbub. This was her husband's real triumph. For the first time since his disgrace in 1717, he was being escorted by a royal guard of Beefeaters, and surrounded by an enthusiastic crowd. Yet Lady Cowper noticed how deeply the occasion had affected him. His eyes were red and swelled, as he generally looked 'when he is mightily ruffled'. He then dismissed the company, ordering Lady Cowper to return at 5 p.m.

She duly obeyed; and found the Guards at his door, with Leicester Square full of coaches, the rooms full of company, 'everything gay and laughing; Nothing but Kissing and wishing of joy.' The Prince had recovered his equanimity; and when Lady Cowper was summoned into the Princess's closet to seal a letter to the Archbishop of Canterbury, he embraced her and kissed her several times. The Princess burst into hearty laughter, exclaiming, 'So! I think you two always kiss upon great occasions.'

Meanwhile the King was advised to go and see the Princess, muttering crossly, '*L'occasion se trouvera!*' each time. They met the following morning in the apartments of the young Princesses at St James's Palace, withdrawing into an inner room and remaining together for over an hour. Afterwards she diplomatically told everyone that she was enchanted with his 'mighty kind reception' of her. To Walpole, she confided rather more bluntly that he had been very rough with her, scolded her, 'adding that she might say what she pleased to excuse herself; that she could have made the Prince better if she would, and that he expected from henceforward she would use

all her Power to make him behave well'. Lady Cowper also described, with
great relish, 'great hugging and kissing between the two old and two new
Ministers'. While Sunderland, Stanhope, Townshend and Walpole could put
on a display of unity, walking 'with their arms around one another, to show
they are all one,' this was confined to the chief ministers. The rest of the
two courts were 'like two armies drawn up in battle array'. The Prince
'looked down and behaved prodigious well', while the King glowered.
Walpole, Lady Cowper recorded, had 'undertaken to make the Prince do
everything the King pleases. The Prince knows nothing of this, but thinks
he governs everything.'[12]

This display deceived the public and the Jacobites into thinking that all
was well once more, but nothing had really changed. The King made it clear
that he was indignant at having to receive the Prince, and would not make
any more concessions. He refused to allow them to use any of the royal
palaces, and would not let them come back to live under the same roof as
him. Nor would he part with his granddaughters. Bernstorff told Lord and
Lady Cowper privately that the King might allow them to spend the summer
with their parents, but he would insist on them returning to him when he
came back from Hanover. In fact they remained nominally in the King's care
till his death, though he gradually eased all restrictions until the Prince and
Princess of Wales were allowed to come and see them as often as they wished.
As Lady Cowper wrote bitterly, 'Townshend and Walpole have agreed for
themselves only, exclusively of all the world.' Contrary to their promises, the
ministers did not pay the Prince's debts, which were not settled until he
ascended the throne. Yet at least a formal notification of reconciliation could
be sent to foreign courts, and the domestic quarrel which had virtually
become a public scandal was officially over.

'You English are none of you well bred'

In the summer of 1720, King George and Stanhope left for Hanover. The King hoped to stay for longer than usual, as England seemed in a more peaceful state than ever before; the royal family were more united, albeit superficially; and the Jacobite threat had been reduced, if not entirely eliminated. It proved to be the calm before the storm – the bursting of the South Sea Bubble.

In 1711 Robert Harley, then Chancellor of the Exchequer, had launched a scheme to convert part of the government's short-term debt, created by war with France, into a permanent debt at fixed interest. The holders of a substantial amount of this debt were invited to exchange their securities for shares in the new joint-stock company. In return the government guaranteed interest on the debt taken over by the company, which was granted a monopoly of trading rights in South America to be obtained from Spain when the war ended. It was intended to strengthen the Tory party against the support the Bank of England always gave the Whigs, and to persuade City merchants to support the peace by the prospects of fresh profits from Spanish commerce. The company's trade did not turn out to be the success originally hoped for, and after disappointment with its commercial activities and outbreak of war with Spain in 1718 the directors were ready to extend its scope as a financial corporation holding government securities. A Sinking Fund was established, into which the proceeds of various taxes were paid annually for gradual reduction of the debt. Its success encouraged Sunderland, First Lord of the Treasury, to consider and adopt a scheme put forward in 1720 by the South Sea Company to take over the greater part of the National Debt. The company expected to gain from increased prestige, and from the profit it would make in offering its shares for the surrender of government securities, since the terms on which the exchange was to be made were left intentionally vague.

To obtain parliamentary approval for the scheme, the Company directors distributed shares at nominal prices to ministers, members and the King's favourites, during the passage of the act legalizing the arrangements. The directors could only make a profit and cover these large bribes if the shares

fetched a high price. Company shares began to rise during negotiations with the government. The South Sea Act received the royal assent in April, and over the next few months £100 shares rose steadily, due partly to the Company purchasing stock illegally in the open market and sanctioning loans on the security of South Sea stock. A few individuals made large fortunes, and speculators were attracted with several new companies being formed to cater for the demand.

The Prince of Wales became a Director of the Welsh Copper Company; though Walpole warned him that he was playing with fire, he insisted that as Prince of Wales it was his duty to take an interest in a venture connected with the principality. He resigned after the company was threatened with prosecution in order to avoid implication and subsequent scandal – but not before he had made a profit of £40,000 in the process. By this time, June 1720, Parliament was so alarmed at the number of new rival companies to the South Sea Company that it passed the Bubble Act, making companies without a royal charter illegal. The South Sea Company directors took advantage of this Act in August by applying for writs against four companies, thus alarming the market and precipitating an inevitable decline in the over-valued shares of their own and other companies. By mid-September shares were falling, panic set in, and many people suffered severe losses or came to the brink of bankruptcy, while several banks and other companies closed their doors.

King George I returned in November to a capital in turmoil, but his appearance did nothing to quell disquiet. At the same time Walpole returned from a well-timed holiday in Norfolk. No blame could be attached to him for the proceedings, as he had been in opposition in 1711 when the Company was granted its charter, and in opposition again when it took over the National Debt. Moreover he could count himself a victim as he had lost as a result of South Sea investments, albeit money he could well afford to lose. Yet he saw the political dangers and lack of stability that might follow. A hunt for scapegoats might not stop short of the dynasty itself. The King and the Prince of Wales had been involved; the King's mistresses had been among recipients of shares offered as an inducement to use their influence in favour of the directors' proposals. Even while the King was still in Hanover, it was rumoured that the Prince and Princess of Wales were about to flee the country, or had been advised to, and if they did the Hanoverian dynasty might fall. It was their good fortune that no Germans had been involved in setting the schemes up, and that blame could be laid entirely at the door of English financiers.

Walpole aimed to preserve the dynasty by whitewashing the King; to allow public confidence to recover by minimizing the directors' errors; and to restore whatever could be restored to those who had suffered. As a reward for handling the crisis so effectively, in April 1721 he was appointed First

Lord of the Treasury, in place of Sunderland, and Chancellor of the Exchequer. Less respectfully he was known behind his back as 'the Skreen Master General', for shielding the guilty men involved in the South Sea Bubble. For the next twenty years his mastery over Parliament was unprecedented.*

Another son, Prince William Augustus, was born to the Princess of Wales on 15 April 1721 at Leicester House. Particularly special to his parents after the death of Prince George William, and his mother's subsequent miscarriage, he was always the apple of their eye. Ironically in view of his subsequent career, the doctor in attendance was a known Jacobite. King George expressed particular interest in his new grandson, partly perhaps to continue helping to build a bridge with his son and daughter-in-law, and partly as the child might be King one day should Prince Frederick, still in Hanover, die before his time. That the new baby was named and always known as William, after the trouble surrounding the naming of his short-lived little brother, was in itself a sign of better personal relationships within the family. King Frederick William of Prussia was invited to be godfather, and the Grenadier Guardsmen on parade at the christening were ordered to let their sidewhiskers grow as a compliment to His Majesty. To their irritation, the King never arrived.

At the age of four Prince William started his military career with formal entry as a grenadier in the 2nd Foot Guard Regiment, and was made a Knight of the Bath. In July 1726, at the age of five, he was created Duke of Cumberland, Marquess of Berkhamstead, Earl of Kennington, Viscount Trematon, and Baron of Alderney.

Meanwhile Princess Anne, the talented one of the family, was growing up with 'not a little of her father's arrogance'. Her face scarred by smallpox, and in figure taking after her plump mother, she was less attractive than the blonde Amelia, renowned for her charm, or the even prettier dark-haired Caroline.

Within three years the family was complete. Two more daughters were born, also at Leicester House; Mary, on 22 February 1723; and finally Louisa, on 7 December 1724. When courtiers came to congratulate the

*Robert Walpole was effectively Prime Minister from 1721 until his resignation in 1742, and is generally recognized by posterity as being the first in British history, and a direct consequence of the retreat of the crown under King George I and his son from constitutional initiatives. The term 'Prime Minister' was initially intended as an expression of mild abuse, suggesting that one particular minister was abrogating power to himself at the expense of the King. In the nineteenth century the power of the 'sole minister' increased as a result of the sovereign ceasing to attend cabinet meetings. The office of Prime Minister was officially acknowledged for the first time in 1905, when its holder was granted a place in the Table of Precedence.

father, who had particularly wanted another son, he said a little testily, 'No matter, 'tis but a daughter'. The last birth proved difficult; the Princess of Wales was forty-one years of age at the time, and suffered an umbilical rupture. The trouble was not fully appreciated at the time; she made light of it, but increasing ill health in later life, and death almost thirteen years later, could be partly attributed to this.

The household of the Prince and Princess of Wales during these years of waiting included various kitchen servants and hands, including cooks, scullions and grooms; over forty appointments of a higher social status, with salaries ranging from £100 to £1200 a year, including the Treasurer of the Household and the Master of Horse. Certain appointments were pure sinecures or partly honorific. Gentlemen of the Bedchamber, peers and sons of peers, and Grooms of the Bedchamber, young gentlemen of good county families, were supervised by the Groom of the Stole, receiving £600 and £400 a year respectively for not very demanding duties generally performed in rotation. Gentlemen in Waiting were of equivalent social status but drew smaller emoluments, as did equerries and pages of honour who accompanied the Prince out of doors, riding and hunting.

The Princess had ordinary domestic servants, as well as Ladies of the Bedchamber and Maids of Honour supervised by the Mistress of the Robes. Various officials administered the estates of the Duchy of Cornwall. Despite the number of servants, royal palaces left much to be desired in the way of comfort and hygiene. Ventilation was poor, and owed more to the persistent draughts from broken windows than anything else. St James's was described in 1740 by Baron von Bielefeld as 'a King's lodging-house, crazy, smoky and dirty'. Washing facilities were almost non-existent, while chamberpots were frequently used, by ladies as well as gentlemen, 'amongst a Cloud of Witnesses'. Only later in the eighteenth century were they put into 'closets' for greater privacy.

It was on household appointments that the Prince of Wales's political influence was founded. The unpopularity of the King's court in the aftermath of the South Sea Bubble also attracted some support for the Prince. A less scrupulous heir to the throne might well have taken advantage of his father's low standing in the kingdom, but he behaved with circumspection, prepared to wait his turn. In any case, any open manifestations of a new rift between them would have been meat to the Jacobite cause.

During the King's regular visits to Hanover, his son took no political initiatives. Though he had a loosely comprised shadow cabinet of gentlemen to whom he had awarded the reversion in various offices, he was unperturbed when the leading figure among them, Sir Spencer Compton, accepted the job of Paymaster General to the Forces in 1722. However the Prince seemed to resent Walpole's promotion to high government office,

though the latter remained on friendly terms with Princess Caroline. The Duke of Devonshire, a hunting and drinking crony of Walpole, was also a member of the Leicester House set. It was largely through him that the Prince was kept unofficially informed of government policy and even 'secret' despatches.

In 1723 'young Hanover brave' celebrated his fortieth birthday. With the passing of the years, the Prince of Wales was becoming more and more like his father. Losing the resiliency of youth, he was developing an obsession with regularity and punctuality; everything had to be done at a set time, for no better reason than it had been done like that in the past. While the King visited Hanover regularly, he and the Princess continued to bide their time, holding court at Leicester House.

They retained cool but correct relations with His Majesty, who permitted them no duties and only rare official appearances. The Princess was a regular hostess at his drawing-rooms, and occasionally the Prince went to Windsor for some shooting with the King. He seemed to be mellowing a little in his declining years, and though he still loved Hanover more than England, his German advisers appeared to be losing something of their influence after 1720, in inverse proportion to the increase of that of Walpole, whose efficiency and skilful management of the House of Commons were valued and appreciated by his sovereign. Minister and sovereign spent many an evening in the royal hunting lodge at Richmond enjoying supper together, then talking politics over a pipe and bowls of punch. As Walpole spoke no German and only a little French they conversed mainly in Latin, their sole common language. Later he would say jestingly that he governed the kingdom by means of bad Latin.

Though personal relations between father and son were never warm, and they rarely spoke to each other in public, a slight improvement gradually came about after 1720. The Prince had learnt to live with his father's coldness. It would have been easier to accept if he had been granted more responsibility, but there was no question of his being designated Regent or Guardian of the Realm again on his father's absences in Hanover, or even appointed one of the Lords Justices. The apparent desertion of those whom he had termed his friends and who might have helped him, notably that 'great rogue' Walpole and the 'choleric blockhead' Townshend, embittered him. He chafed in his position of enforced leisure, powerless to side with an opposition largely comprising Jacobites and pro-Stuart Tories.

In addition he became increasingly parsimonious. With a growing family, his allowance of £100,000 a year from Parliament and the £7,000 or £8,000 a year which the Duchy of Cornwall produced did not go far. Rather than add to his debts he economized. His only living establishments were Richmond Lodge and Leicester House. He went to Richmond each year for five months, and during these rural sojourns he never held any parties nor came

up to London, and never invited anyone to stay. As a result, gossips said, 'all additional expenses of cold loaves, firing, diet and candles were saved. His diet [was] so plain and the quality of his roasts and dishes so little and the ingredients for dressing them so little.'[1]

Meanwhile 'England's daughter, darling of the land', becoming ever more portly, busied herself in her intellectual and gardening interests. When not reading or engaged in conversation with the great minds of the day, she oversaw improvements and the planting of new trees in Hyde Park and the gardens at Kensington, St James's and Richmond.

Like her husband she was angry with Walpole, having placed her confidence in him and found he was unable to fulfil his promise of getting their children back to her. It was evident that the 'reconciliation' had been almost an unconditional surrender, with the King gaining far more than his son, as they stayed in his household, under the care of Lady Portland, till the end of his reign. In addition to the free access to her daughters at all times guaranteed at the reconciliation, they were permitted to visit their mother at Leicester House and Richmond Lodge, and sometimes to appear with her at the opera in the royal box. Although the Princesses always retained great affection for their mother, they assimilated some of the contempt for their father freely expressed at the King's court. With the exception of the placid, sweet-natured Caroline, they were inclined to speak of him with a lack of respect thereafter. They liked their grandfather, and enjoyed walking with him around the gardens of Kensington while he inspected improvements in progress, such as the building of new paths alongside the lawns, and rare plants being cultivated in the nurseries for transferring to Hampton Court.

The heir's court was not the lively place it had been. In middle age the Prince and Princess were losing their zest for social life; and many of the various ladies, whose high spirits and mischief had made the court such fun, had left, usually through marriage. Molly Lepel had married Lord Hervey; Mary Bellenden was now the wife of Colonel John Campbell, the future Duke of Argyll. The glory of Leicester House had worn off; the reconciliation robbed it of its attraction as a centre of opposition, and courtiers who had supported the Prince and Princess of Wales with an eye to reaping their reward in the next reign had to admit disappointment.

The elderly King's court was even more dull than before. As a result of the South Sea Bubble many of the nobility, who had lost heavily, retired to their country seats to retrench, and had to give up the pleasures of town life. 'So many undone people will make London a very melancholy place this winter,' Lord Berkeley wrote prophetically in 1720.

Mrs Howard remained the Prince's mistress, and he still visited her apartments punctually of an evening, often pacing up and down outside her doors, watch in hand, if he arrived early. On one occasion Mr Howard went to call at Leicester House to play the part of a cuckolded husband and

demand his wife's presence. He had neglected her for so long, and his boorish behaviour towards her was no secret, so nobody took his complaints seriously. It was believed that the King had sent him, and a crowd gathered outside to come and mock him until he went away in a temper. The Princess of Wales continued to accept the presence of 'my good Howard' gracefully. When her husband became particularly querulous or tiresome, it was a relief to know that other female company was around to take him off her hands for a while.

Otherwise there was little else for the heir and his wife to do but wait for their accession. Neither relished unpleasantness for its own sake, and they were not prepared to cross the King a second time. They attended occasional balls and concerts, and put in an appearance at the Lord Mayor's civic procession up the Thames to Westminster, where 'some Liverymen offering wine to Their Royal Highnesses, they accepted the same and drank prosperity to the City of London, which was answered by acclamations'.

In their enforced obscurity the Prince became fussy, critical and carping. The more philosophical Princess was content to occupy her time with the children and with her reading. Among works she devoured eagerly were Defoe's *Robinson Crusoe*, and Swift's *Gulliver's travels*. She laughed uproariously, Dr Arbuthnot reported to Swift, at the account of the hobbling prince, who wore one heel higher than the other in a country where one party in Lilliput wore low heels but the other high, and the King only used the low-heeled party for his government. She was not in the least offended at the satirical quip about her husband and his supposed Tory leanings. Swift, never one to tug the forelock, met the Princess and told Mrs Howard afterwards that 'every grain of virtue and good sense in one of her rank, considering their bad education among flatterers and adorers, is worth a dozen in inferior persons'.[2]

Although the King still gave his gold and jewellery to Schulenburg and Kielmansegge, as one mark of generosity he gave his son and daughter-in-law an unusual present – a 'wild boy' captured in the forest of Hanover. This creature walked on all fours, ran up trees like a squirrel, feeding on twigs and moss. He would not lie on a bed at night, but sat and slept in a corner of the room. He was carried into the drawing-room at St James's in the presence of the King, royal family and nobility one night. When the Princess of Wales gave him her glove he tried to put it on his own hand, but seemed more pleased with a watch, particularly when it struck on the hour and he held it up to his ear. Not being house-trained, he was soon removed from the company. The Princess entrusted him to the care of Dr Arbuthnot to see whether he could be 'brought to the use of speech and made a sociable creature', but it is doubtful whether the experiment succeeded.

Princesses Anne and Amelia were delicate children, causing no end of parental anxiety about colds, catarrh, bronchitis, swollen neck-glands and

convulsions. At a time when gin was commonly given as a sedative, and when laudanum was an everyday medicine, when bleeding by applying leeches or cutting veins was a popular treatment for a number of ills, the Princess of Wales had an unashamedly modern approach to medical matters. She and her husband refused to accept without question the treatments recommended by the court doctors.

While Edward Wortley Montagu was Ambassador at Constantinople in 1717, Lady Mary sent home reports of how the Turks in their thousands 'ingrafted' smallpox to render it harmless. A minute wound was infected with pus taken from a smallpox sore to produce a mild attack, which gave immunity and had no more than a minute risk of proving fatal. In 1721 she allowed her small son to be inoculated in like fashion by her physician, Dr Charles Maitland, but very few others followed her example. Most doctors in England gloomily predicted dire consequences, and clergymen preached on the ills of meddling with the ways of Providence. The Princess of Wales thought otherwise. Smallpox was a merciless disease; she, her husband and their eldest daughter had been lucky to survive attacks; she had lost her stepfather and stepmother from the disease; Queen Mary, the wife of King William III, had died from it. She begged for the lives of six condemned criminals from Newgate, who had not had smallpox, to be spared on condition they agreed to undergo inoculation. The experiment proved such a success that six charity children underwent the same treatment, and in April 1722 the Princess had her daughters Amelia and Caroline inoculated. The following year Dr Maitland was sent to Hanover to treat Prince Frederick in like fashion. Inoculation became an established practice as a result.

Although affectionate parents, they were never excessively indulgent. One day the Duchess of Marlborough came into Leicester House just as the Princess had been administering healthy corporal punishment to one of her daughters who was lustily roaring her head off. When the Duchess tried to comfort the child and make a fuss of her, the Prince snapped, 'Ay! see there, you English are none of you well bred, because you was not whipt when you was young.'[3]

The Princess ensured that her children's living quarters were run smoothly. Though they were still under the King's supervision, he allowed her more and more say in their upbringing. At the time Mrs Howard was in overall charge; Lady Portland was governess to the youngest, and she was assisted by a French Huguenot, Lady Charlotte de Roucy, who was 'the Princesses' companion'. Mrs Howard organized matters meticulously, budgeting for miscellaneous items such as tuning the harpsichord and food for the pet birds, and keeping them within an allowance of £50 per annum. The mother looked after her daughters' wardrobes, sending regular orders to lacemakers who were paid between £20 and £60 for lace-trimmed bibs,

aprons, caps and ruffles. On special occasions such as birthdays, the children's little dresses and suits were made entirely of lace; older children generally dressed like their parents. For the Princesses, petticoats were spread over hoops, long dresses and coats were made of rich brocade; flowered silk, damask or velvet were required. Prince William had his own small hats and wigs. All the royal children had a new set of underclothes every two years, and the old ones were handed down to the maids. Their shoes, which could not have been very hardwearing, had to be replaced every week, and fans cost eight guineas a year.

Any tendency to arrogance had to be checked, especially in the case of Anne, Princess Royal, who had somewhat exalted ideas of her own importance. One day she blandly informed her mother that she wished her brothers 'out of the way', so that she could succeed her father on the throne; 'I would die tomorrow to be Queen today.'

At the age of sixteen the chance of wearing a consort's crown came into view. King Louis XV of France was anxious to marry, and a betrothal with the Princess Royal of England seemed a good way of helping to reconcile the two countries, so often enemies in the past, on opposite sides of the channel. A marriage contract was drawn up, and matters were virtually regarded as settled until the French court insisted that the future Queen Anne of France should be received into the Roman Catholic Church. Even if her queenly ambitions were enough to make her consider changing her religion, the house of Hanover could be seriously compromised by such a Catholic connection, and no more was heard of the matter.

Servants felt the full force of Princess Anne's character. As a young girl she made a lady-in-waiting stand beside her bed every night, reading aloud until she fell asleep. On one occasion she took so long to do so that the unfortunate lady went to sleep herself in the middle of a chapter. The Princess of Wales deplored this high-handedness, but instead of scolding her decided first to give her a taste of her own medicine. The following night she called Anne to her bedside and asked her to read aloud. When the Princess reached for a chair, she stopped her. 'Read to me standing,' she commanded, 'I can hear better.' The reading began, with Anne pausing from time to time, complaining that she was tired, or her throat was dry. She could have saved her excuses; the Queen said that the reading entertained her, or that she was not yet tired of listening. At last the Princess started crying; she felt very faint. The Queen decided that perhaps she had learnt her lesson, and remonstrated with her for having behaved so badly the night before.

If she was imperious, she was also talented and very clever. At five years of age her governesses had noted that she 'speaks, reads and writes German and French to Perfection, knows a great deal of History and Geography, speaks English very prettily and dances very well'.[4] Painting, embroidery

and fluent Italian were soon added to her list of accomplishments, but music was always her first love. She sang, played the harpsichord, and later composed instrumental pieces. Handel had been appointed her music master when she was eight, a post which he did not accept lightly. Since he had left Hamburg, he said, nothing on earth could make him teach music; 'I make the only exception for Anne, flower of princesses.'*

During his thirteen years as Prince of Wales, Prince George Augustus never visited Hanover. Maybe the King feared that he would attempt to see his mother, still confined at Ahlden. Yet it would surely have augured better for family harmony in the next reign if some provision had been made for him to meet his elder son, Prince Frederick, on a regular basis. The boy had spent a lonely childhood, with no relatives, except his great-uncle Ernest Augustus, and his grandfather who used to visit sometimes. He had no real friends of similar rank, relying mostly on grooms and pages for company. They must have initiated him into good living at an early age, for he was barely into adolescence before his governor was writing to the Princess of Wales to complain of his addiction to drink and cards. She was reportedly more amused than shocked; but with such a distance between them, there was nothing she could have done, short of coming over to Hanover to take part in supervising him herself.

He was the centre of ceremonial, rather precociously presiding over levées at Herrenhausen at the age of nine. His education had been entrusted to a succession of tutors, who evidently did their work well. As an adult he would display a love of the arts quite at odds with his father's philistinism. His health was indifferent during adolescence; he was prone to feverish attacks and recurrent attacks of glandular pain. A diet of asses' milk was prescribed for him, and he was allowed to wear stays strengthened with whalebone, instead of steel which pressed painfully on his nerves. On his eighteenth birthday in 1725 he was appointed an adult's household instead of governors.

During his reign King George I returned to his homeland for the summer seven times, each visit (except the last) averaging six months in length. After 1720 there was little criticism in England; his subjects now accepted them as quite natural. In Hanover he was reportedly a very different person to the dour figure of St James's Palace. Welcomed with enthusiasm 'at home', he went back to his old life of stag hunts, galas and operas so happily, his entourage considered, that he seemed to have forgotten the accident that happened to him and his family in August 1714.

*On his accession to the throne, King George II made Handel an additional grant of £200 a year for his services as music master to Princesses Amelia and Caroline.

As he saw his grandson Frederick from time to time, a close bond developed between them. In 1725 Walpole told the King that unless he brought his grandson over to England, Frederick would never set foot in the country. He believed that the Prince and Princess of Wales were intent on making him Elector of Hanover after his (George Augustus's) death, and nominating Prince William as his successor in Britain. However King George I dismissed the scheme, saying that it would be unjust to do so without Prince Frederick's consent; and, as he was now of an age (eighteen) to judge for himself, the matter could be allowed to rest.

By this time the matter of a wife for Prince Frederick was beginning to concern the King. His views coincided with those of his daughter Sophie Dorothea, Queen of Prussia, a determined woman known disrespectfully to foreign ambassadors as 'Olympia'. Marriage to the ill-tempered Frederick William, who had ascended the throne of Prussia in 1713, had done nothing to alter her opinion – and perhaps even reinforced it – that the house of Hanover was far superior to that of Hohenzollern. The cultured court of Herrenhausen was more to her taste than the barracks-like atmosphere at Berlin, and her insistence on raising their children in the French manner, rather than the German, led to many a scene between husband and wife.

Prince Frederick, the Queen had decided since he was barely out of the cradle, should marry her daughter Wilhelmina; and her artistic, dreamy son Frederick should marry one of his cousins in England, either the Princess Royal, who shared his passion for music, or Amelia, a hoyden who cared for nothing but horses. The idea found little favour with King Frederick William, who angrily told his wife that he would not have a daughter-in-law 'who carries her nose in the air and fills my Court with intrigues as others are already doing',[5] or at the court of Vienna, where the Emperor looked askance at a strengthening of the Protestant alliance between Hanover, Prussia and Britain. Nevertheless King George I proved agreeable. On one of his visits to Germany he came to the court of Berlin and examined Princess Wilhelmina carefully, holding a candle under her nose to see her better and ascertain for himself that she had no facial imperfections. Deciding that what he saw was satisfactory, he told her parents that the marriage should be postponed on the grounds that both parties, aged seventeen and fifteen respectively, were too young. When the Queen of Prussia pointed out that Prince Frederick already had a mistress, her father relented, assuring her that the marriage should take place on his next visit to Hanover in 1727. The Prince and Princess of Wales were not consulted.

Another family matter had assumed a matter of some urgency. In 1725 the Prince of Wales's sister, the Queen of Prussia, was approached by her mother's representative and chief financial adviser, Count Bar, to negotiate her liberty. After all this time, the Queen thought that an amnesty might be

1 King George I, c. 1714, from the studio of Sir Godfrey Kneller. By courtesy of the National Portrait Gallery, London

2 Princess Sophie Dorothea. © Hulton Getty Picture Collection Ltd

*3 George Augustus, Prince of Wales,
c. 1716, from the studio of Sir Godfrey
Kneller. By courtesy of the National Portrait
Gallery, London*

4 Caroline, Princess of Wales, engraving after a portrait by Sir Godfrey Kneller

5 Hampton Court Palace, early eighteenth century

6 Kensington Palace, early eighteenth century. © *Greater London Photograph Library*

7 Queen Caroline and William, Duke of Cumberland, c. 1730

8 Silver medallion depicting the royal family, 1732, struck by order of the King for distribution to foreign princes and others. © British Museum

9 Worcester mug, c. 1759–60, featuring a print of King George II adapted from a painting by Thomas Worlidge. Museum of Worcester Porcelain

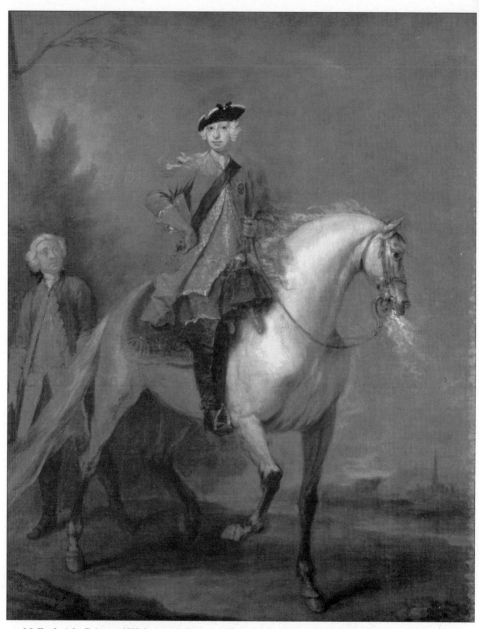

10 Frederick, Prince of Wales, and Captain Thomas Bloodworth, his Groom of the Bedchamber, 1732, by Bartholomew Dandridge. By courtesy of the National Portrait Gallery, London

11 Sir Robert Walpole

12 'The music party': Frederick, Prince of Wales, and his sisters. Left to right: Anne, Princess Royal; Princess Amelia; Princess Caroline, c. 1733, by Philippe Mercier. The setting is the Banqueting House, Hampton Court; an otherwise identical group by the same artist has Kew Palace in the background. The Royal Collection © Her Majesty The Queen

feasible. To her dismay Princess Sophie Dorothea wanted more than her freedom; nothing short of a repudiation of the verdict of 1694, declaring that she had been ill-treated, would suffice. If this was not forthcoming, she would rely on the plans of 'trusted friends' to provide her with her freedom. Fearing a Jacobite conspiracy, the Queen of Prussia sadly let the matter drop, at least until the marriage plans uniting the houses of Hanover and Hohenzollern had been pursued further.

There would be no more chances for Sophie Dorothea the elder, for on 13 November 1726 King George I became a widower. The woman who would have been his Queen Consort died in her castle at Ahlden after thirty-three years of comfortable if lonely imprisonment. Had the choice been left to him, the King would have allowed the news to pass unnoticed. However an emissary arrived in England with an account of her last moments, and with confirmation of court mourning at Hanover and Berlin for the late Princess whose daughter was Queen of Prussia. Reluctantly the King authorized a brief announcement of her death in the *London Gazette*. At the same time he countermanded court mourning at Hanover, and no official notification was made to foreign sovereigns. He forbade any such acknowledgement at the court of St James's, and also expressly refused to let the Prince and Princess of Wales assume mourning or make any public allusion to her death.

On the night of the announcement he defied public opinion by going to the theatre. His defenders at court said that he had looked pale and fidgety throughout the play, to which others retorted that they had heard rumours to the effect that he had been warned of a prophecy that he would survive her by less than a year.

How did the Prince of Wales react to his mother's death? It was said that he had always intended to release her from prison when he ascended the throne, bring her to England and have her recognized as Queen Dowager; and that now she was dead he would have put Leicester House into mourning if he had not been forbidden to do so. Hervey's assertion that he never recalled hearing the Prince refer to his mother need not be taken at face value. Whether he remained indifferent to her fate, or whether he took the sad news like a man and choked back his tears, is not known. But it is difficult to imagine the Princess of Wales receiving the news of her mother-in-law's passing without sadness. She was a kind-hearted woman, and if she believed that Princess Sophie Dorothea was guilty of adultery, then she surely felt just as strongly that the unhappy woman had suffered enough for her sins. It is inconceivable that similar feelings did not penetrate the heart of Prince George Augustus as well.

Maybe the death of the wife who had long since ceased to mean anything to the old King gave him a new lease of life. Within a few weeks he had taken another mistress in addition to 'the Schulenberg', Anne Brett, the

daughter of the divorced Countess of Macclesfield by her second marriage, to Colonel Brett. Perhaps the monarch was more ready to admit to the virtues – or one might say the attractions – of his adopted nation than he was prepared to admit. Evidently keen to feather her nest, and perhaps aware that her elderly beau might not last for much longer, she was soon demanding a title as the price of her favours. He installed her in a suite of rooms at St James's Palace, awarded her a pension, and promised her that she would have her title when he returned from his imminent visit to Hanover.

Accompanied by the Duchess of Kendal – who had apparently accepted Anne Brett, possibly believing the younger woman was only a fly-by-night – and Townshend as Minister in attendance, on 3 (OS)/14 June (NS) 1727 the King left St James's Palace to board his yacht at Greenwich for another visit to Hanover. Some observers thought he seemed more emotional than usual as he said farewell to the family. Others found him in a good mood, looking forward to a series of family reunions. He would see his youngest brother Ernest Augustus, Prince Bishop of Osnabrück; and he would also meet his daughter, the Queen of Prussia, in order to finalize plans for the marriage of Prince Frederick and Princess Wilhelmina. The young Prince had always looked forward to his grandfather's visits to Hanover, and throughout his life he revered the memory of 'a good and great King'. He was looking forward eagerly to the marriage, for although they had never seen each other, he had heard that she was a bright, intelligent girl who shared his artistic interests. His bride-to-be had also warmed to the idea, especially as it would mean escape from an unhappy home life, rendered almost intolerable by the bullying of a mentally unsound, drunken father.

To all appearances, the King seemed in good health and spirits as he crossed the North Sea. On the road to Hanover, as legend would have it, a letter written by his late wife reminding him of the prophecy was thrown into his coach. Next morning he told his suite that he had had a bad night with severe stomach pains, which he blamed on eating too many strawberries and oranges at supper. When advised to rest until he was sure he was well, he insisted that he was fit enough to travel. Later he became pale and fainted, and a surgeon travelling in a coach behind him diagnosed a stroke. Although the King recovered consciousness, he was very lethargic and becoming weaker. The surgeon assured his anxious attendants that the coach's movements would be unlikely to worsen his condition, and there was nothing to be done but make haste to Osnabrück. They arrived shortly after 10.00 p.m. and the King removed his hat in greeting; it was to be his last conscious movement. The servants put him to bed in the room in which he had been born sixty-seven years earlier, but he had sunk into unconsciousness again. Shortly after midnight on the night of 9/10 (OS) 20/21 June (NS), he died.

PART THREE

1727–37

CHAPTER TEN

'The right sow by the ear'

Four days after King George I expired at Osnabrück, the news reached
England. A messenger with sealed despatches from Lord Townshend arrived
at Sir Robert Walpole's house in Arlington Street at midday on 14 June, to
be told that the minister was at his Chelsea villa. Walpole was having his
dinner, but he mounted his horse at once and set off with the despatch for
Richmond Lodge, where the late King's son and daughter-in-law were
taking their customary afternoon nap. As the King's health had generally
been good, they were all taken by surprise, and the man who had just
become King George II was reluctant to believe it at first. Was it some kind
of practical joke? His first reaction, so posterity claims, was a dismissive 'Dat
is one big lie.' Having been summoned from his bed and buttoned up his
breeches, he read the despatch, his face betraying nothing.

When Walpole asked humbly for his immediate instructions, the King
told him curtly to go to Chiswick and take his directions from the Speaker
of the House of Commons, Sir Spencer Compton. Accepting what looked
like a peremptory dismissal as calmly as possible, Walpole bowed gracefully
and retired from the royal presence.

One of King George II's next acts was to order that two portraits of his late
lamented mother, which he had treasured but kept hidden from his
unforgiving father, should now be brought out and hung in a place of honour.

Meanwhile news was spreading throughout the City, as the King and
Queen drove from Richmond to Leicester House. The walls were hung with
purple and black mourning, and the Queen was dressed in black
bombazine. Otherwise there was little sign of gloom; the mood of the
crowds was closer to rejoicing and congratulation. Soon after reaching
Leicester House the new King and Queen held the first court of their reign,
the rooms thronging with nobility and officials, while people arrived keen
to kiss the hands of Their Majesties, professing loyalty and devotion. Still
recovering from their surprise, the King and Queen recalled privately how
their receptions had been so thinly attended at Leicester House during the
previous few years, and must have reflected with amusement on the irony of
the situation.

Most observers were ready to welcome the King as an immeasurable
improvement on his predecessor, although the Jacobites were naturally

disinclined to be charitable. Within a few days the Earl of Strafford was writing to the Pretender of his conviction

that the same violent and corrupt measures taken by the father will be pursued by the son, who is passionate, proud, and peevish, and though he talks of ruling by himself, he will be just as governed as his father was. But his declarations that he will make no distinction of parties, and his turning off the Germans make him popular at present.[1]

Meanwhile Walpole acted as if his days of power were over, and kept up appearances philosophically. 'Everything is in your hands,' he told Compton. 'I neither could shake your power if I would, nor would if I could.' Promising the minister his unstinting support, he said that all he wanted for himself was one of the white sticks, the insignia of Compton's previous office as Comptroller of the Household, or failing that employment of any kind. A shrewd judge of personality, he probably realized that for the time being there was nobody – least of all Compton – who could take his place, and with careful manoeuvring his position would be safe. It was not a foregone conclusion, for he knew that the King had often spoken contemptuously of him to others in the past, believing him too ready to keep on the right side of his father. Yet Compton was regarded by his peers as 'a plodding, heavy fellow, with great application but no talents', least of all the talent required to fill the highest office of government.

Emerging from his first audience with the King, Compton drove back to his residence, Devonshire House. He found that Walpole had finished drafting the King's accession speech, which he immediately copied in his own handwriting. Accompanied by Walpole and other privy councillors, who were to be present at the accession council, he returned to Leicester House to hand it to the King. The latter liked the speech, but found fault with one paragraph and asked for it to be altered. Flustered, Compton had no idea how to reword it, and said he wished it to stand as it was. The King did not take kindly to being opposed, making it clear he wanted it to be changed. Without thinking, Compton rashly asked Walpole to go to the King's closet and see what he could do. As Walpole had written the speech the request was perhaps not an unfair one, but it sealed Compton's fate. Walpole made the necessary alterations, and declared to the King his willingness to serve him in or out of office. Having just demonstrated that he was far more able to deal with matters of state than Compton, all he had to do was play a steady hand and wait.

At the end of the week the court moved to Kensington. The Queen had been been speaking well of Walpole to the King, and suggested he should send for the politician to ask him about the Civil List, which was his

responsibility as Chancellor of the Exchequer. On their meeting the King mentioned such a large sum that Walpole was taken aback, although he did not flinch, still promising to do his utmost to serve His Majesty. Next he had an audience with the Queen, who told him that Compton had proposed only £60,000 for her jointure, thus enabling Sir Robert to outbid him, 'thereby gaining her good grace'. He promised her that he would ask for, and obtain, considerably more. The following morning he went to the King with a Civil List which, he assured him, he would carry through Parliament. The King took him by the hand, said that he had considered the matter, and would permit him to continue in office if his promise could be met. 'Consider, Sir Robert,' he said, 'what makes me easy in this matter will prove for your ease too; it is for my life it is to be fixed, and it is for your life.'[2] At the same time Horatio, Sir Robert's younger brother, Ambassador in Paris, returned to London. Although the King scolded him for leaving his post without appointing a deputy, he was instantly disarmed by a favourable and concise account of Anglo-French relations, and by friendly messages from the court and ministers at Versailles. The Walpole family had wasted no time in consolidating their position at the start of the reign.

At a drawing-room that night, Lady Walpole came to pay her respects to the King and Queen. She could not make her way to the royal dais, for the backs of all the lords and ladies who had previously befriended her were turned on the wife of the fallen minister – or so they supposed. She struggled to get through, and suddenly the Queen caught sight of her, noticed her predicament, and called out, 'There, I am sure, I see a friend!' She was ignored no longer, and commented afterwards that when the gathering broke up, she could 'have walked over the heads' of those who had been scorning her before.

As Walpole put it bluntly to his friends, in having the Queen as an ally he had 'the right sow by the ear'. Only the Chancellor of the Exchequer, it was becoming evident, could manage the House of Commons in such a way as to be useful – if not indispensable – to Their Majesties. When he introduced his proposals for the Civil List at the beginning of the parliamentary session, he declared that King George II should be treated with greater generosity than his father on the grounds that he had a larger family to provide for, and members were reminded that the cost of living had increased since the List was last set. His late Majesty had received £700,000, with an additional £100,000 going to the Prince of Wales. Now, he proposed, the Civil List should consist not only of the £700,000 paid to the late King, but also of £100,000, which had been paid directly to the Prince of Wales in the last reign but which would now be vested in the King to make what allowance he thought fit to his eldest son and heir; and an additional increase of £130,000 arising out of certain funds. The Queen's jointure should be fixed at £100,000, and Somerset House and Richmond Lodge were made over to her.

Only one voice dared to speak against the proposals. 'Honest' William Shippen, a diehard Tory, rose to his feet in the House of Commons to remind his fellow-members that 'that excellent princess' Queen Anne had taken a much smaller List, finding it possible at the same time to make generous benefactions on behalf of her subjects. What she had done so graciously, he said, could be done by her successors. But he found no seconder, and Walpole's figures were voted almost unanimously. Shippen had been sent briefly to the Tower in 1717 for declaring in the Commons that King George I 'was a stranger to our language and constitution'. His frankness had earned him Walpole's respect, and he used to say that Shippen was the only man in Parliament whose price he did not know. Shippen maintained that he and Walpole were both honest men; 'he is for King George and I am for King James, but these men in long cravats only desire place under King George *or* King James.'[3] Once Parliament had passed the Civil List, it was dissolved by the King in person. At once it was seen that he had one great advantage over his father in that he could read his speeches in English.

Walpole had thus carefully worked his way back into royal favour and paved his way for a return to pre-eminence; but Queen Caroline's influence was decisive. Like her husband, she had not cared much for him during the previous reign. Gossips had made her well aware that he referred to her behind her back as 'a fat old bitch'; his own figure, she mused, was hardly slender. Moreover when relations with King George I had been at their nadir, she deplored the Minister's weakness in being unable to secure the speedy return of her children from their grandfather's surveillance. Nevertheless, during the first few days when Compton seemed to be the man of the moment, Walpole had worked assiduously at cultivating a good relationship with her. In personality they had much in common, and she was impressed by the way in which he had kept her informed on public affairs. If it is being cynical to suggest that he was using her as a pawn in the game of safeguarding his own position during the new reign, she was certainly no fool, and any suspicion that he was taking undue advantage of her would not have escaped her. If she had ever had cause to distrust his motives, at the same time she respected his attentiveness, and also appreciated that the country was in safe hands as long as he remained at the head of government. Should her husband attempt to assert his prerogative on coming to the throne for the mere sake of it, and appoint another, less experienced Member of Parliament to take charge of matters, she would be more than prepared to try and influence him otherwise.

The King had promised Compton the chief post, and was reluctant to renege on his promise. Therefore Compton was assured that he was the King's choice, and Walpole undertook to serve under him. When Compton burst into tears, and declared he was not capable of such a job, it was

apparent that the status quo would be restored. On 24 July Walpole was reappointed First Lord of the Treasury and Chancellor of the Exchequer, while Townshend received the seals of the Southern Department. The need for a new general election within six months of the death of the monarch, according to contemporary convention, provided the opportunity for Compton to retire from the House of Commons and move to the Lords as Baron Wilmington, retaining the office of Paymaster-General.

As the King entered excitedly on his inheritance, he naturally took full advantage of his new-found freedom to examine his father's papers, and it was understandable that he should want to settle one or two old scores. Although not vindictive by nature, for almost thirteen years he had lived in a shadow. Among the documents he discovered was a memorandum from Charles Stanhope, Sunderland's private secretary, which had suggested ten years before that the Prince of Wales should be taken and conveyed by Admiral Berkeley to a distant country 'whence he would never be heard of more'. Admiral Berkeley had been one of King George I's favourite English ministers, following a successful naval career with various legal appointments and at one stage First Lord of the Admiralty, but evidence of his collusion in such business could not be overlooked. He was accordingly ordered to resign his offices and retired to the continent, while Stanhope was dismissed from his offices in the royal household. Apart from these, there was no purge of King George I's ministers. Even the once-hated Duke of Newcastle, whose unwitting role at the christening in 1717 had led to the royal rift, was borne no malice and remained in office.

At an early council meeting in the new reign the Archbishop of Canterbury, William Wake, produced King George I's will. Without a word King George II put it unopened in his pocket, and walked out of the chamber. His action seemed rather peremptory, and the councillors thought he was exceeding his brief; some boldly suggested that he did so to avoid payment of his father's legacies. Only later did it emerge that the document also included King George I's scheme for dissolving the personal union of Great Britain and Hanover after the death of his grandson Frederick. The former would go to Frederick's elder son, the latter to his younger. If Frederick was to die without issue, Hanover would go to the Duke of Wolfenbüttel. In addition to the copy produced by the Archbishop, another had been deposited with the Holy Roman Emperor, and a third in the Hanover archives, this one later being transferred to the Duke of Wolfenbüttel in his capacity of executor as head of the House of Brunswick.

Jurists in both territories doubted whether the late King, or any of his successors, could have changed the law of succession in respect of his German estates, and the Hanoverian lawyers held that the will was 'illegal and invalid'. The Emperor had advised that the electorate of Hanover could

only pass from the eldest son by voluntary renunciation. While the British government might favour the separation of both states, it had foreseen constitutional difficulties. King George II's personal position on the subject was open to doubt. He consulted his Hanoverian privy councillors, who agreed with the general verdict that the scheme was not feasible. It was therefore quietly shelved. In suppressing the document and therefore forestalling any further legal argument, the King acted wisely. Perhaps he was doing no more than following precedent, for King George I was said to have destroyed the will of his ex-wife, and also that of his father-in-law the Duke of Celle some years before, thereby doing his son and daughter out of a tidy inheritance.

If the word of his son and his sister is to be believed, King George II behaved similarly with the will of his uncle Ernest Augustus, Duke of York and Bishop of Osnabrück, on his death the following year. Prince Frederick and the Queen of Prussia protested that they would have benefited substantially from his bequests, but Queen Caroline indignantly denied that her husband had done any such thing. All the Duke of York had had to leave, she insisted, was a small inheritance for the King, and his jewels which had been bequeathed and sent to the Queen of Prussia.

The only person who dared to challenge King George II's actions, a few years later, was Lord Chesterfield. The Duchess of Kendal had probably lost more than anybody else by the destruction of her regal protector's will, but she did not complain. Perhaps she was thankful for small (or not so small) mercies, for during his lifetime she had profited handsomely from his gifts of finance, jewellery and other worldly goods, and at least King George II made no attempt to ask her to surrender anything. Her daughter by the late King, Petronella Melusine, a former maid of honour to the Electress Sophie who had come to England with her mother and was created Countess of Walsingham in 1722, was made of sterner stuff. In 1733 Lord Chesterfield married her in the mistaken belief that she had inherited a considerable family fortune. To his disappointment she confided in him that King George I had left her £40,000 in his will but she never received a penny. Out of favour at court at the time, Chesterfield threatened to institute legal proceedings to recover the legacy, but the case never came to court and he was bought off with exactly half the sum. Such a compromise did nothing to make the marriage a success; he promptly took a new mistress and installed his wife in a house next door.

Another casualty of King George I's death was the pre-eminence of Anne Brett. Her rooms in St James's had adjoined those of the Prince of Wales's daughters. When she ordered a door leading from her rooms to the garden to be broken down, the Princess Royal summoned the workmen and told them to block the door up again. Miss Brett lost her temper and had them pull down the barriers, only to have Princess Anne call them back and

restore their work. This dispute might have continued indefinitely had the news not come from Osnabrück. Anne Brett was sent packing at once.

In accordance with his wishes King George I was buried at Herrenhausen, in the Leineschloss Church, close to the Electress Sophie. The funeral did not take place until three months after his death, and his son did not attend, but was represented by his uncle the Duke of York. That King George II did not go to Hanover for the obsequies not only showed a pleasing lack of hypocrisy, but was also commented on favourably in England as proof of his English predilections.

Court mourning ended soon after the funeral, and preparations were made for the Coronation to take place at Westminster Abbey on 11 October. King George II had been bedazzled by the splendour of his father's ceremony, and determined that if anything his should be even more spectacular. Early in the morning the Queen was taken in her chair, attended by Mrs Howard and two other ladies, to an apartment in Westminster, where her servants awaited her. She was dressed in her state robes and ready to meet the peeresses at 9 a.m. At the same hour the King drove in state from St James' Palace to Westminster Hall, and his gracious responses to the rounds of applause from spectators were well received.

A raised gangway had been built between Westminster Hall and the Abbey, and soldiers lined the sides to keep everyone in order. Along this herb-scented platform the procession of peers, peeresses, bishops and knights, walking in pairs, provided a blaze of colour, scintillating jewellery and ornamentation. The jewellers of London had been besieged for days before to meet the demand for precious jewels.

Their Majesties walked under a canopy, the Queen thrusting herself forward to display her petticoat adorned with £2,400,000 worth of precious stones, bought, borrowed and hired. Only a single pearl necklace from Queen Anne's collection had escaped the plundering hands of George I's followers or not been given to Schulenburg and Kielmansegge. The Queen also carried a sceptre and an ivory rod, but she herself declared that 'the weight of the jewelled dress was the worst thing I had to bear'. Her train-bearers were her daughters Anne, Caroline and Amelia, in purple robes of state with circlets on their heads; their coronets were borne behind them by three peers. With her flaxen hair and fair skin, she was a regal figure amongst the procession of gleaming pageantry.

The King was attired in royal robes of crimson velvet, furred with ermine and bordered with gold lace. On his head was a cap of estate of crimson velvet, adorned with large jewels, and turned up with ermine. He was supported on either side by bishops, his train borne by four eldest sons of noblemen and the Master of the Robes. At the great west door of the Abbey the procession was met by the Archbishop of Canterbury, the Dean of

Westminster and other ecclesiastical dignitaries. It proceeded at a stately pace up the nave to one of Handel's anthems.

Once the King and Queen had seated themselves on chairs of state facing the altar, the service began. Archbishop Wake proceeded with Holy Communion, followed by an address from Dr John Potter, Bishop of Oxford. Next the King took the Coronation oath, approached the altar, and knelt to be crowned. As the Archbishop placed the crown on his head, the spectators shouted, trumpets sounded a fanfare, upon a given signal the guns in the Park and Tower were fired, and the peers put on their coronets. Next the Queen was crowned, and they both received Holy Communion. There were also four anthems composed for the occasion by Handel, namely *Let my hands be strengthened, My heart is inditing, The King shall rejoice,* and the most enduring, *Zadok the priest,* all sung by a choir of twelve boys and thirty-five male choristers. Handel had been appointed *Kapellmeister* by King George I in Hanover while he was still Elector, and despite any anxieties he might have had that he would still be welcome at the English court after the death of his patron, King George II was happy to continue the association, appointing him music master to Princesses Amelia and Caroline, as well as commissioning music from him for state occasions.

After the service the King and Queen proceeded to St Edward's Chapel, where the King was arrayed in a vesture of purple velvet, and the Queen retained her robes of state. Still wearing their crowns, they returned on foot to Westminster Hall, followed by a long train of peers and peeresses, all wearing their coronets. The hall was illuminated by two thousand candles in chandeliers. The King and Queen took their seats on a dais at a high table across the upper end of the hall, with the three princesses sitting at one end of the table. The nobility and others invited to the feast seated themselves at tables running down the hall for the banquet, a cold luncheon consisting of 130 dishes. After the first course was served the King's Champion entered to proclaim the challenge and throw down the gauntlet. The Hall was crowded to capacity, and guests who had not taken part in the procession were seated tightly in galleries round the edge of the hall. Many friends and relations of the main diners had come prepared with hooks and pieces of string to try and catch refreshments from the tables below. The royal family returned to St James's before the end of the feast, their departure the signal for an undignified scramble for souvenirs from the hall.

During the evening crowds stood outside the palace, shouting for another sight of the King and Queen, who gladly obliged time after time, waving and bowing as they smiled at this demonstration of loyalty. Firework displays, bonfires, ringing of bells and illuminations testified to the Londoners' mood, on such a night of celebrations as had not been seen for a very long time. Various social functions followed over the next few days – levées at court with men and women eager to pay their respects to the King and

Queen, dances featuring Handel's 'new minuet music', and various theatre productions, including a royal command performance of Shakespeare's *Henry the Eighth* at Drury Lane. The play ended with the coronation of Anne Boleyn, a scene on which the theatre proprietors had lavished £1,000. Fortunately for their extravagance it drew considerable crowds, both those who had been present at the 'real coronation' and those less privileged. The King and Queen came several times with the young Princesses, expressing their approval every time.

The royal family also watched the Lord Mayor's Show, and later that day took part in a banquet at the Guildhall, a sumptuous meal at which 279 dishes were provided at a cost of £5,000. No sum, it must have seemed, was too much to spend in honour of Their Majesties.

'You may strut, dapper George'

King George II's relations with most of his children as adults were frequently strained, and though he was not a particularly paternal man, he often boasted that he was 'well blessed with family'. With a King on the throne, a vivacious Queen Consort, and a family of two Princes (one, admittedly, still in Hanover) and four Princesses, aged between twenty and three years old, the crown assumed a more human touch than it had possessed for many years. Of the five other sovereigns regnant since the Restoration in 1660, none had had anything like a full nursery.

As for the royal parents themselves, they made a striking couple. Though it would be flattery to call the King handsome with his protruding blue eyes and dark red complexion, his friendly, genial manner did much to make up for any physical shortcomings. If his natural pomposity soon reasserted itself, during the first weeks of his reign at least he was affable and pleasant to those around him. The Queen had become fat in middle age, her features somewhat coarsened, but again her affable demeanour compensated for much. Her fair hair still retained the lustre of youth, and her eyes, described as 'keen and intelligent', reflected her character.

On their accession to the throne the King and Queen gave up Leicester House, and the court made St James's Palace its headquarters in London. All the Hanoverian mistresses and favourites who had lived there during the previous reign were unceremoniously turned out. The court always came into residence there a few days before the King's birthday on 30 October, for which loyal courtiers 'made new clothes' to congratulate His Majesty at one of the drawing-rooms, displaying their finery at the ball that night, receiving graceful royal compliments upon their outfits and dancing. Similar festivities regularly marked the Queen's birthday on 1 March.

When the court was at St James's, drawing-rooms were held several times a week, or public days as they were called, and the King and Queen gave frequent audiences and court balls. They attended divine service at the Chapel Royal in state, with the Great Sword carried before the King. They walked in St James's Park, followed by a large suite, the way kept clear by guards, rarely driving out in public unless preceded by an escort. Visits to the theatre and opera were announced beforehand, and their coming and

going always caused a small flurry of excitement. The people loved these sights, and were glad that there was once more a court in London.

The King and Queen also revived the custom of dining in public on Sundays. One large state room at St James's Palace was set apart for the occasion, and at a flourish of trumpets the King, Queen and the royal family entered and sat down to table, surrounded by officers of the household. The courses were served with much ceremony on bended knee, the table decked with magnificent plate, and a band played all the while. The enclosure was railed round, the public were admitted by ticket, and allowed to stand behind the barriers and watch the royal personages eat.

Having been forbidden to set foot inside most of the royal palaces for several years, the King and Queen wasted little time in making a tour of them all. King George I had rarely visited Windsor Castle, finding the grandeur oppressive as well as too steeped in English tradition for the comfort of himself and his German mistresses. George II disliked it as well, and excused himself from going regularly on the grounds that it was too far from London. He went there chiefly to hunt in the forest. On the other hand it appealed greatly to Queen Caroline, and she often stayed there during her husband's absences at Hanover. In one of the recesses of the picture gallery, later the library, she arranged an extensive and valuable collection of china.

They loved Kensington Palace most of all. The muddy roads through Hyde Park made it an inconvenient winter residence, and it always suffered from damp, but its homeliness reminded them of Herrenhausen. Kensington promenades were now revived, the family pacing down the walks between an avenue of bowing and smiling courtiers. King George and Queen Caroline would single out acquaintances for a bow and a few gracious words. He walked very fast with a curious strutting step, while she, taller and stouter, panted behind him 'regal but with increasing *embonpoint'*. The King was an enthusiastic walker; neither frost nor snow would stop him, much as attendants might dread his imperviousness to bad weather.

People were admitted to the gardens by ticket obtainable from the Lord Chamberlain. Alterations had been in progress at Kensington when King George I died, and Queen Caroline entered with enthusiasm on the idea of landscape gardening. With the advice of William Kent and Charles Bridgeman, who had been gardener to the two previous sovereigns, considerable improvements were made. Parterres to the north and east, laid out in Queen Anne's time, were swept away. In their place came the Broad Walk, a small stream which became the Serpentine, and the octagonal Round Pond (originally called the Great Basin), occupied the centre of a semi-circular lawn bordered by trees. From here three long avenues, planted with young trees, radiated into the distance. Gravel was taken from pits in Hyde Park to make the new walks. At first the gardens were

vulnerable to dust from coaches travelling between Kensington and Hyde Park Corner, till in 1735 the Queen had a new road built outside the Boundary Wall.

Bridgeman was paid for his work at the rate of £15 an acre, and earned £2,220 for tending all the royal gardens. Out of this he provided tools, seeds and labour, as well as all new fruit and forest trees. The King paid for structural repairs, tubs and shrubs or trees that grew in them, greenhouse plants and the carriage of the produce. Between 1728 and 1731 Bridgeman was paid an additional £5,000 for new works at Kensington. The Queen always used the Palace as her headquarters during her Regencies when the King was at Hanover. In the gardens she kept a collection of animals, including tortoises sent by the Doge of Venice, and several squirrels.

Richmond Lodge was now the Queen's personal property, and she gave £500 for railing and improving Richmond Green. The court went there for a quiet month every May after the end of the parliamentary session. A small house for banqueting and hunting was built in Richmond Park; enlarged several times, it later became White Lodge. Summer was usually spent at Hampton Court.

At one stage the King intended to build a new London palace, and he commissioned William Kent to design him one. Kent produced a pearwood model for an imposing palace in the Palladian style with grand pavilions and statuary on the roof, similar to Walpole's Norfolk residence at Houghton, and to be built in Hyde Park. The King was pleased with the concept, but on learning the price he suddenly lost his enthusiasm.

Nobody could question King George II's personal courage, particularly on the battlefield; in time he would reveal a certain shrewdness and a vein of caution which generally kept him from making serious errors. Nor could his vanity or pomposity, avarice or temper, be in much doubt. On the other hand, those who knew him thought he had little will of his own. Much as he might scold or contradict his wife in public whenever she was bold enough to express any opinion, in private he always deferred to her. Posterity would record that His Majesty 'was so completely swayed by her in affairs of state that the King may be said to have been merged in the Queen'.[1] Just over a century later, their great-great-granddaughter Queen Victoria and her Prime Minister Lord Melbourne discussed Queen Caroline's 'great cleverness, rigidness, learnedness; of no person succeeding who tried to gain favour with the King by paying court to *other people* than the Queen'.[2]

Yet he was at pains to create the opposite impression. Queen Caroline's mission in life was to manage the King without his being aware of the fact. People must not think they have got a Stuart on the throne, he would say, or they would find themselves mistaken. He claimed that Charles I had been governed by his wife; Charles II by his mistresses; James II by his priests;

William III by his ministers; Anne by her women favourites; and his own father 'by anybody that could get at him'. Who, he would ask with a rhetorical flourish, governed now?

A much-circulated verse, one of many the Queen and Walpole tried but in vain to keep from him, readily provided the answer he did not want:

> You may strut, dapper George, but 'twill all be in vain;
> We know 'tis Queen Caroline, not you, that reign –
> You govern no more than Don Philip of Spain.
> Then if you would have us fall down and adore you,
> Lock up your fat spouse, as your dad did before you.

Someone at court was rash enough to inform him of it, though he would inevitably have met it somehow sooner or later. Distinctly unamused, he asked Lord Scarborough if he had seen it, and Scarborough admitted that he had. The King asked who had shown it to him, but he said he had promised not to tell. The King flew into a towering rage, and commanded him to tell him who had placed it in his hands. Scarborough protested that he had given his word not to betray anyone, which roused the King to greater anger. 'Had I been Lord Scarborough in this situation and you King,' he retorted, 'the man would have shot me, or I him, who had dared to affront me, in the person of my master, by showing me such insolent nonsense.'[3] Not for some months would he speak to Lord Scarborough again. Moreover he was more than unusually short-tempered with the Queen, contradicting her flatly in front of the court whenever she ventured an opinion, snubbing her, pooh-poohing her wishes, and treating her with unusual rudeness. The Queen held her tongue and took it all meekly, realizing that it was done largely for show.

If the King lost his temper, it was rarely for long. Family and ministers soon learnt that his peppery behaviour, his kicking his periwig around the room, and his expletives were more or less routine. His heir was 'a puppy and a knave'; any politician who was out of favour, 'a rascally liar'. Such expressions of disapproval did not necessarily indicate lasting ill will.

His deference to Queen Caroline sprang from weakness, which could be attributed partly to parental influence. From early days his father had bullied him mercilessly and bred insecurity in him, possibly from a well-meant if clumsy paternal desire to toughen the lad and 'make a man of him'. Instead the result had been to exacerbate his uncertain temper. To do justice to King George I, he had been saddened by the breach between them in 1717, and a mixture of pride and shyness on the part of both men had made the reconciliation no more than a partial success. Yet the suspicion still lingers that, in his darkest moments, Prince George Augustus feared that his father would attempt to deny him the succession.

Another explanation is that he recognized his wife's superior intellect and her talent for dealing with people. Much as it wounded his pride (as did the fact that she was taller than him), he was intelligent enough to accept the fact, although he hated anyone to recognize it, and was infuriated that impudent versifiers should dare to make fun of him by drawing attention to the state of things.

Lady Mary Wortley Montagu considered him 'entirely under the government of his wife'. Queen Caroline, she observed rather uncharitably,

> had that genius which qualified her for the government of a fool, and made her despicable in the eyes of all men of sense; I mean a low cunning, which gave her an inclination to cheat all the people she conversed with, and often cheated herself in the first place, by showing her the wrong side of her interest, not having understanding enough to observe that falsehood in conversation, the red on the face, should be used very seldom and very sparingly, or they destroy that interest and beauty they are designed to heighten.[4]

In contrast to his father, his mistresses never had any influence over him, except occasionally Lady Yarmouth in his last years. Queen Caroline was always his greatest love, and his foremost influence. From the early days of his reign, ministers soon learnt that if anything needed the King's consent, Walpole had to be persuaded. He would convince the Queen of the argument, she would speak to the King and convince him that the idea was his, and the minister's recommendation would come back to him in the form of a royal command.

For the next ten years Queen Caroline effectively reigned and ruled, governing the kingdom with Walpole. Queen Regnant in all but name, she regarded Queen Elizabeth as a good example to follow. Yet where Elizabeth Tudor had exercised her power directly, Caroline ruled indirectly through Walpole. Apart from Walpole and Lord Hervey, few realized as much during her lifetime. She had to be careful not to arouse the King's jealousy, for like many weak men in high positions, he relished the outward semblance of authority. As long as he had the show, Queen Caroline had the substance.

She and Walpole soon evolved a system with regard to ruling both the King and the kingdom. Walpole discussed affairs of state with her, and together they planned what should be done. When everything was decided between them, the Queen made it her mission to bring the King round to their point of view. This was usually done in private, but if the matter was urgent, the Minister would confer with the Queen overnight, and next morning when he was summoned by the King, Queen Caroline would time her 'accidental' entry into the royal closet with care. She would immediately offer to withdraw; the King would tell her to stay, and she would take a

chair, occupy herself with knotting, reading or something similar, apparently taking no interest in the conversation. When the King asked her opinion she would say, 'I understand nothing of politics, Your Majesty knows all.' Delighted and flattered, he would press for an answer to his question, and the game would begin. From certain secret signs agreed between her and Walpole, the Queen spoke or remained silent, gave a qualified opinion or expressed herself plainly. It was so skilfully managed that neither the King nor any other ministers who might be present noticed anything. Walpole played with his hat, fidgeted with his word, took snuff, pulled out his handkerchief or played with his shirt frill – all little gestures with their own secret meaning.

Without the Queen, Walpole would never have managed to deal with the King. She would always appear to agree with her husband, even when he announced his intention of doing something foolish, yet she would unfailingly bring him round gently to her point of view. If he took issue with any appointment or plan of Walpole's, the latter would leave the matter in the Queen's hands, and by and by the King would suggest to him the very appointment he had proposed, as if it had been his idea all along.

The Queen's restraining hand worked well on Walpole. He had always been one to argue for the impeachment or exile of his political opponents during the previous reign, or the execution of Jacobite peers. Queen Caroline's policy was to urge mercy wherever possible, and respect freedom of speech in Parliament, and the freedom of the press. She was always careful to conciliate members of the opposition who professed themselves loyal to the Hanoverian dynasty. Her theories about democracy, the popular will and civil liberty had been learnt in her youth from Sophie Charlotte, Queen of Prussia; with such principles and a remarkable gift of tact, she knew how to dissuade Walpole if he should ever persist with any measures which seemed unsound.

The new King's military training had given him a passion for order and routine. He rose between 5.00 a.m. and 6.00 a.m. every morning and took an hour's siesta in the afternoon. The rest of the day was divided carefully between business, pleasure and exercise. Evenings were set aside for cards or his mistresses. While his relationship with Henrietta Howard lasted, every evening at 9.00 p.m. the King went to her apartments, priding himself on his punctuality. If he was ten minutes early, he would pace up and down the gallery with his watch in his hand until the hour struck. Supper was at 11.00 p.m. and bed at midnight.

Shrewd rather than clever, he was indisputably well informed on anything which interested him. Fascinated by foreign affairs, as befitted a German-born King of Great Britain, in an age when such matters were often governed by dynastic considerations, his detailed knowledge of every royal family in Europe was an asset to his ministers. Although it was some years

since he had seen active service, he was still enthusiastic about the army. Talking 'army shop' and reminiscing over military campaigns never bored him (much as he might exhaust company on the subject), and his mastery of regiments, establishments and drill movements was encyclopaedic. It was by his express command that all Guards' reports and returns were sent to him every week. On the subject of promotion in the army, he resented the fact that this was often achieved by purchase, rather than genuine ability. This view was advanced for the time, and did not make him popular with reactionary commanders who saw their control of army matters as their business alone.

Like most Kings he was a stickler for etiquette, and deeply resented the most trifling breaches of convention as a reflection on his royal dignity. As an authority on dress and court ceremonial, such matters as the precise width of gold braid to adorn the coat of a gentleman of the bedchamber, or the number of buttons required for the vest of a backstairs page, assumed an air of importance which courtiers found hard to comprehend. The Queen was content to encourage such petty preoccupations, as they left her free with Walpole to arrange the more pressing concern of governing the country.

In an age when infidelity was the norm, his relationship with his *maîtresse en titre* Henrietta Howard was entirely to be expected. She had been installed in the suite of apartments at St James's Palace formerly inhabited by the Duchess of Kendal. This arrangement, some have assumed, was more a mere formality than a matter of full-blooded passion on either side. Lord Hervey believed that the King's taking a mistress was more 'a necessary appurtenance to his grandeur as a prince than an addition to his pleasures as a man'. No established mistress of a sovereign, said Walpole, 'ever enjoyed less brilliancy of the situation' than Mrs Howard.

Shortly after King George's accession, her husband tried to turn the situation to his own advantage. He ordered her to return to her conjugal duties, and obtained a warrant from the Lord Chief Justice authorizing him to seize her person wherever he should find her. To avoid this she was obliged to remain day and night within the palace. The King's sense of honour obliged him to do what he could to protect her from any kind of assault from her husband. It was an ironic situation, torn between a husband who did not really want her, and a sovereign and lover who was keen to be free of her.

For the palace days of 'my good Howard' were numbered. Other ladies at court noticed that 'somebody who shall be nameless had grown sour and cross' towards her. A more probable explanation lay in her clandestine relationship with another courtier, Lord Bathurst. If this was the case, the King was less jealous than offended at not being kept informed. Increasingly deaf, at length she was too honest to disguise her tedium at the regular prospect of two or three hours closeted with the King.

Although Queen Caroline had long regarded the presence of Mrs Howard as something of a mixed blessing, she was reluctant to see her depart. If she left, the Queen knew, she might be succeeded by someone more ambitious and less manageable. Matters were made more pressing by Mr Howard's threat to seize his wife from Her Majesty's carriage, if that was the only way for him to get her back. At length the King agreed to pay Mr Howard £1200 a year during the lifetime of his brother and heir, the Earl of Suffolk. In return Howard signed a bond by which he promised 'to give her as little trouble in the capacity of husband as he had ever given her pleasure'.

The King and Queen were regular churchgoers, and if indisposition prevented them from attending divine service they received the Sacrament in their bedroom. One morning the Queen asked her chaplain to begin prayers in the room next to her bedchamber. Suddenly he caught sight of the picture of a naked Venus over her fold-stool, and remarked, 'And a very proper altarpiece is here, Madam!' Irritated, she ordered the door to be closed. The prayers stopped, and she asked why. The chaplain refused, he declared, 'to whistle the word of God through a keyhole'.

While King George's command of English was adequate for most purposes, French still remained the main language of the court, as it was at most European courts. When the King or Queen wanted to communicate privately before company or were particularly moved to fury, they would revert to German.

One of the King's favourite pastimes was hunting. In the summer of 1728 he discovered the delights of sport at Windsor, and subsequently increased the stock of game in Windsor Great Park. He also hunted from Hampton Court, where he and the Queen generally spent two months every summer, the King and elder children always riding to hounds, the Queen sometimes following in a coach, Walpole attending regularly, 'clothed in green as a ranger'. Mrs Howard was less enthusiastic: 'We hunt with great noise and violence, and have every day a very tolerable chance to have a neck broke.'[5] Stag hunting was preferred, as King George thought the fox was mere vermin. When the Duke of Grafton told him he was going down to the country for foxhunting, the King told him he thought it 'a pretty occupation for a man of quality, and at his age, to be spending all his time in tormenting a poor fox, that was generally a much better beast than any of those that pursued him; for the fox hurts no other animal but for his subsistence, while those brutes who hurt him did it only for the pleasure they took in hurting.'[6] Princess Amelia, at that time a tomboy of seventeen and the hardest rider in the family, spent much of her spare time in the stables helping to feed and groom the horses.

Hunting apart, contemporaries regarded the court as hardly more lively than in the previous reign. The main indoor recreation was gambling, and most evenings there would be a large quadrille table for adults, and another

where the young people, even young Prince William, would play with the bedchamber ladies at lottery ticket, maybe winning and losing up to £100 in an evening. Maids of honour gambled with the King, until he and the Queen retired to bed. Some found the routine tediously predictable. 'All things appear to move in the same manner as before,' Lady Pomfret complained, 'and all our actions are as mechanical as the clock which directs them.'[7]

By middle age the Queen suffered from gout, and with regular pain in her ankles, she found walking increasingly difficult. Mindful of her husband's impatience with illness in himself and in others, she kept her aches to herself as far as possible. When they were particularly severe she would bravely plunge her hot, swollen feet into a bowl of cold water to reduce the swelling in order to fit her walking boots on and trail obediently round the gardens with him. Augustus II, Elector of Saxony, whom she had known in her youth, sent her a wheelchair which she sometimes used at drawing-rooms when the effort of standing around proved too much.

As Prince of Wales, the talkative Prince George Augustus had been known behind his back as 'Young Rattlebag'. As King, conversation and small talk came to him less easily. Lord Egmont complained that 'His Majesty, knowing his dignity, is careful of what he should not say rather than of what he should.' He 'speaks so very little, and to so few.' He was criticized for 'not speaking to the country gentry when they came to Court, which tries them, and makes them declare they have no business to come there, and so they betake themselves to the discontented party. . . . It were to be wished the King had more affability, and that the sincerity in showing his resentment where he is displeased with his subject's conduct did not prejudice his Majesty's affairs after this manner.'[8] If he found it difficult to chat in a crowd, among his own circle he was still thought to talk too much, and with too little discretion.

Unlike him, Queen Caroline possessed the supreme royal gift of always saying the right thing. To her, it was second nature to inquire after other people's children or their activities, interests and welfare. When guests were invited to dine, she did not shrink back from pointing them out to the servants by name if she felt they had not drunk enough. Her intention was not to force company to imbibe themselves into insensibility, so much as the perfect hostess's belief that a man who was conspicuously sober had obviously spent a very disappointing evening. Yet those who could not hold their liquor could not expect preferential treatment. One man (whose anonymity was evidently respected by posterity) was thrown out from a party for being extremely drunk 'which made him saucy'. The Duke of Newcastle was more fortunate. Somewhat the worse for drink while deep in conversation with the Princess Royal one evening, he had sufficient good manners to apologize to her for his condition next day. She was affability itself, assuring him that he had been charming: 'you have never been so entertaining in your life, I would always see you thus.'[9]

'The knowledge of my dear parents' goodness'

King George I and his son and heir had been separated by a formidable gulf. Between that son and heir, now King George II, and his eldest son and heir Frederick Louis, Prince of Wales, there would be even less love lost. Parents and son had not seen each other since 1714, and had become virtually strangers to each other. For their first seven years in England, the Prince and Princess of Wales had resented King George I's policy of keeping the boy in Hanover, and they had repeatedly urged in private and public for him to be brought over. After the birth of William in 1721 they changed their minds. On this youngest son they lavished the affection which they might have had for his brother, and seemed prepared if not positively anxious for Frederick to stay in Hanover. Walpole had stressed upon the old King the necessity of bringing his grandson to London, and it seemed that his efforts were about to bear fruit once he obtained a tentative decision that the King would bring him back on his return in 1727. King George I's sudden collapse and death put paid to that.

It had also virtually put paid to the marriage plans. Prince Frederick was eager to find freedom and connubial bliss, and postponement of his marriage increased his impatience. Moreover he had always been much closer to his grandfather, the only one who had been able to show any paternal affection for him. Whether King George I had actively taught or merely encouraged the young man to speak out against or despise his parents is open to question. At any rate his mourning for the death of King George I was sincere, as he wrote to his sister Princess Anne from Hanover (27 June 1727):

> I should be lacking in filial duty and the most ungrateful of men if it had not caused me great sorrow, for he treated me with especial affection and friendship. I was so overcome by sadness when they told me the news that I could not leave my bed for two days and fainted twice. My only consolation in this sad affliction is the knowledge of my dear parents' goodness. I flatter myself that I shall always conduct myself in a manner deserving of their esteem and friendship for me.[1]

In his wish to see the marriage negotiations fulfilled there was probably an element of intention to honour his beloved grandfather's plans. Though he had never set eyes on the Princess, he regarded himself as more or less formally betrothed. King George II and Queen Caroline did not reject the idea out of hand, but refused to be bound by King George I's word. They stipulated that their daughter Amelia should marry the Crown Prince of Prussia as well. Queen Sophie Dorothea was eager for her niece to wed her son, but the King of Prussia did not want her for a daughter-in-law, and Princess Wilhelmina shared her father's lack of enthusiasm. From what she had heard of his character and his mistresses, she felt she could do better for herself. Increasingly impatient at the delays, Frederick sent an aide from Hanover to plan an elopement. The operation was to be kept secret, but tongues wagged and an envoy was sent to London to warn the King, who promptly ordered a stop to it. Princess Wilhelmina, he expostulated, had a madman for her father, and he did not think that 'ingrafting my half-witted coxcomb upon a madwoman would improve the breed.' He sent Colonel de Launay to fetch the Prince, who was acting as host at a court ball at Herrenhausen when the Colonel arrived. Although it was a bitterly cold winter night, he insisted that it was the King's command that they should leave for England at once.

Their journey was a hazardous affair. During a blizzard the Prince's carriage slipped off the road and into a frozen marsh, where it broke through the ice. No sooner was it extricated and on its way again before the coachman drove them into thick fog and off a dyke into deep water. By the time the party reached the coast to set sail for England, they were ready for anything. It was just as well, for a full gale was blowing and the boat almost came to grief among swirling ice floes.

The Prince's welcome to England was little warmer. Though he had resented his parents' delay at bringing him to England on their accession, and their refusal to pay his debts at Hanover, he was prepared to forgive and forget. Full of good intentions, he had innocently planned and hoped to please the parents whom he had not seen for fourteen years by an unannounced arrival, which was unavoidable as nobody knew exactly when to expect him. Nobody, and no royal coach, had been sent to meet him, so he had to take a hackney carriage to St James's Palace where he walked to the Queen's back stairs.

Despite an unfavourable report from his tutor in Hanover, the King and Queen treated him reasonably enough at first. He appeared in public from time to time with the Queen, who seemed to take pleasure in his company, and regarded his practical jokes indulgently. The King regarded him with some reserve, until he decided that the young man seemed inoffensive and mild enough. Above all, the Prince did not seem anxious at first to set himself up as any kind of rival to his father, for which the latter was grateful.

To Walpole, he confided that the young man was 'not a son I need be much afraid of'.

Courtiers were impressed by the heir's charming manners and generosity. He seemed more tactful and gracious of manner than his father. Lady Irwin found 'a frankness and affability in his way very different from his rank and very engaging', while Hervey's mother, Lady Bristol, found him

> the most agreeable young man it is possible to imagine; without being the least handsome; his person little, but very well made and genteel; a liveliness in his eyes that is indescribable, and the most obliging address that can be conceived. But the crown of all his perfection is that great duty and regard he pays the King and Queen, with such a mixture of affection, as if obliging them were the greatest pleasure of his life; and they receive it with the utmost joy and satisfaction; and the father's fondness seems to equal the tenderness of the mother; so that, I believe, the world never produced a royal family so happy in one another.[2]

If Lady Bristol genuinely believed this, the King, Queen and Prince of Wales must all have kept up appearances well to give such a false picture to those around them. Alternatively it might be assumed that family differences had not become common knowledge by then. As the son and his parents hardly knew each other, it was only to be expected that his behaviour to them should be deferential yet cautious, and inevitable that the father, being his King, should be overbearing, perhaps even mildly bullying, less out of malice than from a desire to assert his authority.

Prince Frederick was an artistic-minded young man. If he had been less shy and withdrawn, less fond of literature and fine arts, and more of a military caste like his courageous if uncouth younger brother William, he might have found more favour with his father. A skilled viola and cello player, he loved giving concerts to family and friends. He wrote verse in English and French and songs for masques. In private life he shared the usual tastes of young bachelors of the day; he was an enthusiastic womanizer and an equally keen if hardly successful gambler, thinking nothing of losing £1,000 a night, which he often did. Detractors suggest that he never really matured during what was to be a comparatively short life. Nevertheless, the testimony of impartial contemporaries to his charm of manner and bearing suggests that, unlike his brother, father and grandfather, he was at least a gentleman.

At this stage it was clear that his parents disliked him, evidently preferring Prince William, Duke of Cumberland, and his sisters showed him little affection. Fourteen years younger than his brother, William had been petted and spoilt by his parents almost since birth. He had furthermore had the advantage in not having spent his adolescence apart from them, and

thus never been a stranger in the family. The missing thirteen years in Prince Frederick's life created a handicap of understanding which could never be bridged.

At first he was on satisfactory terms with his mother, as long as their father was not around. Before long, though, he came to distrust her. Significantly he always retained respect for his father, who might suffer from a choleric temper but never resorted to subterfuge. His mother was more devious, and relations between mother and son soon soured.

Where the Queen failed in her dealings with him, and how she came to forfeit his respect, lay in her efforts to control and influence him through her devoted protegé Lord Hervey. John, Lord Hervey, was the son of the Earl and Countess of Bristol. Soon after arriving in England in 1714 Prince George Augustus had made him his Gentleman of the Bedchamber. He married Molly Lepel, maid of honour, in 1720, and in the new reign he was promoted to be Vice-Chamberlain to the Queen, and made himself unofficial court jester. Though a married man his attentions could just as easily be swayed by good-looking young men, and after a severe attack of epilepsy he went abroad for a rest cure with a young friend (and probably lover) Stephen Fox, with whom he carried on a particularly intimate correspondence for some years. Pulteney, a former friend of Hervey and later one of his many enemies, called him 'pretty Mr Fainlove', and 'a delicate Hermaphrodite, such a pretty little Master-Miss'. A martyr to ill health, principally poor digestion and a severe gall-bladder condition, this added to his warped nature, but he was a notorious troublemaker and not renowned for faithful friendship. The one exception was Queen Caroline, with whom he remained on the best of terms.

Once the Prussian marriage project was cancelled, or at least held in abeyance, King George II decided that there should be no change to his son's circumstances for the foreseeable future. There would be no need for more grooms of the bedchamber, or other servants, to be appointed to his household. Such steps were taken partly to avoid facilitating his son's contact with the Opposition and prevent him from making a political nuisance of himself. Under pressure from the government, the King reluctantly created his son Prince of Wales in January 1729. Even so, he declared that the young puppy should have no official functions.

Walpole disliked Frederick, as much on political as personal grounds. The Prince of Wales was an obvious enemy, for within the conventions of Hanoverian politics the King's heir was inevitably a focus for the centre of opposition to the King's government. Nor did the controller of the King's Privy Purse, Colonel Schütz, have any great opinion of the heir to the throne. The Prince, he wrote, lacked serious interests. Apart from his numerous mistresses, he had a tendency to be childish, liked flattery, and declared himself familiar with the business of government although he

attended to none. Schütz did however concede that he was 'extremely dutiful to his parents, who do not return it in love, and seem to neglect him by letting him do as he will, but they keep him short of money'.[3] That such praise should come from a man who was otherwise very critical suggests that whatever his other faults, at least the Prince of Wales was a good son.

Not for the first or last time, the heir to the throne was not being treated properly as a King-in-waiting, but instead left to drift with no proper leadership or employment, squandering any gifts he may have had. He certainly did not want to spend his time in total idleness. At one stage he wanted to make a progress through the country, a sensible enough suggestion as it would have given him the chance to see his future subjects and the country at first hand. Presumably jealous of how it would improve his reputation, his father forbade him to consider the idea, 'his popularity having already given offence.' Other heirs after him had sufficient strength of character to make the best of a bad situation; Prince Frederick was less fortunate.

Contrary to Schutz's strictures, he had plenty of interests. His devotion to sport was evident; his interest in the arts was pronounced. At Cliveden he played the country gentleman in fishing and shooting, in village cricket and rowing on the Thames. He was passionate about cricket, teaching his sons, and expecting guests at Kew and Cliveden to join in. He captained the Surrey team for several seasons, though this could have been a tribute to his rank rather than proficiency. In childhood and youth he had sat for a number of minor German portrait painters. Soon after his arrival in England he visited the studio of Philippe Mercier, a Frenchman who had studied art in Berlin. His rococo style, described by Horace Walpole as a 'genteel style of his own with a little of Watteau', appealed to the Prince, who appointed him his Principal Painter in February 1729. His informal conversation pieces marked an innovation in English royal portraiture. His best-known work 'The Music Party' portrayed Prince Frederick on the bass viol, accompanied by the Princess Royal on harpsichord, and Princess Caroline on mandora, with Princess Amelia reading a volume of Milton's poems. In view of the Princesses' antipathy to their brother by the time the pictures were painted, the happy family atmosphere conveyed reveals a certain measure of artistic licence. Even so they marked a change from the grand manner so prevalent in royal portraiture at the time, which generally sought to present the sovereign and his heir as virtual deities. Mercier was also art teacher to the Princess Royal before her marriage, and perhaps to Princess Caroline as well. She drew and painted a number of pictures, some of them copied from Mercier's work.

Over the next twenty years the Prince of Wales also patronized English, French and Italian painters such as George Knapton, Charles Philips, John Wootton, Jean-Baptiste Van Loo, Jacopo Amigomi, and Barthélemy du Pan.

A discriminating and well-informed collector, he acquired several fine Italian, Flemish and French paintings. Although some of the purchasing was done on his behalf by minor artists, craftsmen and designers, they bore ample testimony to his feeling for and serious appreciation of fine art. 'No Prince since Charles the First,' said the engraver and antiquary George Vertue, 'took so much pleasure nor observations on works of art or artists.'[4]

At Cliveden 'the People's Prince' would call in at The Chequers and The Three Feathers for a glass of ale. Many stories were told of his affability with all classes, his readiness to visit the cottages of the poor, listen patiently to their tales and experiences, and 'partake with relish of their humble fare'. He would walk the streets on his own with no apparent fear for his safety, or attend Bartholomew Fair by torchlight, with a party of Yeomen of the Guard clearing the way; then several more bearing flambeaux and flanking the procession, and then appear 'dressed in a ruby coloured frock coat very richly guarded with gold lace, and having his long, flowing hair curiously curled over his forehead and at the sides with a very large bag and courtly queue behind'.

At first Hervey and the Prince of Wales were good friends. The Prince became godfather to Hervey's third son, born in August 1730. They shared literary aspirations, although enthusiasm exceeded ability. A joint collaboration on a comic drama, under the pseudonym of Captain Bodkin, was staged at Drury Lane in October 1731. The theatre's actor-manager, unaware of the authors' real identity, observed with restraint that 'if the two last acts, which he had not seen, were exceeding better than the first three, which he had, the play might last one night'. The paying public were even less impressed. Although the management had had the forethought to place soldiers in the gallery to maintain order, the audience made their feelings noisily evident. Once order was restored, one ebullient gentleman stood up and addressed the assembled company, asserting that 'the highest power on earth could not force the free-born subjects of England to approve of nonsense'. The audience had their money refunded, and a second performance went off peacefully, but it proved to be the last. It was also the last attempt of 'Captain Bodkin' at writing drama.

At about that time they also shared a mistress, another joint venture which proved to be the undoing of their friendship. One of Hervey's mistresses was a Miss Anne Vane, or 'Vanella', described by Horace Walpole as 'a Maid of Honour who was willing to cease to be so – at the first opportunity'. Vanella fell in love with the Prince, a liaison which Hervey initially condoned, perhaps in the hope that she would obtain and pass on to him useful secrets about the heir to the throne. Evidently drunk with his sense of power, Hervey sent the Prince a rhyming, rather ribald letter about the Queen and the Princesses. Though he might have his private differences with his mother and sisters, the Prince rightly resented such impertinence from a man who, though he might be a close friend, owed

almost everything he had to his position as a member of the royal household.

Shortly after Christmas 1731, by which time Vanella was expecting a child, the Prince took another political adviser, George Bubb Dodington. Hervey found himself treated with increasing coldness. He reproached Anne Vane in an angry letter sent through a third party, 'upbraiding her with the ill-services she did with the Prince, and if she did not repair them he would discover what he knew of her and use her as she deserved'. Bitterly upset, she complained to the Prince. After that Frederick and Hervey were enemies. Snubbed by the heir to the throne (for which he only had himself to blame), and denied the comforts of one of his mistresses, Hervey's pride was hurt. Even the King, Queen and Walpole were angry with him, and considered that he had ill-used his former mistress. Not for several months was he restored to favour at court.

In June 1732 Anne Vane gave birth to a son, named FitzFrederick Vane. The Prince of Wales thought he was the father, though Hervey or Lord Harrington, with whom she had also had an affair, might equally have claimed paternity. At the same time, it was believed that she fanned the Prince's latent resentment against his parents.

The reputation of Prince Frederick was done incalculable harm by the destruction of the pages of Hervey's memoirs which dealt with his short-lived friendship with the Prince. It did not help Frederick's reputation that Hervey was high in the Queen's estimation, and also a friend of Walpole. He never hesitated to use his position as an unseen power in the land to further his feud against the hapless Prince. His prowess as a writer of letters and memoirs was vigorously expended in chronicling life at the court of King George II, but his malice at the expense of King and Prince has not boded well for the historical reputation of either.

The stage was set for another lengthy spell of conflict between King and heir. While some contemporaries might share the verdict on the Prince of Wales of Lord Hervey (the last person to be relied on as an objective witness) as 'false . . . never having the least hesitation in telling any lie that served his present purpose', others were impressed by his affability and friendliness.

Not surprisingly Prince Frederick was soon drawn into the political opposition of the day. Soon after his arrival in England he had been introduced to Bolingbroke, who no longer held office in public life or parliament; impeached and attainted for his part in a Jacobite conspiracy, he had fled the country in 1715 but later purchased a pardon for £12,000 from Schulenburg. Though now living in France, he returned briefly once a year to England to keep himself acquainted with political affairs. He still cherished hopes of recruiting young politicians for a 'Country Party', its objective being a national non-partisan government which would reform

and reconstruct the state under a 'Patriot King' with himself as the power behind the throne. Though officially in disgrace with the crown and government of the day, he still wielded the indefinable aura of the elder statesman, particularly to a young Prince of Wales who was eager to learn what he could.

They took an immediate liking to each other. At their first meeting Bolingbroke slipped, and the Prince caught him as he fell, saying as he helped him to his feet, 'My Lord, I trust this may be an omen of my succeeding in raising your fortunes'. In the course of conversation, the Prince was soon dazzled into believing that Walpole and his allies were intent on overthrowing the British constitution, and that it was the duty of the opposition – dissident Tories and disenchanted Whigs – to defend the causes of honour and liberty by forming a national government. A bored or discontented heir to the throne who saw himself as the figurehead of parliamentary opposition, King George II and Walpole knew, need not be feared, but had to be watched all the same.

In May 1729 the King ventured back to the ancestral home for a *Hanoverreise* for six months, taking Lord Townshend as minister in attendance and a large retinue. Three days before his departure he gave the royal assent to the Act of Regency for Queen Caroline. He had not left England since his arrival in 1714, and by returning to Hanover he forfeited much of the popularity which had been his in the first months of his reign. Whereas he had once been voluble in his praise of England and all things English, it was now evident that he had only done so in opposition to his father, whom with age he increasingly resembled. The people hoped they had heard the last of these visits across the North Sea, but the new King was obviously going to follow the family tradition.

Once he was there, one matter had to be settled as privately as possible. The previous year his sister, the Queen of Prussia, had written to point out bitterly that neither of them could ever have persuaded their father to let their mother leave Ahlden. Soon after reaching Herrenhausen he sent for his mother's papers, including letters seized from Königsmarck's desk, went through them carefully, and had them burnt. He never spoke of his mother again. Did he believe in her innocence, and was he filled with regret that it was too late to do her justice? Or was he convinced of her adultery, sadly disillusioned, and aware that his father had been right after all? In later years, it is said, albeit on the none too reliable evidence of Walpole's grandson Horace, his attitude to the memory of his mother had undergone a profound change as a result of reading these documents. Lord Hervey likewise found him at times of tension – and subsequent talkativeness – voluble on his own past and on the difficult relationship with his father, but silent about his mother.

At Hanover, as in England, the King followed a strict routine, or in the words of one of his retinue:

> our life is as uniform as that of a monastery. Every morning at eleven and every evening at six we drive in the heat to Herrenhausen through an enormous linden avenue; and twice a day cover our coats and coaches with dust. In the King's society there is never the least change. At table, and at cards, he sees always the same faces, and at the end of the game retires into his chamber. Twice a week there is a French theatre; the other days there is a play in the gallery. In this way, were the King always to stop in Hanover, one could take a ten years' calendar of his proceedings, and settle beforehand what his time of business, meals, and pleasure would be.[5]

While he was away the dispute with King Frederick William of Prussia came to a head. The King of Prussia had always resented King George's marriage to Caroline, as he had once been a suitor for her hand. Bad-tempered and vicious, he regularly beat his wife and children. King George despised him for his violent behaviour, even though he did not particularly like the Queen of Prussia, his own sister. Both Kings gave each other contemptuous nicknames; King George was 'the comedian' or 'my brother the dancing master', while King Frederick William was 'the Archbeadle of the Holy Roman Empire', or 'my brother the drill sergeant'. King Frederick William claimed King George had swindled his own sister out of her rightful share of their father's inheritance; and when Prince Ernest Augustus, Prince Bishop of Osnabrück and Duke of York, bequeathed most of his property to his nephew, King George II, and only his jewels to his niece, Queen Sophie Dorothea of Prussia, the Prussian King was convinced that his brother-in-law was a villain.

When Emperor Charles VI called upon them to help restore order in the state of Mecklenburg, neither the King of Prussia nor the Elector of Hanover would act in unison. It was as if they were determined to disagree with each other for the sake of it. Matters came to a head when Prussian recruiting officials who had illegally crossed the Hanoverian border to recruit tall Hanoverians for the Prussian army were arrested. Not only did King George take mischievous if understandable satisfaction in crossing Prussian territory on his way to Hanover without informing the court of Berlin of his movements, as courtesy generally demanded, he also insisted that the officers would not be released until the Hanoverian soldiers just recruited into the Prussian army were released. King Frederick William's anger was exacerbated by his learning of the arrests through newspapers instead of his woefully inefficient diplomatic sources. When Hanoverian farmers helped themselves to hay cut at Clamei meadow, on the Prussian

side of the frontier with Hanover, and orders were given for the arrest of all Prussian soldiers travelling in Hanover, whether they carried passports or not, the King of Prussia's temper knew no bounds. He announced that he would challenge his brother-in-law to a duel at Hildesheim. King George was eager to accept the challenge, adding that he would make his adversary bite the dust for his insolences.

Ministers in London and Berlin realized that the time had now come to tell their sovereigns that to settle their differences in such a way could not be tolerated. The duel was called off, but instead troops were massed on either side of the Prusso-Hanoverian border. War seemed imminent, and not until King Frederick William consented to arbitration were relations patched up with his cousin. In due course negotiations were opened again regarding a marriage between the Prince of Wales and Princess Wilhelmina. Impatient to get his daughter off his hands, the King of Prussia only made one condition; that Prince Frederick was to be made Regent of Hanover, and 'allowed to direct the management of the electorate' till his death, and if provision was made for his maintenance. This was too much for King George, and negotiations ceased.*

King George II would have no Regent at Hanover while he was in England. Instead he ordered that the electorate should be governed by a Council of Regency, and as a substitute for his presence at the levées, his portrait as Elector should be placed on the vacant throne in the state room at Herrenhausen. Every Saturday a levée was held as though he was present; the courtiers assembled and made their bow to the picture on the chair of state as if it was the Elector himself.

In England the Queen enjoyed a respite from her husband's continued presence, for her time was now her own. Townshend was jealous of Walpole's favour with the Queen, and tried to induce the King to modify her powers as Regent, urging him to send a despatch from the Hague to that effect. Knowing better than anyone else that royal interests were safe in her hands, the King declined to do so.

Five days after his departure she held her first Council meeting at Kensington Palace. Her Commission of Regency was read, and the Prince of Wales and all others present dutifully kissed her hand. Her powers included opening and proroguing Parliament, signifying the royal assent to acts and

*They were opened again a couple of years later rather half-heartedly, when the Crown Prince of Prussia was betrothed to Princess Elizabeth of Brunswick-Bevern, niece of the Empress of Austria. The court at Vienna demanded that Princess Elizabeth should marry the Prince of Wales instead, while the Crown Prince of Prussia should marry Princess Amelia, as had been previously discussed. King Frederick William of Prussia angrily put a halt to further speculation by ensuring that his son's marriage to Princess Elizabeth took place at once.

measures, appointing bishops, and making other important appointments. She also received overseas ambassadors and envoys in place of the King, and corresponding with foreign sovereigns. Each post and special messenger from Hanover carried a mass of official correspondence for her perusal. The King's absence multiplied the secretarial work. Townshend with the King, and Newcastle at home, wrote to each other by every mail, enclosing for their respective Majesties' information copies of everything they had received and written. Each continued to transact the business of his own Department of State. Their letters dealt mainly with foreign affairs, because the King 'left all domestic matters to the Regent'. Townshend requested that documents marked 'Private' should be seen only by the Queen and 'those Lords of the Council who are consulted upon the most secret foreign affairs'. Decisions on policy were left entirely to the Queen 'with the advice of the Lords of the Council'. Her skilful diplomacy averted an incident that summer with Portugal, which placed an embargo on a British ship in the Tagus. Her firm but friendly representations to the Portuguese minister were successful in getting it lifted, and Townshend wrote that 'the King likes extremely what Her Majesty said to the Portugal envoy'.

During this time the most important negotiation in foreign affairs was the Treaty of Seville, virtually concluded during Queen Caroline's regency though not signed till November, after the King's return. The treaty terminated the long dispute between England and Spain. By its provisions English trade with America, which had been interrupted, was restored. England was given back everything that Spain had captured during the war, including Gibraltar, tacitly relinquished.

The Queen publicly marked her approval of Walpole by dining with him at his house in Chelsea. She was amused by his respect for ceremony, as he waited on her himself, and entertained his other guests in a separate room. He paid due attention to her connoisseurship by arranging for his best pictures to be brought from Houghton House specially for the occasion.

Another evening found the royal party at Cliveden, as guests of the Earl and Countess of Orkney. Lady Orkney was fearful lest the Queen should find the dinner ill-dished and poorly dressed, and the tables badly set. That there were no complaints, she thought, 'shows the greater goodness in the Queen to be so very easy'. As the party did not come home until 4 a.m. the following day, it was evidently a great success.

The Queen held state while at St James's, and on the anniversary of the King's accession, 11 June, she summoned a court which was one of the best-attended of the reign. At Windsor she occupied the rooms which had been used by Queen Anne, and she had drawing rooms in the state apartments. From Windsor she returned to Kensington, which remained her headquarters for the rest of the summer. With its fine gardens and views it had become her favourite of the palaces, as a home second only to

Richmond Lodge in her affections. From here she paid occasional visits to Hampton Court, Richmond, and Windsor.

On 11 September the King landed at Margate. When the outriders reached Kensington to announce his approach, the Queen and the royal family walked to St James's Park to meet him. Their Majesties embraced heartily, and drove back to Kensington followed by their suite and cheered by their subjects. The next day at a meeting of the Privy Council the Queen delivered her commission of regency back into the King's hands.

The Prince of Wales had accepted the situation without demur, and his behaviour to his mother was beyond reproach. Unhappily the opposition wasted no time in attempting to turn the situation to their advantage. The Earl of Essex, one of the Prince's friends, suggested to him that he ought to be at the head of the regency, reminding him that his father had taken a similar point of view in the previous reign. As long as Walpole remained at the head of government, the Earl continued, it would be impossible for His Royal Highness to enjoy to the full his due rights as heir to the throne. Convinced of the enduring obstinacy of his parents, and of his own popularity, the Prince's vanity increased. It would have taken a strong, very level-headed young man in a similar position to realize he was being used by the opposition; and to the lasting misfortune of all, Prince Frederick was not such a character.

CHAPTER THIRTEEN

'Something mean and below him'

King George II was notorious for his self-confessed hatred of 'all boets and bainters'. He had never cared for learning, proclaiming that he had 'hated all that stuff from his infancy' as he despised it and 'felt as if he was doing something mean and below him.' The only reading matter that interested him, it was said, consisted of his gamekeeper's reports. His preference for the card table as a means of recreation was typical of his age. 'Books! prithee, don't talk to me about books,' was the judgment of Sarah, Duchess of Marlborough. 'The only books I know about are men and cards.'[1] Eminent men of letters, who soon knew better than to expect royal encouragement, felt alienated from court as Walpole shared the King's contempt for them, thus denying them patronage and employment.

Any inborn royal prejudices against literature were exacerbated by the likes of rebels such as John Gay. As one of the 'opposition circle' to gather at Leicester House shortly after Prince George Augustus and his wife were ordered out of St James's Palace in the previous reign, Gay had been in high favour, and responded by writing a book of fables for the infant Prince William. Once his patron came to the throne, however, it was a different story. He was offered a sinecure at court as Gentleman Usher to Princess Louisa at a salary of £200 a year, which he felt was a gross insult to his talents and refused. A year later he produced and staged *The Beggar's Opera*, a witty, satirical and successful musical about highwaymen and whores, set at Newgate. Its mockery of political corruption, and by implication the methods of Walpole himself ('Bob the poet's foe'), brought disapproval from the King and Queen.

The next year he wrote a sequel, *Polly*, which satirized governmental corruption again and included as one of the leading characters a highwayman, evidently modelled on Walpole. Convinced that the writer had gone too far, the minister persuaded the Lord Chamberlain to ban the production. Gay promptly rewrote part of it, adding 'some supplemental invections', and had it printed by subscription. One of his most ardent supporters at court, the Duchess of Queensberry, promised to help him by soliciting subscriptions, even to the extent of persuading the King's servants to contribute. When the King asked her what she was doing, she curtseyed and without flinching told him that she was assisting in an act of charity, so

humane that she hoped she would bring His Majesty to contribute as well. Her audacity earned her a verbal message forbidding her to come to court in future. She replied in writing that she was surprised 'and well pleased' to be given such an agreeable command, as she never came to court for diversion, 'but to bestow a great civility on the King and Queen'. When she handed the message to the Vice Chamberlain he asked her if she would give him 'an answer less rough', but when she wrote an even more disrespectful one he decided the first was safer. To his credit the King bore the family no lasting grudge, and though the embarrassed Duke of Queensberry offered to resign his sinecure at court, the King refused to let him.

Queen Caroline had always been a voracious reader, and it was unfortunate that in this aspect she never managed to influence the King and Walpole. Only in the days at Leicester House had she been free to meet her favourite authors and poets. When she was Queen, Pope pilloried her in his caustic couplets, and Swift resented not being promoted beyond an Irish dean when he had fondly expected that his patroness would do much more for him. Both men were friends of Bolingbroke and thus earned the unyielding resentment of Walpole. From then on, the royal doors were closed to them. Swift was particularly bitter at not being sent a medal which he claimed she had promised him as a token of appreciation for his writings. The grievance rankled, and some years later he wrote a caustic poem on the subject of his death and the effect he imagined it would have on her:

> The Queen, so gracious, mild and good,
> Cries, 'Is he gone? 'Tis time he should.
> He's dead you say? Then let him rot;
> I'm glad the medals were forgot.
> I promised him, I own, but when?
> I only was the Princess then;
> And now, the Consort of the King,
> You know, 'tis quite another thing.

Others were more fortunate. She awarded a pension to the impoverished granddaughter of the late John Milton. To Richard Savage, she brought a reprieve from a sentence of death for murder in a drunken fray, and a pension of £50 for his poem *The Bastard*. She went through books at a prodigious rate, if without discrimination. With her remarkable memory, she could recall everything she read. The King was unimpressed, rebuking her for dabbling 'in all that lettered nonsense', calling her a pedant and saying that she loved to spend her time more like a schoolmistress than a Queen. She showed a particular if somewhat misplaced appreciation of Stephen Duck, an uneducated Wiltshire farm labourer by profession who

taught himself the rudiments of grammar, history and science in his spare time and then started writing poetry, which a country clergyman helped him to publish. The Queen was impressed with his industry, and asked that he should be brought to court to meet her. Taking an immediate liking to him, she granted him a pension of £200 a year, and made him one of the Yeomen of the Guard. In time she also made him custodian of her 'folly' at Richmond, Merlin's Cave.* When he took Holy Orders, she made him Chaplain of Kew and Rector of Byfleet. But his verse was cruelly mocked by the jealous Swift and Pope; out of his depth in such exalted circles, he did not long survive his royal patroness, and a few years after her death he died by his own hand.

More memorable was a literally priceless discovery by Queen Caroline. The library and collection of porcelain at Kensington Palace belonging to Queen Mary II, consort of King William III, had long been dispersed, but her cabinet and bureau had remained in the state apartments. While examining the contents in 1728 Queen Caroline found it packed full of prints, drawings and old medals, probably put hastily into the bureau when fire broke out at Whitehall in 1698 and destroyed the Palace. The drawings comprised nearly thirty separate lots, some on loose vellum, others pasted in albums, drawings by Italian masters, Indian sketches, and prints by Wenceslaus Hollar. Most exciting of all were two books of drawings by Leonardo da Vinci, and about a hundred sketches by Hans Holbein. Drawn on flesh-coloured paper, the latter were studies of notables from the court of King Henry VIII which he had used for his oil paintings, long since believed lost, destroyed, or given away. George Vertue called them 'the greatest treasure of its kind now in England', believing that only the cartoons of Raphael at Hampton Court surpassed them. The Queen had them framed and hung at Richmond Lodge, and later took them back to her closet or dressing room at Kensington, which became her private picture gallery as well. The room measured 23 feet by 12 feet, and treasures were crammed side by side into this space from floor to ceiling. Among them were miniatures by Samuel Cooper and Peter Oliver; a Madonna and Christ by Dolci; flower studies by Maria van Osterwyck; and mundane portraits of little-known relatives, as well as a considerable quantity of Japanese ware presented to her by the East India Company.

William Kent was commissioned to build two extraordinary dwellings at Richmond for the Queen. One, a thatched cottage, was known as Merlin's Cave; the other, a four-roomed Gothic cottage, was a grotto. She intended this to be a temple to the great geniuses of British learning, and to furnish it

*See p. 151

she commissioned statues from the sculptor Guelfi. He completed one and then left England. A little later she heard the work of Michael Rysbrack was highly praised; she visited his studio in 1735 and saw him working on an equestrian statue of King William III, commissioned by the corporation of Bristol. She accordingly asked him to finish her gallery of Whig heroes, to include Sir Isaac Newton, the chemist Henry Boyle, the essayist Francis Bacon, and the political philosopher John Locke. These were followed by another royal order, for terracotta busts of every King of England from Alfred the Great to the present, King George II – and herself. Sadly she did not live to see the completed results.

King George II doted on the work of the German enameller and miniaturist, Frederick Zincke. When he first came to paint and draw the royal family, the Queen took him aside and advised him 'to make the King's picture young, not above 25'. The portraits he painted of them at the start of their reign remained among their favourites.

The work of William Hogarth, the *enfant terrible* of the art world, never appealed to the King. One day he was shown a Hogarth engraving, in which soldiers were shown kissing their girls goodbye. 'A bainter burlesque a soldier?' he asked indignantly. 'He deserves to be picketed [tortured] for his insolence. Take his trumpery out of my sight.' The more discerning Queen commanded Hogarth to paint a conversation piece of the royal family, and he produced two large preparatory oil sketches, one showing them out of doors near a circular garden temple, and one in a grand interior.* He was not granted sittings by all members of the royal family. The impossibility of getting everybody to sit for him put paid to the project, so that neither he nor any other painter succeeded in producing a finished group portrait of the King, Queen and children together.

When it came to having his portrait painted, King George II was a reluctant sitter. In the competitive art world of the eighteenth century it was an advantage in securing illustrious sitters to have previously painted a member or members of the royal family or other persons of eminence, and painters used every effort to do so. Joseph Highmore, who had worked in the academy of the late Sir Godfrey Kneller, tried but failed to get a sitting from King George II and Queen Caroline. It is recorded that he 'did by stealth draw them first on paper . . . and afterwards by Memory in some parts & copying those pictures before painted by Sir G Kneller'.[2] The pictures he subsequently engraved gave the misleading impression that they had been a royal commission.

The principal Crown Painter on the accession of King George II was

*The exterior portrait is in the Royal Collection; the other is in the National Gallery of Ireland. See p.134.

Charles Jervas. He was succeeded by the multi-talented William Kent, a Master Mason to the Office of Works, a versatile designer and restorer of paintings as well as artist and architect himself. Not all his skills were universally appreciated. At Kensington Palace he designed and decorated a suite of rooms, the effect of which was called 'poor stuff', and 'a terrible glaring show' by Vertue. Queen Caroline appreciated his enthusiasm for gardening, but his ideas were sometimes unorthodox. To follow nature faithfully he endeavoured to plant dead trees in the gardens 'but was soon laughed out of the excess'.

Though they had little in common, the King and the Prince of Wales both loved music. Despite his general contempt for most of the other fine arts, King George II was genuinely moved by the work of Handel.* The Prince of Wales shared his passion up to a point, but with the contrariness of youth he could not resist teasing his parents by finding fault with the works of Handel – or affecting to – and set up a rival opera company under Giovanni Buononcini, an Italian composer and musician whose talent, most contemporaries agreed, was not commensurate with his vanity. Opposition politicians and the Prince's friends followed him into the opera house in Lincoln's Inn Fields to hear Buononcini, while the King, Queen and Princess Royal and their dwindling supporters continued to patronize Handel's far superior music at the half-empty Haymarket Opera House. One day Lord Chesterfield claimed that he had gone to the German opera, 'but finding the King and Queen there alone had come away assuming that they had gone there to talk business.'[3] Ever the loyal daughter, Princess Anne said she soon expected to see half the House of Lords playing in Buononcini's orchestra in their robes and coronets. The King exclaimed with disdain that he did not think setting oneself at the head of a faction of fiddlers a very honourable occupation for a person of quality.

At the height of the rivalry, when Handel's fortunes were at a low ebb, the King had told him reassuringly that 'these Italian discords' were finished in London. His words were prophetic, and before long Buononcini had gone in disgrace. In a moment of over-confidence he presented the Academy of Ancient Music with a madrigal in five voices which, it came to light shortly afterwards, had plagiarized a piece by the Venetian composer Antonio Lotti published some twenty years earlier. Discredited and broken in spirit, he fled to Paris and little more was heard of him.

*Handel's major modern biographer, Newman Flower, asserts that the King 'had a poor sense of music, but he realized that to throw over Handel would be to alienate himself from the musical coterie which was so firmly rooted now in the town [London]'.[4] However it is unlikely that the King would have made such efforts to champion or patronize the composer so ardently if he had remained completely unmoved by his music.

The Prince's financial dependence on his father forced him to live in St James's Palace, though by this time his mother rarely spoke to him and his father never. When father and son were in the same room, so it seemed, wherever the Prince was standing, the King might walk past him, but ignore him completely as if the young man 'filled a void of space.'

The Prince constantly resented his father's parsimony. Parliament had voted the King £800,000 a year for his Civil List on the understanding that he would make the Prince of Wales an annual allowance of £100,000 and allow him a separate establishment. The King angrily refused, preferring to keep the Prince dependent on him by paying and engaging his household staff, reserving the right to appoint and dismiss his son's servants, and giving him a mere £24,000 per annum as pocket money. The opposition did not shrink from attempting to exploit the heir's bitterness, much to the alarm of Walpole and Hervey. People who made their fortunes under a Prince, they declared, would 'submit to being snubbed and ill-used; and people who were caressed by a Prince, cajoled with good words and treated with kindness, would serve him without great hire'. Although he disliked the Prince, Hervey advised the Queen that it would be in the King's own interests to give the Prince a regular allowance with which to maintain his own establishment. The Queen was not receptive; 'Ah! that people will always be judging and deciding upon what they know nothing of.'[5]

Yet the Prince could console himself with the knowledge that his father was tight-fisted towards everybody. Walpole later said that the only present the King gave him was a cracked diamond. Gossips asserted that once he spent some time turning over a pile of logs to discover a lost guinea, which belonged to somebody else. When asked by some maids of honour for a gift to raffle, he agonized for a while before producing a handful of small, deeply flawed amethysts and topazes. When he gave the Queen some fine Hanoverian horses, it was said, he used them himself while charging her for their upkeep. 'Blessed with family' far more than his father, he provided his daughters with inadequate allowances and Queen Caroline had to supplement them herself. She included the three eldest in her lease on the Dutch House at Kew, where they could entertain and give their own private concerts. The gardens played host to a masque devised to celebrate the Princess Royal's twenty-first birthday, where the decorations included a thousand lamps suspended from the trees,[6] naturally at the Queen's expense.

In May 1732 the King paid another visit to Hanover, and invested the Queen with full powers of Regent as before for the four months that he was away. This time the Queen managed to advance a cause dear to her heart. Knowing the injustices and anomalies of the criminal law, she was always on the side of clemency. Reluctant to sign death warrants in her capacity as Regent, where possible she chose to exercise her prerogative of mercy. She took a close personal interest in reform of the prison system. When it was in

her power she released prisoners, and made penalties easier for debtors and other offenders. Determined that something should be done to remedy the deplorable condition of public prisons, she had taken up the matter soon after the King's accession. During her second regency an inquiry was instituted into the prevalent system of abuses; particularly gaolers and warders conniving at the escape of rich prisoners, while subjecting the poorer ones, who could not pay their extortionate demands, to every sort of cruelty, insult and oppression.

Revelations of Select Committees of the House of Commons of ill treatment and inadequate nourishment in men's and women's prisons horrified her. She repeatedly urged on Walpole the necessity of reform, and the revision of the criminal code. But he was averse to any legislation unless demanded by political expediency, and the most she could hope to achieve was a more vigorous inspection of prisons, and the punishment of gaolers whose cruelty could be proved.

Of much greater importance to him was the excise scheme the following year, in which he proposed to bring tobacco and wine duties under the law of excise, and so ease the land tax. During the wars of Marlborough land tax had risen to four shillings in the pound, but during the last few years, as a result of peace and prosperity, this figure had been halved. Walpole's proposed excise scheme would have reduced it further or even abolished it. Custom duties had long been levied on wine and tobacco, and his changes basically affected the method of collection. He envisaged that they would probably lessen if not stop smuggling altogether (despite his own readiness to replenish his cellars at Houghton and Chelsea by purchasing from smugglers), and excise duties would rise by one-sixth, more than sufficient to meet the deficit caused by easing the land tax.

His proposals had the support of the court, as the King's Civil List depended to some extent on the duties on tobacco and wine. He was confident that he would also have the support of Parliament, but events proved that he had seriously miscalculated both parliamentary and public opinion. People regarded the proposed extension as the first step in a scheme of general excise in which every necessary of life would be taxed, and in which private houses would be at the mercy of over-zealous excisemen. Many of Walpole's friends and colleagues, as well as rivals who had long waited for an opportunity of undermining him, opposed the scheme. When he introduced the Excise Bill in Parliament in March 1733, the opposition attacked him furiously. Lord Carteret, one of the first to find fault, declared that 'it would place it in the hands of a wicked administration to reduce the English people to the same condition as the people of Turkey; their only resource will be in mobs and tumults, and the prevailing party will administer justice by general massacres and proscriptions.'[7]

For four weeks Walpole defended it while opposition steadily mounted, despite the support of the King and Queen. The monarch admired his chief minister's courage in the face of persistent parliamentary attacks: 'he has more spirit than any man I ever knew!' All the same, it was soon evident that spirit alone was not enough. Always more willing to compromise, at length the Queen asked Lord Scarborough, whose opinions she always trusted. 'The Bill must be dropped, or there will be mutiny in the army,' he warned. 'I will answer for my regiment against the Pretender, but not the excise.' At once she acknowledged that it must be dropped. After a private conference with the King and Queen at St James's Walpole reluctantly agreed, and offered his resignation from office which he knew they would not accept. Privately he admitted that the dance 'will no longer go', and later that week in Parliament he announced calmly his intention of postponing the measure for two months – a graceful and subtle way of conceding defeat.

'There is baboon enough for you'

Though Anne, Princess Royal, might side with her parents against her much-disliked eldest brother, she did so largely out of boredom with life at home. She complained regularly to Hervey about her father's vanity, his boring military reminiscences, his boasting of his success with other women, his bullying the Queen, and his insistence on other people coming to him with new conversation while his was always 'the same things over and over again'. While he could bear major misfortunes tolerably well, she said with asperity, when in his worst humours he was the devil to everybody who came near him, and it was usually for some trivial reason such as a page powdering his periwig badly, or a housemaid setting a chair in a different place. Proud and domineering, she was a Princess of talent and industry. Long before the rest of the family rose each morning she was up herself, busy with her paints, her books or her sewing. She was a keen reader like her mother, a competent painter, and spoke several languages fluently. Equally enthusiastic at the card table, she irritated others by rapping her knuckles as she played, especially if they were too slow for her ever impatient spirit.

The second daughter, Princess Amelia, or Emily, was an active, extroverted young woman. Though several minor German princes offered their hand in marriage after her betrothal to Prince Frederick of Prussia failed to come about, she rejected them all. Prettier than her eldest sister and regarded as even cleverer, she was also the family flirt. Brief affairs with the Duke of Newcastle and the Lord Chamberlain, the Duke of Grafton, a grandson of Charles II, caused endless gossip and a whiff of scandal, not to mention intense irritation to Queen Caroline. Princess and Duke would go hunting together two or three times a week, riding away from the rest of the party. Once at Windsor their attendants lost them altogether, and they did not return to the castle until long after dark. Everyone imagined that they had gone together to a private house. As the King was in Hanover at the time, the furious Queen scolded her daughter thoroughly and threatened to tell the King on his return. Walpole dissuaded her, saying that it would do the Princess harm, and that the Duke would not care.

Happiest when hunting, she became increasingly eccentric and shocked fellow members of the congregation at Hampton Court church by arriving

in riding clothes and carrying a dog under each arm. Like her father she was impervious to cold and enjoyed the fresh air. It was no coincidence, perhaps, that her health was far better than that of her sisters, all of whom she survived. She found the sickly Hervey and his constant presence at court grated on her nerves, and the feeling was mutual. Nobody knew Emily, Hervey would declare, without disliking her. He considered her an evil-tongued shrew, 'glad of any back to lash and the sorer it was the gladder she was to strike'.[1] Lady Pomfret was more charitable, though her praise was somewhat qualified; Emily, she said, was 'one of the oddest princesses that ever was known; she has her ears shut to flattery and her heart open to honesty. She has honour, justice, good-nature, sense, wit, resolution and more good qualities than I have time to tell you, so mixed that (if one is not a *devil*) it is impossible to say she has too much or too little of any; yet all these do not in anything (without exception) make her forget [she is] the King of England's daughter, which dignity she keeps up with such an obliging behaviour that she charms everybody.'[2]

The third sister, Princess Caroline, was prettier but too fat. Shy, good-natured and passionately loyal to her eldest sister, she was happiest with her reading and drawing. After Anne married, she willingly became her mother's constant companion. Her admiration for Hervey bordered on semi-avuncular infatuation. The Princesses, all of very different temperament and not really liking each other very much, did not care for their elder brother. Soon after his arrival in England Frederick had taken them into his confidence, but they repaid him by betraying him to the Queen and to Hervey.

Prince William was petted by his sisters. A boy after his father's heart, he was very grave and solemn from an early age. Instead of wanting to play with others of his age, he preferred to pore over books on the army, or study military uniforms. His ready turn of phrase delighted his mother. One year on 30 January, a fast day in remembrance of the execution of King Charles I, he clamoured for his dinner. Did he think it seemly to do so, she asked him reprovingly, and did he think it right for the people to execute their King? He answered back that he could not tell what the King's crime was until he had read his history.

By 1733 King George II was determined to marry off his eldest daughter Anne, the Princess Royal. She was equally set on finding a husband. Smallpox had disfigured a long face with bulbous eyes that had never really been attractive, and she was taking after her mother in running to fat. Bored with life at her father's court, she was anxious to avoid the nightmare of spinsterhood under the reign of a brother whom she detested.

Her choice of prospective husbands was limited. Most of the King's brother monarchs were Roman Catholics, and the few German princelings

who might have been suitable for his daughters were thought too insignificant, particularly for someone as arrogant as Anne.

Among the few eligible Protestant Princes was William IV, Prince of Orange, Count of Nassau, Stadtholder of Friesland, Groningen, and Guelderland. Nearly two years younger than his future wife, he was hardly a catch. His deformity remains something of a mystery; he may have been born with part of a vertebra missing, which resulted in an increasing curvature of the spine, or he might have suffered from a tubercular condition which attacked the back.[3] Hervey, no physical paragon of the human race himself, described him as being almost a dwarf, and 'as much deformed as it was possible for a human creature to be; his face was not bad, his countenance was sensible, but his breath was more offensive than it is possible for those who have not been offended by it to imagine.' As ever, though, he exaggerated the young man's faults. The less malicious Lord Chesterfield praised his 'ease of freedom that is seldom acquired but by a long knowledge of the world,' admitting that 'his shape is not so advantageous as could be wished, though not near so bad as I had heard represented.'

Despite the Princess Royal's personal and physical shortcomings, she had 'an excellent warm animate constitution', which made her 'now and then remember she was a woman'. Her lack of enthusiasm for her husband-to-be was evident, but as Hervey remarked cynically, her choice lay between Hell and Holland. Either she would be 'wedded to this piece of deformity', or live and die an old maid in St James's. She vowed that she would marry the Prince 'if he were a baboon'. Her father replied with disarming honesty, 'Well, then, there is baboon enough for you.' The betrothal was organized, and Parliament voted the Princess Royal a dowry of £80,000.

Prince William arrived at Greenwich early in November, and was lodged at Somerset House in the Strand. His reception was icy in the extreme; not one single salute gun was fired, nor did one soldier appear on parade. Only with difficulty was the King persuaded to send Lord Hervey to present his compliments to the Prince. On his return the chamberlain was summoned by the Queen, curious to know 'what sort of animal she was to prepare herself to see'. Hervey assured her tactfully that she must not expect to see an Adonis; 'that his body was as bad as possible but that his countenance was far from disagreeable and his address sensible, engaging and noble.'

The Princess Royal's demeanour was equally detached. Far from expressing any excitement at the arrival of the young man who, whatever his faults, was to provide her with some release from her tedious existence at home, she sat in her apartment at St James's playing her harpsichord.

As if to compensate, the people of London turned out to welcome him, the streets heavily decorated with cockades of orange ribbon. A royal wedding was a royal wedding, and that was diversion enough. Everything

was ready for the nuptials, to take place a few days hence. St James's prepared its wedding finery; a covered wooden gallery to seat 4,000 was built to lead the processions from the Palace to the adjoining French chapel for the ceremony. The widowed Duchess of Marlborough, watching from her windows, called it the King's 'Orange chest'.

The wedding was to take place on a Monday. At divine service at the Dutch Church in London on the day before, the bridegroom walked out from the overheated atmosphere into the cold winter air, and promptly collapsed. For three weeks he lay seriously ill with pneumonia. His indisposition, the gossips said, had been brought on by the glacial atmosphere of the London court, and he had contracted an almost fatal chill from the frosty glares of his future in-laws. For several weeks his life was in danger, and none of the royal family came to visit him. Hervey asserted that the King thought it below his dignity, but in view of his feelings about illness and the fear of infection, this was not the only reason. Even the Princess was forbidden to see him. To add to his gloom, smallpox was raging throughout the city and claimed the life of one of the Prince's suite.

Once he was well enough to be moved, the Princess Royal invited him to the Palace incognito for cards with her and her sisters. Even King George II, having reconciled himself to the fact that this ugly but evidently forbearing young man was not going to die after all, unbent sufficiently to play backgammon with them. A period of convalescence at the more salubrious Kensington followed, after which he went to Bath, hoping that the waters would complete the cure. At Bristol he was received ceremoniously by the Mayor, and returning to London via Oxford he was wined and dined and awarded an honorary degree. Back among his bride-to-be's family his greeting was less effusive. At a formal Sunday dinner the King ordered him to join the gentlemen-in-waiting who stood behind his chair, asking 'What is the Prince of Orange until he has married my daughter?' Tactfully concealing his triumph, he answered that his health would not permit him to stand.

The wedding was rearranged for 14 (OS)/25 (NS) March 1734 and took place at the Chapel Royal, St James's Palace. Since the groom's illness interest had subsided somewhat in the ceremony; unwanted tickets which had been held since November were being offered for sale in local coffee houses. Nevertheless soldiers had been employed day and night at great expense to guard the chapel against opportunist souvenir hunters and thieves.

The Princess Royal looked radiant with her shining blonde hair beneath a twinkling coronet, dressed in robes of silver tissue with a train six yards long. The groom was attired in a suit of cloth of gold, and despite his deformity managed to strike a dignified figure. Even Hervey had to admit that 'as his countenance was not bad, there was nothing very strikingly disagreeable about his stature'.

To the right of the elaborate altar a throne had been erected, with two chairs of state for the King and Queen. Nearby was a canopy of state for the Prince of Wales, the Duke of Cumberland, and Princesses Amelia and Caroline; the two younger Princesses were cordoned off from the others in a separate gallery. All four sisters sobbed quietly throughout the service. The King, so Hervey noted, was equally lachrymose; he gave his daughter 'a thousand kisses and a shower of tears but not one guinea'. After the Bishop of London had performed the rites of holy matrimony according to the Church of England, an anthem, *This is the day*, composed by Handel to a text written by the bride, paraphrased from Psalms 45 and 118, was sung. On leaving the chapel, the royal family went to the Palace drawing-room where bride and groom knelt to receive the blessing of the King and Queen. At 11 p.m. they took supper in the Great State Ballroom, the King and Queen seated under a canopy at the head of the table, with the Prince of Wales, the Duke of Cumberland and the groom on the right hand and the bride with her sisters opposite.

Afterwards, according to custom, when bride and groom were bedded, the King had planned to allow the groom to be behind a curtain, with only the bride exposed to the spectators. Whether this was out of kindness, in order to help conceal his deformity, or whether to emphasize his more lowly status and the King's conviction that his daughter was marrying beneath her, is open to conjecture. All that could be seen was the Prince in a nightcap and long brocaded nightgown.

They enjoyed a brief honeymoon at the Dutch House, Kew, and then returned to London. Though he could hardly be described as handsome, the Princess Royal behaved as though he was a positive Adonis, addressing everything she said to him, and applauding everything he said to everybody else. As far as the rest of the family was concerned, only the Prince of Wales appeared to show any particular civility to his brother-in-law. He, too, knew how it felt to be treated as an outcast.

While he was in London the Prince of Orange was very popular with the Londoners, who cheered him whenever he showed himself in the streets. There was doubtless an element of teasing the King with loyal addresses recalling the Glorious Revolution, and hints that his son-in-law might serve His Majesty as a previous Prince of Orange had done.

William Hogarth had tried to secure the official commission for painting the marriage. He obtained permission from Queen Caroline to attend the ceremony and make his preliminary studies but he had reckoned without William Kent, who as a high official in the Ministry of Works was responsible for the accompanying decorations. Kent had his own plan to record the wedding scene, as well as an old score to settle with the man who had once ridiculed him in caricature. A member of Kent's staff ordered Hogarth to stop work, despite his protest that he had the Queen's authority, and the

Lord Chamberlain called on him in person to withdraw. When the artist appealed to the Queen, all she could say was that she had not realized that the permission granted to Mr Hogarth might interfere with Mr Kent's plans. It was a double defeat, for Hogarth had already produced rough sketches for a future work, a group portrait of the King, Queen and all their children. An individual portrait of the young Prince William, Duke of Cumberland, was the only item so far complete. The family group was halted and never taken further.

Meanwhile the Princess Royal, now Princess of Orange, proved herself strangely reluctant to leave the home from which she had apparently longed to escape by marriage. Queen Caroline was distraught at the thought of 'this monster' sleeping with her daughter, despite Hervey's reassurance that one soon became accustomed to 'the figure of the body one's married to'. She wept for three days prior to the young couple's departure.

The rest of the family were hardly less affected when it came to farewells at St James's. Even the King, in a rare moment of generosity, gave his daughter a magnificent pair of diamond pendant earrings. Only the Prince of Wales refrained from taking his leave of them; according to Hervey, he asked the Prince of Orange to let his sister know that 'the reason for omitting it was the fear of touching her too much'. The Prince had attempted to comfort his mother, agitated and full of emotion at the parting with her daughter. Whether he did so out of genuine sympathy or a desire to make mischief – though it would be only fair to him to assume the former – his offer was indignantly rejected. 'Oh, my God, this is too much!' the Queen spluttered.

Hervey was asked to join the royal escort accompanying the newly married couple as they set out for Gravesend where Prince William's ships awaited to take them to Holland. A letter from Queen Caroline, written to Anne that same day, assured her:

> My sadness is indescribable, I never had any sorrows over you, Anne, this is the first, a cruel one. Caroline behaves so well but our conversations always finish on the same sad note. The King, who sends you affectionate greetings, is worse than us all . . . love me always as tenderly as the most affectionate mother flatters herself that you do.[4]

Foremost in the homesick young bride's mind was the likelihood of her husband's country being involved in a European war before long. If he was summoned to the field of battle, she would have good reason to return to London, albeit temporarily.

After a rough crossing over the North Sea, they arrived on the coast of Holland and took up residence at their new home in Leeuwarden. Once

they had settled in the Princess reverted to her childhood habits of petty tyrannies over ladies-in-waiting and servants, thinking nothing of keeping them standing or reading to her until they were fit to drop. The Dutch were subjected to her customary arrogance, for she never cared to conceal her opinion that they were inferior to the English. As far as possible she kept her own company, surrounded by her music and books. Prince William evidently felt that he had done his duty by marrying and ensuring the succession, and for the sake of peace and quiet he was prepared to leave her to her own devices.

Early that summer he went to join the Holy Roman Emperor's army of the Rhine, leaving his wife increasingly homesick, and expecting a child. She had already decided for herself that any son of hers might one day inherit the thrones of Hanover and England, and it would not do for any such child to be born on foreign soil – in other words, outside England. Aghast, Prince William warned her what a dreadful impression such an action would have on his people. Even so, swearing her servants and attendants to secrecy she planned her return journey, and by the beginning of June she was back at Kensington Palace.

Once again she could enjoy court functions in London, and quarrels with her elder brother. Only now did she realize how much she missed her old home. Handel was so pleased at his star pupil's presence that he extended his Covent Garden opera season until July as a special mark of respect. Queen Caroline was deeply affected at her daughter's return, while the King made no attempt to conceal his irritation. Still on active service, the Prince of Orange swallowed his pride; unable to do anything immediate about his wayward wife's behaviour, he went back to his soldiering. Horace Walpole advised her to consider returning to Holland of her own free will in order to meet her husband when he returned from the war, so he would not need to send for her. On receipt of his letter, she wept for a whole morning.

After a few weeks her husband sent one of his gentlemen to London to let her know that he would be at The Hague in two weeks' time to meet her. More tears followed, but eventually she realized it was impossible to delay the inevitable. In the autumn she set out for Harwich to return to Holland for the birth of her child. As she arrived at Colchester she was handed a letter from her husband regretting that he would be unable to meet her at The Hague as he had been delayed. Back she went to Kensington, to more emotional scenes and paternal impatience. Within a few days she was persuaded to embark at Harwich, but after a few hours' journey she pleaded 'convulsions' and ordered the ship to return to port. Her medical advisers were coaxed into telling her husband and parents that if she put to sea again while she was pregnant it would be at peril of her life.

At this her husband, who had travelled day and night to Helvoetsluys to meet her on her arrival in Holland, lost patience, and ordered that she was to

come at once by the shortest sea crossing through Calais. He backed up his orders with an appeal to the equally angry King George, who commanded her to travel from Harwich to Dover via Gravesend. When she protested that the condition of the roads made it essential for her to come via London, he saw through her motives, and gave his permission only for her closed coach to cross London Bridge without stopping. There was nothing for it but to give in, and her long-suffering husband arrived at Calais to await her arrival. They were at The Hague by the end of the year. For all her prevarication, it looked as if the eagerly awaited heir would be born on Dutch soil.

Alas for their hopes. By April 1735 the *accoucheur* confirmed their uneasy suspicions that there was no child after all. Her misery rekindled the old feelings of homesickness, and she talked hopefully of going back to England that summer. However her extended stay the previous year had done her more harm than good. Even Queen Caroline, more ready than anybody else to find excuses for the daughter whom she greatly missed, warned her sternly that she did not belong in England any more: 'You are now William's wife, God has given you skill and judgement, you are no longer a child.'[5]

Queen Caroline's anxiety for her daughter was exacerbated by her own increasing ill health. Added to gout were her sufferings from a hernia incurred by the birth of Princess Louisa in 1724. By the end of October 1734 she was gravely ill. Keeping her woes to herself she attended the King's birthday ceremonies as usual, but for once she found the heat and fatigue almost unbearable. Fear of her husband's displeasure had less effect than the instinct of self-preservation, and afterwards she kept to her room for a month.

Walpole lectured her gently on the importance of looking after herself properly: 'your life is of such consequence to your husband, to your children, to this country,' he warned, 'that any neglect of your health is really the greatest immorality you can be guilty of.' His greatest fear was that, should she die suddenly, the King would fall under the influence of some scheming mistress without brains who would draw him towards the opposition. Not hesitating to discuss the matter, she told him that she was sure the King would marry again, and she had advised him to do so on more than one occasion. She seemed resigned to the probability that he would outlive her. This being the case, Walpole need not fear the influence of a second wife. The King's good sense and affection for his family, she assured him, and his unbounded confidence in him (Walpole) would make it difficult if not impossible for a second Queen to disrupt his family life or influence political affairs.

Walpole was less than convinced, insisting ruefully that if he could claim any success in carrying on the King's affairs, 'if it is a success, I am free to own, I never could have had but by the mediation of Your Majesty.' He declared his intention of remaining in London until the Queen had recovered, but she would not hear of it. Much to his relief, she was soon better, but he had had a chilling presentiment of what her loss could mean to him.

CHAPTER FIFTEEN

'As great a political coward that ever wore a crown'

In November 1734 Lady Suffolk, the former Mrs Howard, finally left court. The King's 'nightly visits' had been becoming shorter and more perfunctory for some time, 'and not without sometimes a total intermission'. He found her company ever less congenial, and he distrusted her friendships with Bolingbroke, the ever-mischievous opposition Whig Pulteney, whose name King George II had personally struck from the Privy Council book in 1731 for his lack of respect, and Alexander Pope, whose vitriolic verse was particularly resented. It was rumoured that Walpole heartily disliked her and was anxious to see an end to her influence. At the end of the summer Lady Suffolk asked for permission to take a holiday, her first in twenty years of royal service. She went to Bath for six weeks, where Bolingbroke happened to be staying. Whether they attempted any political intrigue is unlikely, but not wishing to waste an opportunity to make mischief, Princess Amelia suggested that there must be something scandalous in their meetings. She returned to London for the King's birthday in October, but not only did he not visit her apartments; he barely uttered one civil word to her in public.

Two weeks after her return from Bath Lady Suffolk had an interview with the Queen, who would have preferred her to stay, in which she begged leave to retire because of the King's unkindness. The Queen asked Lady Suffolk to take a week to reconsider her decision, promising that she would put her case before the King. He was not anxious for her to remain, asking the Queen why she would not let him 'part with a deaf old woman of whom I am weary'. Ungallantly he overlooked the fact that she was five years younger than him.

If he was glad to see the last of Lady Suffolk, she left royal service with equal relief. The Princess Royal was equally pleased at her departure, remarking candidly how she wished her father would take someone else, 'that Mama might be a little relieved from the ennui of seeing him in her room'. Lord Suffolk had died the previous year, his liver having proved unequal to the demands his love of the bottle made on it. Free to remarry, she took as her second husband, in the King's words, 'that old rake George

Berkeley'. He heard the news when he was in Hanover. 'I would not make such a gift to my friends,' he wrote to the Queen with disdain, 'and when my enemies rob me, please God it will always be in this manner.'[1]

King George II's interest in foreign affairs had been rekindled with the outbreak in 1733 of the war of the Polish succession, and Emperor Charles VI made it clear that he expected British support against the French. Walpole knew it would be impolitic to ask the Commons for financial support for an overseas conflict which concerned Hanover more than Britain, and argued that the latter should remain neutral. King George II would have dearly loved to take to the battlefield. Much as he disliked the Emperor personally, his electoral duty and lifelong hatred of France put him passionately on the empire's side. The hero of Oudenarde was stirred with the vision of covering himself with martial glory a second time. He must do his duty in helping to preserve the balance of power in Europe, he angrily told Walpole. Moreover he knew he was growing old and infirm, and this would probably be his last chance to perform a task for which he felt himself so well suited.

At the same time, he knew more than Walpole about European affairs and the delicate balance of power; and he appreciated that France might defeat the Empire and establish the hegemony in Europe that King William III and the Duke of Marlborough had fought so hard to destroy. The Queen unhesitatingly took the side of her husband, and thought the Emperor was justified in asking for British assistance. Nevertheless Walpole baulked at committing the country to war and levying higher taxes on the people. 'Madam, there are fifty thousand men slain this year in Europe, and not one Englishman,' was his boast.

Another member of the family was also more than willing to prove his martial ardour. In the summer of 1734 the Prince of Wales petitioned the King for permission to serve with the Hanoverian forces against the French on the Rhine, and be given a regiment to command; for a proper allowance as befitted the heir to the throne; and for a suitable marriage. In doing so he protested that he had 'never wilfully done anything' to forfeit the love and confidence of his father. The King told him plainly that what had offended him more than anything else was the Prince's 'particular disregard to his mother and his undutiful conduct towards her'. Until he mended his ways, he could not expect to have the confidence of his father.

As for his demands, the first could not be granted, although for once the Prince had an unlikely ally in his mother, who was proud of him for asking. The matter of his allowance would depend on how he treated his mother in future. Queen Caroline and the Prince had a long discussion the next day, when she declared that she had never done anything to irritate the King against him. Nothing would give her greater pleasure than that they should

be 'well together'. What concerned her most, she told him, was his weakness in listening to people 'who are trying to make a fool of you', and whose main interest in life was to distress the King. In other words, he was allowing himself to be made a tool of the opposition politicians. Penitently he wrote a submissive letter to his father, who told the Queen to tell their son that the sincerity of his words would be judged by his future behaviour.

If a military command was out of the question, and reasons for not granting him an allowance could be found, the problem of finding a Princess of Wales could not be left for too long. Initially the King suggested Princess Charlotte Amelia of Denmark, one of the few Protestant princesses available. That she was said to be deformed, mentally retarded, and a dwarf, doubtless had much to do with her availability. The King had seen her, and admitted that she was 'not handsome and rather small', but such discouraging comments from others were enough to put the Prince off all thoughts of her, and the House of Commons readily supported him. This left virtually nobody else but Princess Augusta of Saxe-Gotha, whom the King inspected in 1735 on his visit to Hanover. He declared himself satisfied with her, and the formalities were put in hand. Five cabinet ministers conveyed to the Prince His Majesty's willingness to demand the hand of Princess Augusta on his behalf, if he desired. The Prince replied without enthusiasm that whatever match the King thought suitable would meet with his approval.

The royal treasurer, Lord Delaware, was sent to ask the Duke of Saxe-Gotha for his sister's hand in marriage. The Duke was apparently pleased that an eligible bachelor had been found for his young sister, and the necessary formalities were soon concluded.

As he was about to be betrothed, the Prince was required to dismiss Anne Vane. The bitter pill was sweetened for her by the parting gift from the Prince of a house in Grosvenor Square and an allowance of £1,500 a year until she found a husband, and £20,000 on marriage. She did not live to enjoy either for long, for the infant son of which he believed himself to be the father died soon afterwards, and she followed him to the grave within a few months. The Prince was genuinely stricken with remorse and grief, much to the surprise of his mother who declared that she could never have believed him capable of such depth of feeling. Meanwhile Lady Archibald Hamilton, a thirty-five-year-old mother of ten, was appointed Lady of the Bedchamber, Privy Purse and Mistress of the Robes to the Princess of Wales's household. Some believed her to be the Prince's mistress, though she was probably nothing more than a respected confidante. On at least one future occasion her plain speaking would reveal that any influence her presence might have had on the heir to the throne would have been to the good.

The King paid another visit to Hanover in the summer of 1735, again appointing the Queen his Regent. This time the Prince of Wales was angry

at not being entrusted with the privilege, and his open disrespect to his mother made his wounded feelings evident. It was not her only problem. Walpole had told the King he did not wish him to go, fearing that once he was back in his electorate he would take an unseemly interest in the war of the Polish succession, without his ministers to restrain him. Lord Harrington, his minister in attendance, was ordered to try and counter any moves which might involve Britain in a continental war. When he heard that the Emperor had offered King George II the command of the Rhine army in return for British support he dreaded the consequences. To his relief, the King's commonsense prevailed. Wiser than he was sometimes given credit for, he respected Walpole's policy of non-intervention and declined the offer.

The conflict came to an end in 1738 and Britain, having taken no part, had no say in the peace settlement at Vienna. Yet although he was not to know it, King George II would eventually be given one more chance on the battlefield; and he would use it well.

Meanwhile Queen Caroline was becoming aware of a new, disturbing influence at work on her husband. His letters to her became shorter, and at Hanover he took over some of the prerogatives which he had previously assigned to her, such as signing commissions. Through Harrington he cavilled at some of her acts, something he had never done before. Harrington's jealousy of Walpole and the Queen were presumably responsible. By embarrassing the Queen, he knew he would embarrass her chief adviser, yet she bore it without complaint. She was afraid to keep up much state, lest the irascible King should become too jealous, so she removed the court to Kensington, holding only such drawing-rooms as were absolutely necessary. These she held rather out of policy than from pleasure, her chief object being to conciliate the powerful Whig peers who were still dissatisfied with the government.

At the same time an even less welcome influence came to make its presence felt. While he was away, the King fell for the charms of the attractive young Baroness Amelia Sophia von Walmoden. A niece of the younger Madame von Platen, she was well aware of the obligations to which she would be subject as *maîtresse en titre*, as well as the advantages. As Queen Caroline had feared, the departure of Lady Suffolk was likely to herald the appearance of someone more youthful, more beautiful, and worst of all more ambitious. Rather oddly, at every stage of his courtship he consulted his wife. Suddenly the letters – so it was said – began to average forty to fifty pages, placing his every confidence in her. In turn she showed most of them to Hervey, who rewarded her confidence by ensuring that they rapidly became common knowledge at the court of St James's. Hervey thought she was hurt, more in her pride than in her marital affection. In that case, one wonders why she did not keep them to herself, but instead 'broadcast her shame'. None of these letters has survived; Hervey was the only one who

claimed to have seen them, and their very existence in the first place remains open to doubt.

Some of the more favoured servants were prepared to joke with the King about his infidelities and such readiness to share the details with his wife. Mrs Selwyn, one of the Queen's bedchamber ladies, told him that he was the last man with whom she would dare to have 'an intrigue', because he always told the Queen.

It proved an unusually trying Regency for her, and she found solace in improving her house and gardens at Richmond, the property in England which was hers above all others. She had already had a dairy and menagerie built in the park, and was now having a series of ornamental buildings erected. The most remarkable was one known as Merlin's Cave, approached through a maze of close alleys and clipped hedges. Dismissed by *The Craftsman* as like 'an old haystack thatched over', it was intended to be a small personal library and museum, its centrepiece being a large circular room housing 'a choice collection of English books' and waxworks of several large allegorical figures, among them 'Merlin at a table with conjuring books and mathematical instruments', and others representing the goddess Minerva, and Queen Elizabeth.

Although contemporaries at court might scorn it as an extravagant eccentricity, local people were fascinated, and once it was completed she threw it open to the public on certain days. Its success encouraged her to create a similar building nearby, called the Hermitage, described as 'very Gothic, being a heap of stones thrown into a very artful disorder and curiously embellished with moss and shrubs to represent rude nature'. Rather incongruously, it was entered via an enormous gilt gateway. Like the rest of the improvements to Richmond Lodge and the gardens, these buildings were expensive luxuries which the Queen was unable to finance from her civil list, and she knew better than to appeal to the King's never over-generous nature. Walpole gallantly came to her financial rescue by making her small secret grants from the Treasury.

The King returned from Hanover rather reluctantly for his 'mean dull island' in time for his birthday on 30 October, arriving just before dinner as the Queen came out of chapel. Unfortunately he was not in the best of health nor tempers. Travelling day and night had brought on a painful attack of piles, to which he had been prone for some years. All the courtiers suffered from his angry outbursts, but far from being afraid, they welcomed them as a badge of honour. All those who had been deliberately 'rumped' by the King, or those on whom he had turned his back, formed themselves into a Rumpsteak Club. In no frame of mind to make light of this, he exploded with wrath at their daring to make such a mockery of him.

In his absence the Queen and Hervey had taken some of their least favourite paintings from the dining room and replaced them with better

ones. When he returned the King noticed at once, and ordered rather crossly that the old ones should be put back. Hervey asked for at least two to be retained, a couple of Van Dyck portraits, one of King Charles I and his equerry, the other of King Charles, Queen Henrietta Maria, and their eldest children. The King indignantly accused Hervey of assisting the Queen with his fine advice 'when she was pulling my house to pieces and spoiling all the furniture.' He did not care whether the Van Dycks were changed or not; but he particularly objected to 'the one with the dirty frame over the door, and the three nasty little children'. Perhaps the young Stuarts were not the most tactful of choices, whatever the picture's artistic merits.

'Would Your Majesty have the gigantic fat Venus restored too?' Hervey asked respectfully, referring to Giorgio Vasari's *Venus and Cupid*. The King may not have known much about art, but he knew what he liked. 'Yes, my Lord; I am not so nice as your lordship. I like my fat Venus much better than anything you have given me instead of her.'[2]

In his later years King George II's Hanoverian blood and upbringing, and Hanoverian superiority, were beginning to reassert themselves. The Prince of Wales who had proudly if inaccurately once bragged about not having one drop of blood in his veins that was not English now chose to find fault with everything about his adopted country:

No English or even French cook could dress a dinner; no English confectioner set out a dessert; no English player could act; no English coachman could drive, or English jockey ride, nor were there any English horses fit to be drove or fit to be ridden; no Englishman knew how to come into a room, nor any Englishwoman knew how to come into a room, nor any Englishwoman how to dress herself, nor were there any diversions in England, public or private, nor any man or woman in England whose conversation was to be borne – the one, as he said, talked of nothing but their dull politics, the other of nothing but their dull clothes. Whereas at Hanover all these things were in the utmost perfection. The men were patterns of politeness, bravery and gallantry; the women of beauty, wit and entertainment; his troops there were the bravest in the world, his counsellors the wisest, his manufacturers the most ingenious, his subjects the happiest; and at Hanover, in short, plenty reigned, magnificence resided, arts flourished, diversions abounded, riches flowed, and everything was in the utmost perfection that contributes to make a prince great or a people blessed.[3]

He condemned all the English as king-killers and republicans, and complained that while in Hanover he could distribute his royal favours as a reward for faithful service, in England he simply rewarded people for not being rascals and bribed them not to cut his throat. It was the English

parliamentary system, and the restrictions on the English monarchy, that he especially resented. It was so different from the benevolent, paternal despotism of Hanover.

To those who dared to complain of his frequent journeys back to the land of his birth, he retorted that his English subjects were continually going to their country seats; Hanover was his country seat.

He was irritated by the custom of giving large tips to the servants of one's host when going out to dinner. Even the Queen admitted she found it a considerable expense to visit her friends in town. It was her fault, the King told her; his father, when he went to other people's houses in town, was never fool enough to go giving away his money. When the Queen insisted that she was only doing what Lord Grantham had told her she should, he retorted that she was 'always asking some fool or other what she was to do, and that none but a fool would ask another fool's advice'. When Hervey pleaded on the Queen's behalf that it was 'polite custom', the King retorted, 'Then she may stay at home as I do. You do not see me running into every puppy's house, to see his new chairs and stools. Nor is it for *you*,' he said, turning to the Queen, 'to be running your nose everywhere, and trotting about the town to every fellow that will give you some bread and butter, like an old girl that loves to go abroad, no matter whether it be proper or no.'[4]

After one such occasion, Hervey alleged (though he admitted to hearing the story at third hand), the Queen finally lost her temper with him. She told him angrily that there was no reason for him to come back to England. He could easily have stayed in Hanover, without returning to torment himself and her, 'since your pleasure did not call you, I am sure your business did not, for we could have done that just as well without you as you could have pleased yourself without us.'[5] Shaking with rage, the King stalked out of the room. The only one to escape the King's wrath was the Prince of Wales, who had the good sense to keep out of the way.

Walpole, for one, believed that his dreams of absolute power were nothing but bluff. With all his personal bravery, the Minister suggested, the King was 'as great a political coward as ever wore a crown, and as much afraid to lose it'.

The Prince of Wales was twenty-nine in 1736, and the matter of his marriage could no longer be postponed. Although the King's previous visits to Hanover had been restricted to once every three years, he had promised Baroness von Walmoden that he would return for her next birthday, 29 May 1736. She was expecting a child which he assumed to be his, and he wanted to be with her then. In the spring she gave birth to a son. If the Prince of Wales was to be married, it would have to be before then, or postponed until the winter; or else the ceremony would have to take place without the

groom's father being present. Although the mutual antipathy between father and son was no secret, for the latter to go to the altar while the former was abroad courting his mistress would surely damage the dynasty by such an unashamed display of family disunity.

Lord Delaware was despatched to Saxe-Gotha to bring Princess Augusta back; still carrying her doll, she landed on 25 April at Greenwich, and stayed the night at the palace there. Nobody from the royal family was on hand to meet her. It was probably the King's way of putting prospective members of the family in their place, for a similar lack of hospitality had been extended to the Prince of Orange two years earlier. The excuse that the King and Queen made was that until she was Princess of Wales, there was no rule of precedence to guide them as to how she should be received. Yet in their present mood of mutual irritability, the only common factor between them appeared to be impatience with their elder son and heir; and the unfortunate bride was caught in the middle of their general wrath.

The Princess was tall but rather ungainly in her movements, shy and gauche; aged seventeen, she had led a very sheltered life. Her mother assumed that as the Hanoverians had been on the throne for over twenty years, everyone in England would be speaking German by now. As a result her education had been rather neglected, linguistically at least; she knew little French and no English.

However everyone was favourably impressed with her quiet and modest good sense. In particular the Prince of Wales was delighted with her, as well as doubtless anxious to make amends for the rest of the family's cold reception of her. He met her at Greenwich, conveyed her up the river Thames in his barge with musical accompaniment, supped and dined with her in public, and did not leave her until 2 a.m. the following day. On being introduced to her future father- and mother-in-law at St James's she sank humbly to their feet, a gesture which made an excellent first impression. Among the Queen's first words to her were to 'avoid jealousy and to be easy in regard to amours'; such caution, she said, had ensured her a happy marriage herself.

The wedding ceremony was performed by the Bishop of London at 9 p.m. in the private chapel at St James's. As the hands of the couple were joined at the altar, a salute was fired in the park to announce the news to the people. Although the Prince's patronage of the unlamented Buononcini had almost been the undoing of Handel, the latter bore the heir to the throne no malice and graciously composed an anthem for the occasion.

At the supper afterwards the groom made himself conspicuous by eating several helpings of jelly, believed to be an aphrodisiac, laughing and winking at the servants every time he took a new glass. Such behaviour, the Queen muttered, made her feel sick. At the ancient ritual of putting the bride and groom to bed the King steeled himself for the task of helping his

son into a nightshirt where he could join his bride in bed. They sat there side by side, surrounded by the royal family, as guests were admitted to come and see them all together. The solemnity presented by this spectacle was somewhat marred by the Prince's tall nightcap which, everyone said, was several inches higher than the cap of any grenadier in the army. Had it not been her own son, the Queen said wryly afterwards, it would have made her laugh.

Princess Augusta was fortunate to make a good impression on everyone. At first nobody had a bad word to say for her. Observing that she had gained the approval of the King as well as the husband whom she barely yet knew, Walpole remarked that these 'were circumstances that spoke strongly in favour of brains which had but seventeen years to ripen'. Despite his aversion to his son, the King 'behaved to her not only with great politeness, but with the appearance of cordiality and affection'.[6] The Prince of Wales must have hoped that not the least of his marriage's results would be to ease the relationship with his parents.

'How is the wind today for the King?'

Now that his son's wedding had taken place, the King was impatient to return to Hanover. Walpole had sworn to the Queen that her husband would not go if he could possibly prevent it. The Quakers' Bill was passing through Parliament and the bishops were making trouble for the government in the House of Lords; the King's departure for his old home again so soon would be an embarrassing inconvenience, but for once neither the Queen nor Walpole could bring him to reconsider. When the bishops' action was offered as an excuse, he exploded with wrath: 'I am sick to death of all this foolish stuff, and wish with all my heart that the devil may take all your bishops and the devil take your minister, and the devil take the parliament, and the devil take the whole island, provided I can get out of it and go to Hanover.'[1]

He left in May 1736, taking Horace Walpole as minister in attendance instead of the troublesome Harrington, whom the Queen and Sir Robert Walpole had decided should never accompany his sovereign again after last time. Before going the King sent his son a kindly message to the effect that wherever his mother resided, there would always be a home for him and his wife. The Prince took this to mean that there would always be a prison. At the same time his allowance was raised to £50,000, and he also received the revenues of the Duchy of Cornwall, amounting to between £8,000 and £9,000 a year. However the King drew the line at paying his son's bachelor debts.

He also left strict instructions that the Prince and Princess of Wales should not dine in public nor attempt any 'progress' through the country, and he appointed the Queen 'Protector of the Realm'. However he sent his son an uncharacteristically generous present of £1,000. This did not appease the Prince's bitterness at, again, not being appointed Regent. He deliberately absented himself from the Council when the Queen broke the seals of the King's commission making her Regent, pretending that he had mistaken the appointed hour.

The King's return to Hanover was celebrated by the birth of a baby son to

Baroness von Walmoden. He believed the child to be his.* The Baroness
was not short of male admirers, however, and a few weeks later when the
King was staying at Herrenhausen and she at the Leine Schloss, where she
returned by night and he visited her sometimes, a gardener found a
ladder leading to the window of her bedroom. Suspecting a burglar, he
found a young man hiding in the garden. Enquiries revealed that he was
an officer in the Austrian service, named Schulemburg, a distant relative
of the Duchess of Kendal, on a visit to Hanover in connection with a
diplomatic mission. He made such a fuss that the captain of the guard
released him at once. Early next morning the Baroness went to the King
before he could hear the story from anyone else, and assured him that she
felt it was part of a plot on the part of Madame d'Elitz, another
Schulemburg relative (and a former mistress of the King, his father and
his son) to try and discredit her. While suspecting the obvious, he was
prepared to give her the benefit of the doubt. Meanwhile young
Schulemburg was urged privately by Horace Walpole to leave Hanover
quickly in order to avert scandal.

The King despatched a long letter to the Queen, telling her about the
incident and asking for her opinion. As he was so fond of 'the Walmoden',
he said, he could not judge the matter impartially himself, and if she was in
doubt would she ask Walpole, 'who is much more experienced, my dear
Caroline, in these affairs than you, and less prejudiced than myself in it.'

A husband whose insensitivity bordered on the farcical was not Queen
Caroline's only family problem. At home the Prince of Wales seemed
determined to put his wife up to various discourtesies in an effort to tease
his mother. She found them tedious, but put her feelings to one side and
invited them to dine once or twice a week, as well as music and cards in the
gallery at Hampton Court in the evening. The Princess came to these latter
functions, but not the Prince, though he was obliged to come to dinner.
Such meals were not very pleasant for any of them. The Queen found her
daughter-in-law dull, her son's silly jokes gave her 'the vapours', and she
complained that an afternoon with them made her feel as tired as though
she had carried them round the garden on her back.

As if that was not enough, the country was restless. There were corn riots
in the West Country, and at Spitalfields the weavers attacked and killed
some of the Irishmen who were undercutting them. In September 1736
Parliament passed the Gin Act to control and restrict the sale of gin which
made one 'drunk for a penny, dead drunk for tuppence', by imposing a tax

*According to Hervey the boy, named Louis, died within a year of birth. Other sources say that
he came over to England with his mother after Queen Caroline's death, was known as 'Master
Louis', and died in 1811.

of £1 a gallon on all spirits, and £50 for a retail licence. It was much resented by the people whom it was supposed to benefit. When the Queen returned to Kensington in her coach one day a mob surrounded her, shouting, 'No Gin! No King!' Calmly she leaned out of the window to assure them that if they were patient, they would have their gin and their King as well. The Queen had given her full support to the Act, as she wanted to abate the scandal of drunkenness, yet much of the odium fell on her and Walpole. In his quest for popularity the Prince of Wales sided with the people, and was said to have been drinking gin publicly in a London tavern on the day the Act came into force. It was sold just as openly under fictitious names, and the ineffective Act was repealed seven years later.

Worst of all, in Edinburgh the Porteous riots shook the forces of authority, when two smugglers, Wilson and Robertson, were sentenced to be hanged. On the day of the execution Captain John Porteous was in command of the town guard, and his men had been issued with ammunition to keep the crowds under control. As expected they surrounded the gallows, jeering and shouting and, after Wilson was executed, they pelted the executioner and the guards with stones. In the ensuing chaos Robertson escaped and on Porteous's orders the troops fired on the crowd, killing six or seven and wounding many more. Only after a fierce struggle did Porteous and his soldiers escape. Through the narrow winding streets they arrived at a tavern where he had arranged to meet the magistrates after the execution. He had intended to give his version of the incident, but some of the mob had forestalled him. By the time he arrived, the magistrates had heard their version of events, and they ordered his arrest on a charge of murder. He had long been notorious in Edinburgh for his violent methods of quelling riots, often wading into the crowds and lashing out indiscriminately with his cane. At his trial by a jury of townsmen he was found guilty and condemned to execution.

The gentry of Edinburgh considered that rough justice had been done, and they forwarded a signed petition for mercy to Queen Caroline in her capacity as Regent. She sent a reply that though she was naturally disposed to show mercy, she would not pardon the prisoner, but instead grant a reprieve for six weeks in order to give her the opportunity to inquire whether he was a proper object for royal clemency. Had the law been allowed to take its due course, Porteous would probably have had his sentence commuted to transportation, but the Edinburgh mob would have none of it. They stormed the prison, dragged him from his cell and hanged him before the troops could rescue him.

Queen Caroline was infuriated at this usurpation of authority. The strain and years of ill health were telling on her, and at last her considerable patience was exhausted. Rather than submit to such an insult, she declared

before the council, she would make Scotland a hunting-ground. The Duke of Argyll answered diplomatically, 'In that case, Madam, I will take leave of Your Majesty, and go down to my own country to get my hounds ready.'[2]

There was a feeling that action should be taken against the city of Edinburgh, such as a nominal fine. Nevertheless Scottish peers in the House of Lords argued firmly in favour of their countrymen, Walpole's cabinet was fiercely divided, and the episode was closed with a measure passed through both Houses of Parliament, disqualifying the Provost of Edinburgh from holding public office again, and the imposition of a nominal fine of £2,000 on the city in order to finance the granting of a government pension to the widow of Porteous.

When the King proposed prolonging his stay in Hanover beyond his birthday (30 October), the people complained that they had not granted him a Civil List in order to defray his travelling expenses to Hanover and the enrichment of his German whores. The Queen was equally disgruntled, and made her feelings clear to Walpole. He advised her sympathetically that if she wanted to retain her power over her husband, she would have to put up with his extra-marital affairs, even to the extent of letting him bring Baroness von Walmoden over to England where she would be far less dangerous than in Hanover. She would soon be everything to the King that Lady Suffolk was – except deaf. Tactlessly he told the Queen that she could no longer keep the King by her side by the arts and charms she had employed as a younger woman, and now she had to make the best of a difficult situation.

Swallowing her pride, she wrote her husband a diplomatic letter suggesting that, 'as nothing was agreeable to him in England, he had better bring over that person who would make it so.'[3] In return she received a tender reply in which the King accepted her suggestion with delight, and favoured her with the fullest description of Walmoden's physical and intellectual perfections. He grovelled his thanks, telling her how unworthy he was of her, and saying that his mistress would stay in Hanover after all. Walpole's unpalatable advice had evidently worked. Less well received, it seems, were the cautious words of his brother Horatio. He was thought to have told the Baroness privately that if she came to England, it would be to her advantage to 'keep out of politics'. This came back to the King, who was so enraged that he kicked him.

The King's prolonged absence was welcome to the opposition. A wreck of an old horse, with broken saddle and pillion, was turned out in the streets of London with a placard around its neck reading 'Let nobody stop me – I am the King's Hanover equipage going to fetch His Majesty and his whore to England'. Notices were displayed in the city announcing that His Hanoverian Majesty planned to visit his British dominions for three months in the spring. A notice was pinned to the gates of St James's:

Lost or strayed out of this house, a man who has left a wife and six children on the parish; whoever will give any tidings of him to the churchwardens of St James's Parish, so as he may be got again, shall receive four shillings and sixpence reward. N.B. This reward will not be increased, nobody judging him to be worth a crown.

Meanwhile the Prince of Wales was becoming ever more popular. He let it be known that once he had gone without dinner rather than keep an opera audience waiting. 'Huzza for the Prince!' people would call in the street, to which he replied, 'Huzza for Liberty and Property'. The City of London granted him its Freedom in a gold box, and made him a member of the Worshipful Company of Saddlers, after which the King would refer sourly to his son as 'the Saddler'. Among the Prince's friends there was a plan to divide Britain and Hanover after the King died, with the Electorate going to Prince William. It would be linked with an increase in the Prince's allowance to £100,000, a price which he thought his parents would pay willingly for William's sake. The idea came to nothing, although Frederick in his will recommended it as 'from that moment Jacobitism will be rooted out.'

Early in December, after giving a ball and farewell supper at Herrenhausen, the King tore himself away at last from Baroness von Walmoden and his equally beloved Hanover. Four days later he arrived at Helvoetsluys, where his yacht was awaiting him. Although the Princess of Orange had just gone through a difficult *accouchement*, with her life in danger for a time, before giving birth to a stillborn daughter, the King was informed (though whether he was told all details is uncertain) but made no effort to go and see her. Either the desire to return to England as soon as possible was greater than the wish to see his daughter – even if she had exhausted his patience during her first months of marriage; or else he had no desire to be embroiled in the political problems of his son-in-law and Holland.

At St James's the Queen was more sympathetic, writing to her daughter:

Words are unnecessary, dear Anne, to tell you how I have suffered and my joy at receiving you back from God, whom I thank with all my soul. I have you and that is enough. May He grant you renewed strength and make you a happy mother of a family . . . and be certain that you will have happier and easier labours in the future.[4]

At Helvoetsluys a violent gale was raging. Nobody in London knew at first whether or not the King had embarked, and the Queen was particularly anxious, while the Prince was possibly less perturbed. Walpole was in gloom at the possibility of his fall from power with the eclipse of the widowed

13 Anne, Princess Royal, c. 1734, by Jacopo Amigomi. The Royal Collection © Her Majesty The Queen

14 Queen Caroline, 1735, by Jacopo Amigomi. By courtesy of the National Portrait Gallery, London

15 King George II, c. 1744, from the studio of Thomas Hudson. Commissioned by the Chief Justice, Sir John Willes, it hung in the Court of Common Pleas, Westminster, until the demolition of the law courts in 1883. By courtesy of the National Portrait Gallery, London

16 William, Duke of Cumberland, engraving after a portrait by Sir Joshua Reynolds.
© Hulton Getty Picture Collection Ltd

17 Princess Mary of Hesse-Cassel

18 Queen Louisa of Denmark

19 Augusta, Princess of Wales

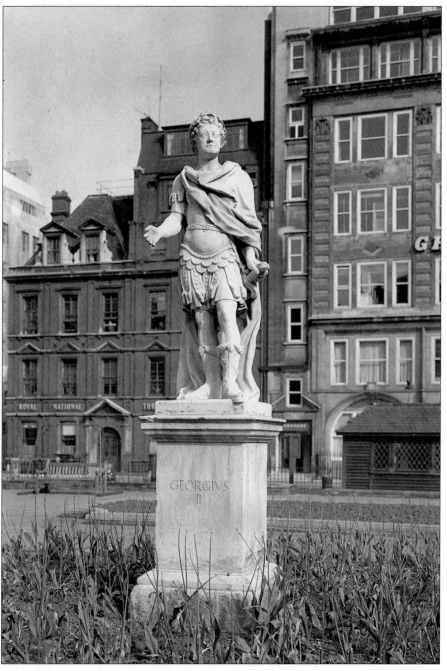

20 King George II, statue by John Van Nost erected in 1753 in Golden Square, London.
© Greater London Photograph Library

Queen. At the height of their anxiety he invited Hervey to dinner, and unburdened himself on the subject. Careful not to stress his anxiety at what his own position might be at the court or government of King Frederick, he pitied the family – the young Duke of Cumberland and the Princesses, forced 'into dependence on a brother that loves them not,' and the Queen, 'falling into the hands of a son who hates her.' As for the Prince, he was 'a poor, weak, irresolute, false, lying, dishonest, contemptible wretch, that nobody loves, that nobody believes, that nobody will trust, and that will trust everybody by turns, and that everybody by turns will impose upon, betray, mislead, and plunder. And what will then become of this divided family, and this divided country, is too melancholy a prospect for one to admit conjecture to paint it.'[5]

The people of England were less moved at the thought that their sovereign might yet be lost at sea. According to a popular joke of the day: 'How is the wind today for the King?' 'Like the people, against him.'

While anxiety in London (at least on the part of the Queen and Walpole, if nobody else) was at its height, the Prince of Wales gave a dinner to the Lord Mayor and Aldermen, and his speech was well praised. He expressed his thanks to the assembled company for 'their duty and loyalty to the King and for their affection to him', and ended with his customary professions of 'his constant zeal for the liberties of his country'. Not for the first time, Hervey managed to twist his words in order to place the worst possible construction on them to the distraught Queen Caroline. As he would have it, when she asked about it the following morning she was reportedly distressed by his insensitivity at what seemed to be such ill-timed hospitality. 'My God! popularity always makes me sick,' she muttered, 'but Fretz's popularity makes me vomit. I hear that yesterday they talked of the King's being cast away with the same *sang-froid* as you would talk of a coach being overturned, and that my good son strutted about as if he had been already King.'[6]

Walpole joined in the chorus against the Prince of Wales, declaring gloomily that when Frederick succeeded to the throne, 'he would tear the flesh off [Queen Caroline's] bones with hot irons.' More magnanimously, Hervey (who could be fair when the mood took him) conceded that he thought the Prince would make use of the Queen's great knowledge and experience in the management of affairs, and her position would not be nearly so intolerable as she feared. In fact it was his considered opinion that within a month of Frederick's accession she would have more influence with him than with anyone else, by skilfully managing him as she and Walpole had managed her husband for the last ten years. Princess Caroline, who had once been the last to speak ill of anybody, proved even more ready than her sisters to condemn their brother. She told Hervey that not only did he hate their mother, but 'he has so good an opinion of himself that he thinks he

wants no advice, and of all advice, no woman's'. The moment he was King, 'she would run out of the house, *au grand galop*'.

A King's messenger, who had been three days at sea and landed at Yarmouth, in a howling gale, arrived at the palace with a letter from the King to say that he was still at Helvoetsluys. At once the Queen's anxiety turned to relief.

By that time, however, the King had ordered Admiral Sir Charles Wager to set sail against his better judgment, swearing that he would sooner spend twelve hours in a storm than another day at Helvoetsluys. 'Well, Sir, you can make me go, but I can make you come back again,' the Admiral protested, adding that he need not wish for twelve hours as four would probably be enough to see him out. They set sail, and in a desperate effort to lighten the ship's load the sailors demolished the King's suite on the quarter-deck and pitched his furniture overboard. Prostrated by sickness, he was in no state to complain at such indignities.

Meanwhile word reached St James's that the ship had been lost at sea with all hands and passengers. The Queen lost all hope, broke down and wept bitterly. In the Prince of Wales's household there was an air of subdued excitement. Hearing this, the Queen and the rest of the family prayed fervently for His Majesty's deliverance at a special service of intercession at the Chapel Royal. While they were still in church a letter arrived from the King saying that he had put to sea but returned to shore, where he was still detained by contrary weather. The Admiral had saved him from himself, although three sailors had drowned. Five weeks later the seafarers arrived safely at Lowestoft, grateful to be alive.

On 15 January 1737 King George II was back in London. Even he could not fail to notice the hisses and absence of cheers as he drove back to the Palace in his coach. He had been away for eight months, and in terms of personal popularity this homecoming surely marked his nadir. Nevertheless, overcome with emotion at being home again he kissed all his family, even his despised eldest son, and complimented Walpole on the way in which he had conducted affairs in his absence. Even the normally uncharitable Hervey noted that 'as last year nobody had the good fortune to catch one smile from His Majesty so now there was nobody who had the mortification to meet with one frown.' Next he made up for lost time by taking the Queen up to bed.

In sharp contrast to his previous bad-tempered return from the ancestral home, this time he behaved uncharacteristically well. His narrow escape from drowning had subdued him, and his last letters to the Queen across the North Sea, far from mentioning Walmoden, penitently described how little he deserved her toleration and goodness which he could never forget. For a while, she was reminded of the same young Electoral Prince of Hanover who had sat by her bedside while her life was threatened by smallpox and thus risked his own.

Once again, it seemed as if his normally robust constitution might give way. Piles, a heavy cold which turned to fever, and nervous strain as a result of the last few months took their toll, and the King who was always so impatient of ill health in others had to retire to bed. A tiresome patient, he made no secret of his resentment with 'troublesome, inquisitive puppies who were always plaguing him with asking impertinent, silly questions about his health like so many old nurses.' Even so, for several days he was too ill to see anybody but the Queen and Walpole. The latter taxed the Queen with concealing the King's true state of health, and thought the chief trouble was 'pining and fretting' for his mistress in Hanover. The Queen, he said, should send for Baroness von Walmoden to come and nurse him, a suggestion the Queen angrily resented.

Meanwhile the Prince of Wales and his friends declared openly that his health and constitution had suffered so severely that he was unlikely to survive for long. It was rumoured that the King had caught the pox in Hanover, or a malignant fever, and on no less an authority than that of the old Duchess of Marlborough he could not possibly live for another year. Such gossip soon came to the King's ears, and had the right effect. Although suffering from a sore throat and in a high fever, he insisted on dressing to attend a levée. As impatient as ever at the thought of anybody being aware of his condition, in a fit of anger he dismissed a Lord of the Bedchamber who was rash enough to inquire after his health.

The opening of Parliament was delayed until February 1737, in order to give the King time to recover. By accident or design, the Prince of Wales chose this moment to lay before Parliament his claims for £100,000 a year. The King had just submitted to the agonizing operation of being cut for the piles, and was in such poor health that perhaps the Prince and his friends hoped the shock might complete what they thought nature had in store for him. His advisers suggested that the opposition, who had been promised support by the Prince of Wales in return for their championing his financial grievances, would support the measure by a majority of about forty votes. Early in the session the opposition brought a motion in Parliament asking the King to grant him the increase demanded from the Civil List and to settle a dowry or jointure on the Princess of Wales. Though the opposition had more than once shown willingness to support his case for a much-needed increase, he had exercised caution until after his marriage. This placed new strains upon his finances; and the King had been in no hurry to make financial provision for the Princess.

Walpole feared that a vote in the Commons might bring him down. He proposed making terms with the Prince; a jointure for his wife, and for himself the conversion into a fixed settlement of his present precarious allowance of £50,000 a year. To Walpole's formal offer of these concessions, conveyed by the Lords of the Council, the Prince returned a curt verbal reply that the matter was now out of his hands.

The King and Queen reacted to their son's stand with anger, vented in part on Walpole and other ministers for failing to settle the business out of the public eye. Walpole was not discomfited, pointing out that he had put the Prince at a disadvantage as it could now be stated that he had done himself a disservice by rejecting his father's gracious offer. The opposition's motion, supporting the Prince's full claims, was defeated.

The King and Queen were delighted. The Queen cursed the very day he was born, while Princess Caroline declared savagely that he was a nauseous beast who cared for nobody but himself, and for nothing but money, was the greatest liar that ever spoke, and would not hesitate to put one arm around a person's neck to kiss him and with the other arm, stab him for five guineas. They wanted to expel the Prince from the palace, but Walpole dissuaded them, and prevailed on the King to settle £50,000 on the Prince, together with £10,000 a year from the Duchy of Cornwall, while the Princess received a jointure of £50,000 from Parliament. The Prince continued to live at St James's, dined at his parents' table, and attended their levées, but the Queen never spoke to him, and the King behaved as if he was not in the same room. Even so, Walpole continued to persuade the King with some difficulty that it would be as well to make the jointure and the settlement of £50,000. The King gave way, but with bad grace.

When Parliament rose in the spring, the words the ministers most dreaded hearing – an announcement by the King that he intended to return to Hanover shortly – were not heard. Hardly trusting the Prince of Wales in his present mood not to intrigue against him in his absence, he knew better than to leave his kingdom again too soon. Moreover the Queen had evidently suffered during the last few months, and the strain had obviously undermined her health. No more for the time being was heard of Walmoden. Instead it seemed that her place had been usurped, in England at least, by the young, pretty but empty-headed Lady Deloraine, who was content to boast to others of her apparent hold over the King. In her case much of it was wishful thinking. As usual the Queen refused to listen to gossip, though perhaps she was grateful for the presence of somebody to distract his attention from 'the Walmoden'.

'I never yet saw a woman fit to buckle her shoe'

By the new year of 1737 the Princess of Wales was pregnant. Her ladies had known since March, when she was reckoned to be in her fourth month. Not until June did the Prince write to tell his mother, informing her that the baby would be born in October. She duly congratulated them, and put some searching questions to her daughter-in-law, only to be greeted with a persistent 'I don't know'. At once the Queen became suspicious. Was her son planning to foist a spurious child on them? The previous summer he had often hinted that his wife was pregnant, but nothing ever came of it. Recalling how he had claimed to be the father of Anne Vane's child when at least two other men might equally have been the father, and bearing in mind the Prince of Wales's glandular problems in adolescence, she privately questioned her son's ability for fatherhood.

The Prince of Wales wanted the confinement to take place in London, while the King and Queen intended the Princess to remain at Hampton Court, where they would be staying when the birth was expected, and could therefore witness the event. In July King, Queen, Prince and Princess all moved to Hampton Court. On the last day of the month they dined together in public as normal. It was one of the few ceremonial occasions on which all four met. That evening the King played his usual game of commerce, the Queen hers of quadrille, and they retired to bed at 11 p.m.

Unknown to them, their daughter-in-law had already gone into labour. The Prince of Wales had made up his mind that nothing would prevent his child from being born at St James's, away from his parents' eye, perhaps out of sheer obstinacy and his refusal to be ordered about; perhaps, as some have suggested (although highly unlikely) because he feared they might try and do away with the child. The latter fear was also apparently expressed by Augusta, who was alarmed if not paranoid about her parents-in-law's undisguised preference for the Duke of Cumberland. Ever since the argument about his allowance earlier that year, the Prince had been completely ignored by his father, while his mother might extend a theatrical hand to him on public occasions but had not addressed a single word to him in private.

Accompanied by a few members of their suite, the Prince drove his wife to London, calming her as she moaned in agony, begging to go back to Hampton Court. He assured her cheerfully that it would soon be over. They reached St James's at about 10 p.m., just in time, and she was carried shrieking with pain up to bed. No sheets were ready in the palace, and a couple of tablecloths had to be used instead. At 10.45 p.m. she was 'delivered of a little rat of a girl, about the bigness of a good, large toothpick-case.' Only two Lords of the Council were present to witness the birth.

At 1.30 the following morning a courier brought the news to Hampton Court that the Princess was in labour. A woman of the Bedchamber, Mrs Titchburne, aroused the Queen, whose immediate reaction at being disturbed at such an unearthly hour was that the palace must be on fire. On being told the news, she said she would go to her daughter-in-law at once, and asked for her nightgown. 'Your nightgown, Madam, and your coaches, too; the Princess is at St James's,' Mrs Titchburne answered. The Queen refused to believe it at first.

By now the King was beginning to wake up. He exploded with rage, venting his anger on the Queen. See how they had outwitted her, he shouted, and put a false child on them. Ignoring him she dressed hastily, and soon they had summoned a party comprising Princesses Amelia and Caroline, Lord Hervey and a few other lords in waiting. Their coach arrived at St James's by 4 a.m. as dawn began to break over the city. Ever ready to widen the breach between mother and son – as if it needed widening at this stage – Hervey offered to make the Queen a cup of her favourite hot chocolate in his own apartments, as he did not suppose she would stay long with the Prince of Wales. She certainly would not stay there long, she assured him, and his lordship need not fear her tasting anything on that side of the house.

At the sight of her daughter-in-law the Queen softened at once, congratulating her and commiserating with her on her sufferings. 'It was nothing,' the exhausted young mother answered stoically. Lady Archibald Hamilton brought the baby in for her to see. Turning to her grandchild, she kissed her, exclaiming; 'Poor little creature, you have come into a troublesome world!' Meanwhile the Prince was trying to make excuses, but the Queen ignored him. She reproached Lady Archibald, the mother of ten children herself, asking her how she could, 'for your own sake as well as theirs, venture to be concerned in such an expedition'. Lady Archibald said nothing to the Queen, but in her presence turned coldly to the Prince, saying, 'You see, sir'. It was evident that she had tried to dissuade him from such folly.

Before leaving the Queen asked the Princess of Wales if there was anything else she could do. Had the Princess asked her to forgive her

husband and herself for their rash conduct, the Queen might have complied. Instead the young mother answered, a little distantly, that she had nothing else with which to trouble her. Getting ready to leave, the Queen warned her son that she could not answer for the consequences if he insisted on seeing his father for several days, and then returned to Hampton Court. Her initial doubts that it had been the Princess's child were appeased. If instead of 'this poor, ugly little she-mouse', her grandchild had been 'a large, fat, healthy boy', she said, she would have suspected the worst.

When Walpole and Lord Harrington arrived at the Palace later that morning she declared that her patience was exhausted, and unless steps were taken to check 'their impertinence', life would become intolerable for her and the King. While admitting that the Prince of Wales's behaviour had been indefensible, the minister sagely advised her not to allow her resentment to get the better of her. People talked enough of the partiality she and the King had for the Duke of Cumberland, he said, 'and should all your anger break out at this time they will be apt to say that your anger is principally occasioned by the Prince's having a child to disinherit your favourite.'[1]

Nine days later she went back to St James's to enquire after her daughter-in-law and granddaughter. In a sullen mood, the Prince spoke not a single word to her in private. He led her to the coach in silence, but on seeing a large crowd gathered round to watch, he knelt theatrically in the mud to kiss her hand as she stepped inside. It was the last time they would see each other.

The King was in no mood for compromise. While he rejoiced heartily at the Princess's safe delivery of a child, he let it be known, he was nevertheless bound to condemn the way in which she had been exposed to such danger, and that their withdrawal from Hampton Court without informing the King and Queen of the matter was a deliberate indignity which they resented in the highest degree. Princess Caroline joined in and sent a message through Dunoyer, the dancing master, that notwithstanding the respect she owed him, 'Your Royal Highness deserves to be hanged'. The Prince spat in the fire, and shrugged that she was 'always like that'.

The Prince of Wales was warned by Carteret and Pulteney, men whom he had previously regarded as trusted allies, that he had gone too far this time. He tried to defend his conduct in letters to his father by pleading his distraught state in extenuating circumstances, an excuse which failed to convince for a moment. In addition he declared that he was wise to hasten the Princess of Wales away to St James's as there were no midwife, nurse nor arrangements for an accouchement at Hampton Court. As there had been false alarms only a few days before, this was even less credible.

Letters to the Queen in which he signally omitted to address his mother as 'Your Majesty' reinforced the King's anger at their son's base ingratitude towards and callous treatment of his mother. Indeed, the Prince of Wales failed to appreciate that the Queen often tried to defend him. She had been opposed to the King's proposal to dissolve the personal union of Great Britain and Hanover so that the Duke of Cumberland could have the electorate. The King told Hervey that he had often had occasion to scold the Queen for taking the Prince of Wales's part, and had more arguments with her on account of her constant excuses for his foolish conduct than he ever had with her on any other subject.

The King and Queen accepted an invitation, which they considered theirs by right, to be godparents to their granddaughter, named Augusta after her mother. Afterwards they felt the time had come to teach their son a lesson. To their credit they were not nearly as vindictive as King George I had been on a similar occasion in 1717 (when the then Prince of Wales's sole 'offence' had been allowing his tongue to run away with him), and had no intention of doing anything as cruel as depriving him and his wife of the custody of their child. The King was wise enough to know that if anything happened to the 'royal little animal', the world would accuse him and the Queen of having murdered it, for the sake of the Duke of Cumberland who would then again be his brother's heir again.*

The Cabinet agreed with the King's decision. Much drafting and redrafting by Hervey, Walpole and others took place before the King's orders to his son could be signed and despatched on 10 September 1737. After a detailed summary of the young man's misdemeanours, notably concealing from him and the Queen all knowledge of the pregnancy until within a month of the baby's birth, and having exposed the Princess and child to the greatest perils by moving her precipitately from Hampton Court, he was no longer to reside in the King's palace. He was to leave St James's Palace with his family 'when it can be done without prejudice or inconvenience to the Princess'. Only when the Prince manifested a just sense of 'duty and submission' would the King consider pardoning him.

The Queen declared her wish that she would never see her son again, while the King told her he could not wait for 'the puppy' to be out of his house, as he could never forgive him for his behaviour to her: 'I must say you have been an excellent mother to all your children, and if any of them behave ill to you they deserve to be hanged. I never loved the puppy well

*Despite the circumstances of her birth, Princess Augusta throve, and lived to be seventy-five. One of her daughters also became Queen Caroline – the notorious consort of King George IV.

enough to have him ungrateful to me, but to you he is a monster and the greatest villain that was ever born.'[2] He solemnly warned all foreign ministers, peers and Privy Councillors that whoever went to the Prince's Court would not be admitted to that of the King. Handel was forbidden to give a concert for the Prince, and his physicians were commanded to refuse invitations to attend his birthday dinner. He was deprived of his guard, and the furniture from his apartments. However the King stopped short of ordering the Prince's servants to leave their master.

Two days later the Prince, Princess and their household left for Kew. Many onlookers were in tears, and the sentry at St James's, having received positive orders not to salute the Prince, said he would have done so if his Captain had not been watching him. City magnates, opposition Whigs and Tories wasted little time in flocking to the Prince's court. Carteret and Pulteney soon joined them, less out of sympathy with the Prince than as a matter of policy, of opposition to the government. When told, the King sighed that they would 'soon be tired of the puppy'. He was not only a scoundrel, but 'such a fool that he will talk more fiddle-faddle nonsense to them in a day than any old woman talks in a week.' Shortly afterwards the family took up residence at Norfolk House, St James's Square, later moving to Leicester House, 'that pouting place of Princes'.

But the King was unforgiving. He mused that his son must be a *Wechselbag*, or what in Germany they called a child put in the cradle instead of another. 'A changeling', Hervey suggested helpfully. The Queen added that 'My dear first-born is the greatest ass, and the greatest liar, and the greatest canaille, and the greatest beast, in the whole world, and I most heartily wish he was out of it.'[3]

The King was concerned not to become involved in 'a paper-war with his daughter-in-law'. On 15 September she wrote to him expressing her regret for what had happened, and to offer her services as mediator in the quarrel. The King replied how sorry he was that she should have suffered on account of her husband's folly, and that only by his actions could he seek forgiveness. Three days later the Princess wrote to the Queen, explaining the 'facts' about the so-called concealment of her condition. Her doctors and the midwife had assured her that she would not be brought to bed until the middle of September, and that when the labour pains began she thought she was only suffering from colic. It grieved her very much to think that her husband's conduct was so misunderstood by his mother and father. Suspecting that the Princess was only writing at the instigation of her husband, the King and Queen refused to accept or believe her explanations, and the letters only made their resentment worse.

The Prince sent his father a submissive verbal reply, and then proceeded to hold a meeting for the benefit of the Lord Mayor and aldermen, and various members of the opposition, at which he gave his version of events

and published the correspondence between him and his father. As it was not fully accurate, the King proceeded to publish the 'official' version, to which the Prince retaliated by publishing the correspondence which had passed between his father and grandfather in 1717.

By the autumn Queen Caroline's health was further declining. For a long time she had kept secret from everyone except her husband the umbilical rupture resulting from the difficult birth of her last child. Since becoming Queen she had fought constantly against gout and physical weakness, though like her husband she hated to admit that she felt unwell. Her daughters, in particular Princess Caroline, her main confidante since the marriage of the Princess Royal, understood her better than the King, but nobody knew more than her favourite woman of the Bedchamber and unofficial private secretary Charlotte Clayton, created Lady Sundon in 1735.

The strain under which she had been living contributed to a general feeling of depression. The last year and its anxieties – the Porteous riots, her eldest daughter's difficult confinement, the fear of losing her husband at sea, and finally the quarrels with her eldest son – took their toll. She blamed her failing health for her decline in influence over the King, his increasing impatience with her, and his passion for 'the Walmoden'.

As usual the King and Queen left Hampton Court late in October, arriving at St James's in time to celebrate the King's birthday on the 30th. For once Walpole was absent, in mourning for his wife who had recently passed away. Though they had been separated for some years, propriety demanded that he show some signs of respect.

Walpole disliked Lady Sundon and had long resented the influence she had over the Queen, which seemed inexplicable. At last he discovered the reason. When she saw him after his wife's death, the Queen asked him several searching questions about Lady Walpole's health, and in particular one complaint from which she had never suffered. At once it all became clear, and on returning home he told his son Horace that now he knew 'by the possession of what secret Lady Sundon has preserved such an ascendant over the Queen'.

Anxious to put the troubles of the last year behind her, the Queen found solace in organizing her personal library. William Kent was designing her a special room overlooking the Green Park, which she could furnish with books and new bookcases to her heart's content. She had ordered busts of philosophers and learned men to be arranged in the corridor, and English ambassadors abroad had been asked to obtain the best French, Spanish and Italian books to make her collection as complete as possible. The result would be the equivalent of the Electress Sophie's apartments at Herrenhausen, where she could surround herself with books, friends and stimulating discussion.

On the morning of 9 November 1737 she walked over there, as she had done for the previous few days, to superintend the work in progress. Suddenly she was seized with violent internal pain. At first she thought it was a recurrence of the colic from which she had suffered earlier that year, but as it gradually worsened, she made her way back to St James's Palace and retired to bed. A drawing-room was to be held that afternoon. Deeply concerned, the King intended to postpone it, but she told him she felt much better, got up and dressed, and insisted on being present. She was her usual affable self, although she could barely stand. It was a relief when everyone had gone and she could return to bed, assuring the King that it was only a temporary indisposition. After sending for the German court physician to come and attend to her, he spent the evening playing cards with Lady Deloraine.

Lord Hervey was also there, and she asked him what she should take to ease the pain. A chronic invalid and hypochondriac himself, he must have wondered where to start, but he recommended a concoction called snakeroot which the German doctor forbade her to take. As she was now in high fever, he called in another doctor. Not knowing what was wrong with her, they administered a number of remedies in turn which not surprisingly made her violently sick. Next came Dr Ranby, who bled her twelve ounces. Suddenly Princess Caroline, who had been sitting with her for most of the day, was seized with severe rheumatic pains, so Hervey produced another of his concoctions, which made her worse as well.

When the King returned he was upset at finding the Queen so ill. He lay on her bed all night outside the coverlet, thus ensuring that both had an equally restless time.

On the next morning she was bled again, and the fever subsided a little. The doctors thought she was better, but she knew otherwise. Commiserating with Princess Caroline, still suffering from the effects of Hervey's pills, she comforted her with the certainty that 'we shall soon meet again in another place'. At her request the King held his usual drawing-room, and Princess Amelia took her mother's place at court. Towards evening the Queen worsened, and cried aloud to Princess Caroline, 'I have an agony which nobody knows of'. Two more physicians were called in, and the purges and blistering continued. The King was increasingly concerned, and once again sat up all night with her.

The next day it was impossible to suppress the fact that she was seriously ill. At Kew the Prince of Wales enquired whether he might come and see his mother. It was just like one of the scoundrel's tricks, the King raged, like his kneeling in the mud to kiss her hand the last time they saw each other, but 'he shall not come and act any of his silly plays here'. He always hated the rascal, he raged, but now hated him worse than ever: 'he wants to come and insult his poor dying mother, but she shall not see him.'[6] In the afternoon

the Queen enquired whether her son had asked to visit. When the King told her she accepted his decision, and told him she had no wish to see him again. Although too weary to argue, she sent a private message of forgiveness to her son through Walpole, saying she would have seen him with pleasure but such an interview would have embarrassed the King.

Her worsening condition the next day did not prevent her from attempting to conceal the true cause of her illness. Desperately worried, the King begged her to let him tell Dr Ranby about the rupture, but she denied it. Nevertheless he sent for Ranby, who had probably guessed the truth, and confided his fears to him. The doctor examined her, and said he must operate. No longer able to keep her secret, the Queen turned her face to the wall, and wept for the first and last time. Two more surgeons were summoned to assist with the operation, but years of reticence and neglect had done their work. It was too late for effective treatment.

On the following morning, a Sunday, the wound was mortifying and gave her great pain. Dr Ranby declared that she could not survive for many hours. She sent for her husband and children (except for the Prince of Wales), and asked them not to leave her until she died. To Princess Caroline she commended the care of the younger children. To the Duke of Cumberland she asked that he should be a support to his father all times, and try to make up for the vexations caused him by his elder brother. To her husband, she gave the ruby ring he had placed on her finger at the Coronation, and said that he must marry again. Between sobs, he promised her that he would still have mistresses. '*Ah, mon Dieu! Cela n'empêche pas,*' she sighed. Then she fell into a doze and everyone feared she would pass away in her sleep, but she woke up feeling better, declaring that she would last three more days, until the Wednesday. Her birth, marriage and birth of her first child had all been on a Wednesday, as had the receipt of news of the late King's death, and her Coronation. She would surely die on the same day of the week.

Next morning Walpole arrived back from Houghton, where he had just attended his wife's funeral. In consequence of his mourning he had not been sent for officially, but when he heard how serious the Queen's condition was he came as soon as he could. The interview was very short, but the Queen said, 'I have nothing to say to you but to recommend the King, my children, and the kingdom to your care.'[5]

For two days she appeared to be holding her own, and the physicians hoped against hope that she might recover after all. On the Thursday a change for the worse took place and she suffered much pain, but she bore it all without complaint. When Dr Ranby came to dress her wound, she asked him in jest what he would give to be cutting up his wife, from whom he was seeking divorce. When a candle set alight the wig of another surgeon assisting in the operation, she asked Ranby to wait a moment so that she

could laugh. If even a groan escaped her under the knife, she would apologize for her complaints, when she knew they were doing all they could to help her.

Some of the bishops remarked on the absence of any services from the chaplain, and courtiers said it was not right that the Queen should suffer without the consolations of religion. On Walpole's recommendation Dr Potter was sent for. Princess Amelia demurred, knowing her mother's questioning attitude towards religion, but he insisted, saying that it would be 'quite as well that the farce should be played. The Archbishop of Canterbury would perform it decently; and the Princess might bid him to be as short as she liked. It would do the Queen neither harm nor good; and it would satisfy all the fools who called them Atheists, if they affected to be as great fools as they who called them so.'[6] Dr Potter came to see her, and prayed by her bedside. On leaving the chamber he was surrounded by inquisitive courtiers, and evaded all questions on whether she had taken the sacrament by the non-committal statement that she was in a 'heavenly disposition'.

By this time the King was frantic with grief and anxiety. To his daughters, Hervey, and the physicians and surgeons, he spoke hour after hour of how she was the most wonderful wife man ever had. Yet this did not prevent him from continuing to scold her. If she kept on constantly shifting around, he would ask how the devil could she expect to sleep if she would never lie still. When she did lie still, he would complain that she was staring like a calf that had just had its throat cut. If he had bullied her into eating what she immediately threw up, he would ask her roughly why she had called for a thing if she did not want it. If she did like it, why give it away? But if he had not behaved in his normal manner, she would have missed the snubs and the bullying.

His constant praise of the Queen's courage was not unmixed with that of his own. She was as brave, her told Hervey and his daughters, as he had been during that terrible storm on the North Sea. 'Is he gone?' Princess Amelia asked crossly when she came in after he had left the room on one such occasion. She was 'sick to death of hearing of his great courage'.

On 20 November Queen Caroline asked one of the physicians how long she was likely to last, and he assured her that she would soon be at rest. She took her leave of the King and thanked him for all her goodness to her. To the hypochondriac Princess Caroline, who had always been her favourite daughter, she said that she would follow her in less than a year. At about 10 p.m., while the King slept fitfully on the floor at the foot of her bed, and Princess Amelia lay in a couch-bed in the corner of the room, the death-rattle began in the dying woman's throat. 'I have now got an asthma. Open the window,' she gasped, followed by 'Pray.' Princess Amelia began to read some prayers, as the last breath left her mother's body. Princess Caroline

held a looking-glass to her lips, but no sign of moisture appeared. ''Tis over!' she said. The King knelt down and kissed the face and hands of his wife several times, before his daughters led him away to their apartments.

After her death the King requested a guard to keep watch beside his bed for several nights. He spoke incessantly about her, weeping the whole time. A few days later he asked Baron Borgman, a Hanoverian officer in his service, to bring a portrait which the Queen had given him and was said to be a better likeness than any others in his possession. When he saw it he burst into tears, and ordered that it should be placed on a chair at the foot of his bed. Nobody should disturb him, he told the page, till he rang the bell. Two hours later, calm and dry-eyed, he ordered the page to take the picture away: 'I never yet saw a woman fit to buckle her shoe.'

He took over payment of all her private salaries, pensions and charities amounting to £15,000 a year, declaring that no one should be the poorer for her death but himself. When the gardener Charles Bridgeman died shortly afterwards, the gardens at Richmond came under the King's care. Her zeal in the gardens had added 188 acres to the royal gardens, more than doubling the cost of their maintenance and requiring separate gardeners for each palace. New contracts were drawn up, and despite the additional expense the grieving King did not mutter one word of protest.

On the night of 16 December, a simple service was held in the room where her body lay, encased in a lead coffin and an outer one of English oak. Only the King, the Duke of Cumberland, and the Princesses attended. The chamber had been transformed into a chapel, the walls hung with purple and black, while tall tapers burned night and day around the bier, the doors guarded by gentlemen pensioners with their axes reversed. Nobody had been allowed to enter the room except the King himself and those who watched by the body. As Dr Potter read prayers of consolation and hope the King, overcome with grief and exhaustion, broke down and wept like a child. Later that night the coffin was taken to the Princes' Chamber at Westminster Abbey.

The funeral took place the following evening in Henry VII's Chapel. King George had ordered a new vault to be made just large enough to contain the Queen's coffin. Then he ordered it to be made twice as large, as he said he would be put in the same vault when he died, and the sides of both coffins were to be removed so that their dust could mingle. At the obsequies the King attended, 'prominent in his grief', while the Princesses sat crying softly in the royal pew, mourning for the mother they had adored. Their eldest brother, needless to say, was not invited. The procession of government mourners was headed by Walpole, who had virtually owed his pre-eminence in government to the woman whom they were burying. Handel composed an anthem for the choir, *The Ways of Zion do Mourn*;

according to the Bishop of Chichester, 'it is reckoned to be as good a piece as he ever made; it was about fifty minutes in singing.'*

Princess Anne was anxious to come to England for her mother's funeral. Her sisters begged Prince William to dissuade her from attending, as they were alarmed at the effect her presence might have on the King. Nevertheless they all wrote to mourn for their mother and console the only daughter denied a last chance to say goodbye, assuring her that the Queen had often spoken of her as she lay dying. Princess Caroline sent her the text of Handel's anthem, remarking on the words 'They shall receive a glorious kingdom and a beautiful crown from the Lord's hand', calling it 'the finest cruel touching thing that ever was heard.' The Duke of Cumberland also wrote to her, united in grief for 'the best of mothers and the dearest of friends'.[7]

Queen Caroline's death was regarded as a national calamity. The mood was summed up in a sermon preached by the Revd Dr Crowe, chaplain in ordinary to the King, and Rector of St Botolph's, Bishopsgate:

> The Lord hath taken away His anointed with a stroke; the breath of our nostrils is taken away. The great Princess is no more, under whose shadow we said we should be safe, and promised ourselves lasting peace – she, whom future generations will know as Caroline the Illustrious.[8]

An intelligent woman and a strong personality, who was wise enough not to dominate her husband, Queen Caroline was one of the most remarkable – and perhaps most underestimated – of British consorts. Yet perhaps the greatest of her achievements, only appreciated in retrospect, was her role in strengthening the Hanoverians' somewhat precarious hold on the British throne. As R.L. Arkell noted, 'by her acumen and geniality, (she) ensured the dynasty's rooting itself in England',[9] while according to W.H. Wilkins, her 'gracious and dignified personality, her lofty ideals and pure life did much to counteract the unpopularity of her husband and father-in-law, and redeem the early Georgian era from utter grossness.'[10] The Jacobites readily recalled that she had always been on the side of mercy, particularly with regard to the matter of granting pardons after the 1715 rebellion.

The King's extravagant grief revealed 'a tenderness of which the world thought him before utterly incapable'. At first he would see nobody but his daughters. When compelled to see Walpole or any of the other ministers, he could talk of nothing but his overwhelming loss. He seemed so cast down and broken in spirit that many thought he would not survive her for long. A

*The same anthem was also sung in 1901 at the memorial service in Westminster Abbey for Queen Victoria.

week after the funeral he ordered a hackney chair to take him across Horse Guards Parade to the chapel, and spent some time in the vault alone with his thoughts beside her tomb. Forcing himself to appear at a drawing-room early in the new year, he stayed barely two minutes 'and had grief still fixed on his face'.

When he opened Parliament in January 1738, he took his speech in his hand, but paused for some time while he tried to regain his composure and speak without breaking down. Even when he began to read he put his hand regularly to his forehead and had tears in his eyes. Government and opposition were united in paying tributes and expressing sympathy to His Majesty, and the Jacobite 'Honest' Shippen rose to his feet to speak of the greatness of the late Queen's character. The King thanked them, saying he was 'so sensibly touched by this convincing proof of your particular regard to me that I am not able in this distress to command myself sufficiently to express the just sense I have of your affection and concern for me upon this occasion.'[11]

For a while the sight of a Queen dealt to the King at the card table was enough to make it impossible for him to continue his game. In deference to his feelings, the family took to using incomplete packs of cards from which Princess Amelia had considerately removed the Queens. At length he regained his composure. Eventually he went to look over a new consignment of fine Arab horses, and cynics said he would soon be looking over some fine women as well.

Who would have the regal ear now? asked the politicians. Newcastle thought it would be Princess Amelia, but Walpole knew better:

Does your Princess Emily design to commit incest? Will she go to bed with her father? Or does he desire she should? If not, do not tell me the King intends to make a vow of chastity, or that those that lie with him won't have the best interest with him. I am for Madame Walmoden, I'll bring her over and I'll have nothing to do with your girls. I was for the wife against your mistress, but I will be for the mistress against the daughter unless you think the daughter intends to behave so as to supply the place of both wife and mistress, which as I have told you before, I know not how she can do but by going to bed with him.[12]

In the meantime Lady Deloraine would have to do, despite the King's objections that she stank of Spanish wine so much that he could not bear her. Walpole told the King firmly that he had to look forward for the sake of himself, his family, friends, and kingdom. He owed it to them not to ruin his health by indulging in vain regret and pity for what was beyond recall. Rather indelicately he told Princesses Amelia and Caroline that, though he had taken the side of the late Queen against Lady Suffolk, he 'was now for

Walmoden'. But until she could come from Hanover, he advised them to send for Lady Deloraine, for the sake of his health; 'people must wear old gloves till they could get new ones.' They were shocked, and never forgave him.

The opposition were confident that Walpole could not long survive the death of his greatest friend and protectress at court. However the King continued to lean on his First Lord of the Treasury as much as ever. The death of Walpole's wife from whom he had been parted for so long meant less to him than that of the Queen, but another sorrow was about to fall. Free to marry again, he made his long-time mistress Moll Skerrett his second wife, but within three months she died in childbirth.

Queen Caroline's death did little to reverse the King's unpopularity. Not long afterwards an epitaph was pasted on the Royal Exchange:

> Oh death, where is thy sting?
> To take the Queen and leave the King?

PART FOUR

1738–60

'The boldest man I ever saw'

Sincere as his grief and mourning were, King George soon recovered from his wife's death. All the same he never ceased to miss her during his remaining twenty-two years, though he disregarded her entreaties to marry again. At fifty-four he was not a young man; with two sons, one already married with one child and a second on the way, there was no pressing need to father more children. As for other reasons – well, as he had promised on her deathbed, he would have mistresses.

Walpole had committed himself to bringing 'the Walmoden' over to England. His move was not prompted solely by altruism and a need to satisfy his master's appetites of the flesh, so much as an attempt to try and maintain his influence over the King through a female intermediary. As he had skilfully managed Queen Caroline and in a sense governed the King through her, so he hoped he could do the same with the Baroness. The bellicose King could find welcome distraction from his bereavement in the European theatre of war, regularly dreaming of dusting down his sword to wield in the heat of battle once again. Would 'the Walmoden' be able to cool his martial ardour? The First Lord of the Treasury believed she might.

To his disappointment Baroness von Walmoden proved a pleasant enough woman but with little character, and even less interest in politics. While the King spent much time in her company, he never discussed the business of government with her and never asked her for advice. Charming though she might be, she could never replace Queen Caroline in his affections. To her credit, the Baroness never attempted to interfere in matters which she knew were beyond her. She behaved with discretion, taking no immediate advantage of her position except for selling a few peerages.

Ironically she came to England at about the same time that an heir to the throne in the next generation was born. People were ready to contrast the domesticity of the Prince of Wales and his family life with the lechery of his father and 'the German whore'. If the King needed a woman of ill-repute, the wags asked, surely he could find an English one and stay at home, as 'there are enough of them to be had and cheaper'.

King George II may have wished the Duke of Cumberland and any heirs that he might have to succeed him, but the prize would go to the sickly,

seven-month-old Prince born on 24 May (OS)/4 June (NS) 1738 in a house rented from the Duke of Norfolk at St James's Square, and christened George William Frederick. The King feigned little interest at first, merely remarking that the saddler's wife had been brought to bed, a reference to the Prince of Wales's patronage of the Royal Worshipful Company of Saddlers, although he could not but feel some pride in the continuation of the male line of succession into a further generation. At first the baby was only expected to live for a few hours, and as a precaution he was given a private baptism almost at once. He defied expectations by living into his ninth decade.

As Walpole had seen and feared, it was impossible to distract King George II from foreign affairs for long. In 1738 the prospect of war with Spain was the greatest danger to peace. Britain's monopoly of the slave trade with the Spanish Main, and conflict between British merchants and Spanish coastguards, led to a deterioration in relations between the courts of St James's and Madrid. Bored with years of peace, the British people wanted war against Spain, as did the King, Prince of Wales (united for once) and opposition. The government and Walpole disagreed, fearing the costs of war and the unpopularity which would accrue to a government which increased taxes.

Robert Jenkins claimed that in 1731, as Captain of the *Rebecca*, he had been caught by the Spaniards, who removed all the instruments of navigation from his ship, and also his left ear. A Spanish officer slit it down the middle with his cutlass, he said, one of his colleagues tore it off and gave it back to him, bidding him to take it home and show King George. Now seven years later he showed his severed ear, carefully preserved and bottled, to the House of Commons. Some alleged cynically that he had lost it in the pillory or in a tavern brawl, while others doubted that he had been to sea at all, and suspected that the shrivelled exhibit was not his own ear, probably not even an ear at all, but a macabre stage prop. Had anybody thought to remove his wig, they asked, and see whether both ears were intact? There were no forensic science testing methods to prove whether he was telling the truth or not, but his words – 'I commend my soul to God and my cause to my country' – struck a chord in the heart of every patriot, and the ear 'which wrapt in cotton he carries about with him in a box made a great impression on the whole assembly'. Despite Walpole's attempts to obtain compensation by peaceful means, the people – or more specifically the opposition – were spoiling for a war of plunder.

The presence of a powerful British force in the Mediterranean was regarded as a major threat by the Spanish. When envoys met to discuss a peace settlement, the ministers at Madrid were reluctant to meet British commercial claims. The British Ambassador in Madrid was requested to demand from Spain an unqualified renunciation of her long-established

right of search, and with the despatch of Admiral Vernon to the West Indies with orders to destroy Spanish settlements 'and distress their shipping' it was evident that most of the British cabinet no longer intended to solve the dispute by amicable means.

War was declared in October 1739. From the steps of the Rose Tavern, Temple Bar, the Prince of Wales toasted the mob rejoicing in the streets, while the King was stirred by dreams of leading his nation to victory. Nothing was talked of but humbling the pride of Spain. A popular masque including a new song, *Rule Britannia,* with music by composer Thomas Arne and lyrics by poet James Thomson, expressed the country's aspirations. The people would ring their bells now, Walpole remarked gloomily, but they would wring their hands before long.' Never a bellicose politician, always cautious enough to avoid committing the nation to war if possible, he faced the crisis at a difficult time. Widowed for the second time in a year, he himself was in failing health and often excruciating pain. 'It is your war, and I wish you joy of it,' he told Newcastle bluntly in an irritable moment. He threatened to resign his office but the King refused to hear of it, asking him, 'Will you desert me in my greatest difficulties?'

Despite the King's personal interest in military matters, the army was ill-prepared for a prolonged conflict. In similar recent instances the government had been content to hire Dutch and German troops to defend British soil. In peacetime British troops numbered around 17,000, but most of these were involved in garrison duties, as well as a small reserve force in case of a new Jacobite rebellion. Within weeks of declaration of war their strength rose to nearly 75,000, thus creating problems for the army's meagre resources of trained officers, equipment and administration. Normally only volunteers were enlisted, and for life, so there were no trained reserves. Pay and conditions did not generally attract men of good quality; too many 'volunteers' were debtors and convicted criminals released from prison on condition that they enlisted in the army.

Good quality officers would have made a difference, but as a result of years of peace and the system of promotion by purchase and political patronage, they were few and far between. Like his father and second son, King George II deplored this scheme of things, but it was difficult to defy custom and political pressures. All he could do, and not without considerable resistance, was to stop the granting of commissions to infants and to lay down a regular tariff for promotion. He made strenuous efforts to make important appointments and promotions himself on military rather than political grounds in wartime, a logical move which his ministers strove to prevent.

In November 1739 Admiral Vernon seized the Spanish American base and treasure depot of Porto Bello, demolishing its fortifications, but similar attacks on other ports failed. He kept the Spanish treasure fleets from

reaching Spain, but otherwise inflicted little damage on them, his achievements being compared by the opposition to 'breaking windows with guineas'. Within three years he was recalled home. On his return he told King George that security lay in being master of the sea, 'and when he ceased to be so, his land army could not preserve him.' As a military man the King took issue with this, insisting that soldiers were necessary.

By this time the war of plunder had merged into a general European conflict, the war of the Austrian succession. Emperor Charles VI, having no legitimate son, had prevailed upon most of the European powers, including Britain, France, Hanover, Prussia and Spain, to abide by the Pragmatic Sanction, a diplomatic treaty which guaranteed that his daughter Maria Theresa would succeed him, even though she as a woman was debarred by the Salic Law from the imperial title. The idea was that her husband, Francis of Lorraine, now Duke of Tuscany, would be elected Emperor, though this was not specially written into the sanctions. Charles VI died in October 1740, and Maria Theresa found herself under attack from King Frederick II of Prussia, who had recently succeeded his father King Frederick William. He invaded and laid claim to Silesia, part of her domains, and then suggested that she should cede the territory to him in return for his support against other hostile powers. Her refusal and armed resistance resulted in the alignment of the main European powers on one side or the other.

The Electors of Saxony and Bavaria declared their support for Prussia. Maria Theresa called on Britain to honour her obligations as a signatory to the Treaty of Vienna in 1731 and support her. Walpole dreaded a war in which Britain would be involved; he hoped the conflict could be kept to Germany, and he persuaded King George II to offer his services as a mediator between Austria and Prussia. But the King, distrusting the ambition of his nephew Frederick, saw danger in a Franco-Prussian alliance. Much against his better judgment, Walpole was persuaded into assisting Maria Theresa, who was very much an object of public sympathy in Britain, with a subsidy of £300,000 and an army of 12,000 Hessian and French mercenaries.

A Franco-Prussian alliance was concluded by the Treaty of Breslau in June 1741, and King George II was increasingly eager for war. That summer he visited Hanover, much against the wishes of Walpole who rightly feared that once back in the land of his birth he would attempt to direct diplomacy himself. One French army captured Prague, and another was poised to invade Hanover, though neither Britain nor Hanover were at war with France. Fearful of the threat to his electorate, in September 1741 in his capacity as Elector he secured a French promise to respect Hanover's neutrality in exchange for his promise to vote for Charles Albert of Bavaria, whose candidature was supported by France. In addition he retained the

12,000 mercenaries sent by Parliament to assist Maria Theresa to protect Hanover.

The treaty was extremely unpopular in Britain, proving as it did that the King cared more for the safety of his electorate than for the good name of his kingdom, and Walpole was blamed for not controlling his course of action. The King was accused of flagrant dishonesty in having obtained a parliamentary subsidy for the benefit of Maria Theresa and then deserting her.

A general election in April 1741 had weakened Walpole's grip. When the new parliament met in December, the unseating of several government candidates by election petitions, combined with arguments about the conduct of the war in Europe and the Prince of Wales's allowance all conspired to wear him down. His health was deteriorating, Londoners were burning him in effigy, and it was rumoured that he and his brother Horace were to be sent to the Tower. King George declared that no harm would befall the minister who had served him so faithfully since his accession, but Walpole knew his position was untenable, and in February 1742 he laid down his seals of office. Kissing hands for the last time as Minister, the King was genuinely moved, weeping and begging to see him frequently. He raised him to the peerage as the first Earl of Orford, and granted him a pension of £4,000 per annum.

Without the Queen, and without the man who had in effect been his Prime Minister throughout his reign, King George II still displayed sound judgment when selecting his ministers. The man who replaced Walpole at the head of a reconstructed ministry was the new Secretary of State for the Northern Department, the Earl of Carteret, for whom the King had the highest regard. A polished speaker and effective debater, he had a perfect grasp of foreign affairs, although less to his credit were his boundless confidence in himself and contempt for public opinion.

With Walpole gone, the Prince of Wales saw his opportunity to press for an increased allowance. Carteret and his friend Pulteney, who had been out of office for several years since a quarrel with Walpole but was now recognized as one of the most capable Members of Parliament, longed for a reconciliation between father and son, and were keen to see themselves at peace with King and heir. For his part, the Prince was keen to see Carteret and Pulteney at one with their former associates, members of the old opposition. King George was not averse to making a new start; perhaps he was prompted by his knowledge of his son's popularity in the kingdom, or by rumours of an impending Jacobite invasion, and appreciated that a house (or in this case a kingdom) divided against itself could not safely stand. Maybe he was mellowing; he still missed the Queen, and sorely felt the absence of young children at the palace. He had looked kindly on his daughter-in-law, and wanted to get to know his grandchildren better.

The meeting between father and son was effected largely by Pulteney, who asked each beforehand not to insist on impossible preconditions which would be unacceptable to the other without loss of dignity. King and Prince met privately for an amicable if brief meeting. The Prince kissed his father's hand, while the King spoke graciously to one or two of his supporters, and the Prince spoke affably to the ministers in attendance. The meeting was followed by a triumphant tour through the City, decorated for the occasion, and the Mayor and Corporation came out to congratulate them. Later in the day the Prince and Princess proceeded by barge to Greenwich, escorted by other gilded and decorated craft, while musicians played them down the river, and hats, hands and handkerchiefs were waved all along the route.

The Prince's Guard, withheld since the quarrel of 1737, was restored, and his allowance was increased. For a while it seemed as if father and son could be friends, but good relations between them did not last long. The habits of a lifetime for each, it seemed, were too thoroughly ingrained.

Meanwhile in Europe King Frederick of Prussia, supported by France, was at war with Maria Theresa, still nominally supported by Britain. Although no state of war existed between England and France, Carteret regarded the latter as a perpetual enemy, and maintained that a relatively strong Austria must be kept thus as a counterweight; the old alliance between Britain, Austria and Holland against France, Bavaria and Spain was vital to the balance of European power. At the same time Hanover had to be protected from the threat of a joint Franco-Prussian invasion. To the opposition, Hanover was no more than a mere encumbrance.

Naturally the safety of the electorate was paramount to King George II. The new government was pledged to come to Maria Theresa's aid. £5,000,000 was voted for the army, while the subsidy to Austria was fixed at £500,000, and an army 16,000-strong was sent to the Low Countries to fight on Austria's behalf. With King George's approval, Carteret set out to engage King Frederick of Prussia on the Austrian side in order to keep France out of Germany, while in Berlin the British Ambassador was asked to prepare the way for a peace agreement. Threatened on several borders and pledged to an unpopular war, King Frederick was amenable, but Vienna was less compliant, while Maria Theresa was desperate for the return of Silesia.

A Prussian victory in May 1742 put King Frederick's star back in the ascendant. Under pressure from Sir Thomas Robinson, later Lord Grantham, British Ambassador at Vienna, Maria Theresa was forced to realize that prolonging war with Prussia would jeopardize Austria's position in Germany. In June Austrian and Prussian representatives signed peace preliminaries at Breslau. King Frederick received Upper and Lower Silesia in full sovereignty, and undertook to give no further support to the enemies of Austria. Parliament increased the subsidy to Britain's allies, and Hanover

was further safeguarded by an Anglo-Prussian defensive alliance in November and an Anglo-Russian pact in December 1742.

With Austria and Prussia at peace King George was assured that as Elector of Hanover he need no longer seek refuge in neutrality, and felt that he could economize by reducing the number of troops kept in the electorate for defence purposes. Carteret was thus obliged to persuade a reluctant parliament to take Hanoverian and Hessian troops onto the British payroll. William Pitt bitterly condemned the proposal to pay the Hanoverians in a speech which the King never forgave, fulminating that 'this great, this powerful, this formidable kingdom is considered only as a province to a despicable electorate; and that in consequence of a scheme formed long ago, and invariably pursued, those troops are hired only to drain this unhappy nation of its money.'[1]

In the House of Lords Chesterfield argued along similar lines, albeit with less bitterness. The regular visits of their Kings to their electoral dominions, he said, 'contrary to the original terms on which this crown was conferred upon them, have inclined the people of England to suspect that they only have the second place in the affection of the sovereign; nor has this suspicion been made less by the large accessions made to those dominions by purchases, which the electors never appeared able to make before their exaltation to the throne of Great Britain, and to some measures which have been apparently taken to aggrandize Hanover at the expense of Great Britain.'[2] He was magnanimous enough to concede that no blame could be attached to the King or his father; the guilty men were those ministers who deliberately concealed from their royal master the true sentiments of the nation. To the King's subjects, it looked increasingly as though the Hanoverian succession had conferred immense advantages on one side, to the detriment of the other – the British. Only half in jest, he quipped that the surest cure for Jacobitism was to make the Pretender Elector of Hanover, 'as the people would never fetch another King from thence'.

Carteret fiercely defended Anglo-Hanoverian policy, asking Parliament if they would submit to France or not; 'I will always traverse the views of France, in place or out of place, for France will ruin this nation if it can.'[3] Nevertheless King George was bitterly hurt and angry when the speeches were reported to him. A parliamentary system which allowed men to speak so insolently about their sovereign and his birthplace incensed him. He stopped short of threatening to abdicate, but the thought was probably not far from his mind. Five years earlier, Queen Caroline and Sir Robert Walpole would have been there to support him in the face of such attacks; now he was alone. Pining for Hanover, he would lament that there were Kings enough in England; 'I am nothing there; I am old and want rest, and should only be plagued and teased there about that damned House of Commons.'

That summer a Pragmatic Army of British, Hanoverian and Hessian troops had assembled in the Low Countries under the command of Marlborough's old officer, Lord Stair. His plan, to wait for the moment to attack the French base at Dunkirk and then advance to Paris, was rejected by the King in one of his cautious moods. Unwilling to provoke King Louis XV, with whom he was not at war, he thought it unwise to make a direct attack on French territory. In the spring of 1743 Dutch and Hanoverian contingents joined the force and began advancing into Germany. In the summer King George and Carteret returned to Hanover and the King, accompanied by the Duke of Cumberland, arrived to take command of the army. It was his first experience of being at the batttlefront since the battle of Oudenarde. The seventy-year-old Stair stayed to keep a professional eye on his sovereign, a mere ten years younger than he was. In high spirits, the King celebrated his arrival with a review of the troops. Ignoring Stair and making it obvious that he preferred the company of Hanoverian staff officers, he managed to give his British troops the impression that he was indifferent to their interests.

A few days later scouts located a French force close to Dettingen, and French guns posted along the riverbank opened fire upon the Pragmatic Army which they believed to be retreating. Battle ensued on 8 (OS)/19 (NS) June, and the King was evidently exhilarated by the danger.

An eye-witness account of his conduct on the battlefield was left by a Mr Kendal, of Lord Ashburnham's troop:

> The French fired at His Majesty from a battery of twelve cannon, but levelled too high. I saw the balls go within half a yard of his head. The Duc d'Aremberg [commanding the Austrian contingent] desired him to go out of danger; he answered, 'Don't tell me of danger; I'll be even with them!' He is certainly the boldest man I ever saw.
>
> The French got into the corner of a wood to flank our right. The King then drew his sword and ordered the Hanoverian horse and foot, and some English, through the wood, and rode about like a lion. He drew them up in line of battle himself, ordered six cannon to the right, and bade them fire on the flank of the French. He stood by till they fired; they did great execution killing thirty or forty at a shot. Then he went to the foot and ordered them not to fire till the French came close and were about one hundred yards distant. Then the French fired upon us directly, and the shot flew again as thick as hail. Then the King flourished his sword and said: 'Now, boys, for the honour of England; fire, and behave bravely and the French will soon run.'[4]

Now the Elector of Hanover could take pride again in the honour of England, and his troops were quick to respond. Cumberland acquitted

himself well, according to a young acting adjutant, James Wolfe, 'he gave his orders with a great deal of calmness and seemed quite unconcerned'. When the Duke was wounded by a ball in the leg, Dr Ranby was quite anxious for a while. Visiting his son afterwards during treatment, the King congratulated him on his bravery: 'if you do well [recover] I shall not be sorry for your wound.'

By evening the French forces had been driven in retreat across the river Main, several hundred being drowned or trampled to death by their own cavalry in the process. The English were victorious, though posterity would contend that it was a victory of courage rather than strategy. The King had emerged elated and unscathed from the battle. Nothing could have pleased him more than to know that he would go down in history as the last King of England to lead his army on to the field of battle, even though he had worn Hanoverian uniform and been present in his capacity as Elector of Hanover rather than as His Britannic Majesty.

He and Carteret returned home in November after the campaigning season was over. Horace Walpole, no great admirer of his sovereign, wrote:

We were in great fear of his coming through the City, after the treason that has been publishing for these two months; but it was incredible how well his reception was; beyond what it had ever been before; in short, you would have thought it had not been a week after the victory of Dettingen. They almost carried him into the palace on their shoulders; and at night the whole town was illuminated and bonfired. He looks much better than he has these five years and is in great spirits.[5]

In London King George II was saluted as a war hero, and the victor of Dettingen. Once again Handel commemorated the triumph with music. Earlier that year he had produced his masterpiece, *The Messiah*, which the King had attended. Moved by the fervour of the *Hallelujah Chorus*, he immediately rose to his feet – as did all the audience at once – and remained standing until the last chord died away. Now, in November, Handel's *Dettingen Te Deum* was performed at the Chapel Royal. Its martial, stately tones, employing 'every kettledrum and trumpet that he could press into service' stirred the King even more deeply than the *Hallelujah Chorus*.

However political strife and a war–weary nation greeted the King. In the Commons William Pitt declared that His Majesty 'was exposed to few or no dangers abroad, but those to which he is daily liable at home, such as the overturning of his coach, or the stumbling of his horse'.[6] He also questioned the wisdom of fighting, save to continue the satisfaction of bestowing four or five hundred thousand pounds on Hanover. The City of London offered congratulations on the birth of another son, Prince William Henry, to the Prince and Princess of Wales, and on the engagement of the

King's youngest daughter Louisa to Crown Prince Frederick of Denmark, but no mention was made of Dettingen. Carteret retained royal confidence as the only minister with a proper grasp of foreign affairs and who understood his feelings for Hanover, but in the government he was politically isolated. The future of the country seemed hopeless, Horace Walpole wrote, 'no union in the court; no certainty about the House of Commons: Lord Carteret making no friends, the King making enemies.'

When Parliament met in December 1743 Pitt led the attack, declaring in the Commons that Walpole had betrayed the interest of his country by his pusillanimity; Carteret 'sacrifices it by his quixotism'. He belittled the result of the battle at Dettingen which he refused to recognize as a victory, preferring instead to dwell on the alleged cowardice of the Hanoverian troops. A continuance of the present policy, he warned, would bring untold disasters, not the least of which would be the landing of the Pretender who would 'be joined by a despairing people as a last hope against an execrable, a sole minister, who had renounced the British nation'.

In the Lords Chesterfield also condemned the Hanoverians' cowardice. The matter of retaining them in British service continued to occupy Parliament, and in January 1744 after the Christmas break, Pitt castigated Carteret as 'a Hanoverian troop-minister' whose only party were 'the 16,000 Hanoverians, the place men by whose means he has conquered the cabinet'. Carteret defended the King and himself, insisting that there was no cowardice on the part of His Majesty. Yet he was unnerved by the endless vituperation, and arguments between himself and the Pelhamites undermined his confidence as well as his position still further. When the Duke of Newcastle dared to criticize Carteret before the King he was soundly rebuked.

King George's approval was not enough to defend Carteret from the consequences of a difficult year. In February 1744 rumours of an imminent attack by a fleet from Brest swept the country, and a few days later talk of riots in Staffordshire and Birmingham, and Jacobite risings in North Wales and Cheshire, added to the panic. The ministers did nothing to calm the nation's fears, but characteristically the King kept his head. Without consulting the government he marched troops into the south-eastern counties, ready to meet any invading French force. The nation rallied around the King, with addresses promising loyalty and obedience coming in from every corner of the realm. Among them was a ninety-coach procession to St James's by the city merchants, offering the King a loan of £6,000,000. Even Pitt moved that an address should be presented to His Majesty 'that he will be graciously pleased in this dangerous and critical conjunction of affairs' to augment forces by land and sea as were proper and necessary, adding assurances that the House would make good any expenses incurred in the defence of himself and the security of the kingdom. In March a fierce

gale in the Channel dispersed the French fleet assembled at Dunkirk, King Louis XV's declaration of war was met with a counter-declaration by Britain, and the threat of invasion by France evaporated.

Meanwhile, in Europe the Pelhamites insisted on appointing the septua-genarian Field-Marshal George Wade as British Commander-in-Chief in the Low Countries, and once he was there refused to send him the extra troops for which he pressed so urgently. The furious King did what he could to speed up despatch of reinforcements, then announced that he would go and take personal command of the combined British and Hanoverian forces. If he did so he would probably take Carteret with him. The Pelhamites realized that their ascendancy in the government would surely suffer, and they told him that Jacobite activity made it imperative for him to remain in England.

That summer the war went badly for the allied forces in Europe. At home Newcastle, his brother Henry Pelham, Chancellor of the Exchequer, and the Earl of Hardwicke, Lord Chancellor, intrigued against Carteret, promising positions in the cabinet to his political enemies once he was out of office. In November they delivered an ultimatum to the King, giving him ten days to dismiss Carteret or accept the resignation of the Pelhamites. 'You would persuade me to abandon my allies,' the King said angrily, 'but that shall never be the reproach of my reign, as it was of Queen Anne's; and I will suffer any extremities rather than consent.'[7]

Yet the King's support could not sustain a minister who had lost the confidence of the Commons as well as that of his own colleagues. He consulted the Earl of Orford, who he did not realize was bound by old loyalties to the Pelhams, and warned him that there was nothing he could do to retain the minister in office. The reproach that the King demonstrated royal political cowardice is undeserved; to have done otherwise would have produced a governmental crisis at a difficult time, and laid him open to charges of excessive obstinacy. Accepting his limitations as a constitutional monarch, on 23 November 1744 he accepted the resignation of Carteret, now Lord Granville (a title recently inherited through his mother), from the office of the Northern Department, to be replaced by Lord Harrington.

King George II accepted his new ministry, led by Henry Pelham, with reluctance. Newcastle thought that he intended 'to suffer us generously to the business this session and to kick us out afterwards'. The Earl of Hardwicke was chosen by the cabinet to try and pacify the ruffled sovereign, who retorted that he had 'put all my power into your hands, and I suppose you will make the most of it.' Hardwicke countered by explaining that 'the disposition of places' would not be sufficient if His Majesty took pains to show the world that he disapproved of his own work. The King answered

that he had been forced and threatened, and that the Pelhamites had threatened to oppose him if their recommendations were not accepted. 'Your instruments, sir, are only your instruments of government,' was the reply.

Meanwhile the army was still engaged in Europe, and problems had to be faced such as command of the Pragmatic Army and the war effort of the reluctant Dutch. In January 1745 Emperor Charles VII (Charles Albert of Lorraine) died, thus paving the way for the reconciliation of Austria and Bavaria. As King and Elector, George II supported the candidature of Grand Duke Francis of Tuscany, Maria Theresa's husband, mainly because of his aversion to his nephew in Prussia. He was elected in preference to the French candidate, Augustus III, King of Poland and Elector of Saxony. The British army would be employed in Flanders against the French, rather than in Germany in support of Hanover. While the King wanted to take command himself, among Britain's allies there was no enthusiasm for such a venture. The choice was between the old and frail Marshal Königsegg and the twenty-three-year-old Duke of Cumberland, and it was decided to appoint both. In March 1745 the Duke became Commander-in-Chief of the Pragmatic Army, with Königsegg as his second-in-command.

Cumberland was a painstaking and competent administrator, who took an enlightened interest in his troops' health and welfare. For all his stern disciplinary methods, his soldiers liked and respected him. He was a skilled strategist, but did not always succeed on the battlefield; never lacking courage, in the face of the enemy he could be hesitant, slow to make decisions, sluggish and unimaginative in movement, incapable of grasping the right opportunity. It was his misfortune to have as his adversary the masterful Marshal Saxe.

In May the Duke led the 44,000-strong Pragmatic Army in an attack on 76,000 Frenchmen entrenched in an impregnable position at Fontenoy. He displayed great bravery, but in the face of heavy French fire the Dutch withdrew from the battlefield, leaving the Anglo-Hanoverian forces to fight on and concede eventual defeat. Delighted with his son's conduct, the King blamed 'the miscarriage of the attack' on the Dutch, agreeing with his son's private verdict on 'the inexpressible cowardice of the Dutch'. Had he been there, the King proclaimed, he would have put some 'resolution' into the cowards. The Princess Royal was bitterly ashamed at the Dutch soldiers' behaviour. She had never liked her philistine younger brother; and his reputation as a brave commander and soldier would always be a thorn in her side. Her poor misshapen husband could never hope to lead his soldiers into battle, and her brother's laurels made her jealous.

Saxe proceeded to overrun most of Flanders, capturing Ostend, one of the ports on the British line of communications, from the Austrians. To check the French advance the government decided that it was essential to

persuade King Frederick of Prussia to withdraw from the war. At the Convention of Hanover in August 1745, the British and Prussian representatives agreed to guarantee each others' territorial possessions and King George II pledged himself to support King Frederick's claims to Silesia. Although Austria strongly resented the move, the Austrians and Saxons were checked in their advance by Prussian forces, and by a threat from Britain to discontinue subsidies unless peace was made with Prussia. Peace was signed at the Treaty of Dresden on Christmas Day. Maria Theresa ceded to Prussia Silesia and Glatz in full sovereignty, and King Frederick agreed to recognize the election of her husband as Emperor Francis I.

'Je sens la mort'

By this time, European affairs were less pressing than the renewed Jacobite threat. Encouraged by the success of Irish pro-Stuart soldiers fighting on the French side at Fontenoy, and spurred on by the promise of help from France, Prince Charles Edward, the Young Pretender, was determined to strike a blow for his cause. On 27 June 1745 (OS) he sailed from Nantes with two ships, one carrying arms, the other himself and seven followers – three Irishmen, three Highlanders, and an English Jacobite. The arms ship was intercepted by an English frigate and forced back to France, but the Prince and his men landed on the west coast of Scotland the following month. Rallying the Highland clans to his banner, he seized Edinburgh and set up his Court at Holyrood.

The news reached London in mid-August and the Council of Regency offered a reward of £30,000 for the Pretender's apprehension, while the Pretender offered the same reward for the apprehension of the Elector of Hanover. King George II was in Hanover, from where he warned the Duke of Cumberland to be ready to bring troops over from Holland if needed. He himself came back to Britain at the end of August in a good humour, refusing to be panicked. Meanwhile the Jacobite army was advancing southwards, and in September met an English force under Sir John Cope at Prestonpans. Fighting lasted about ten minutes, before Cope and his dragoons retreated. About three hundred were killed, and eighty officers, a thousand men, and all their baggage, were captured. Charles Edward Stuart returned to Edinburgh, while Cope rode towards the Border. Lord Mark Ker, governor of Edinburgh Castle, observed that the defeated commander was 'the first general in Europe who had brought the first tidings of his own defeat'. A few weeks later the Pretender and his ever-growing force, neither well armed nor disciplined though full of enthusiasm, invaded England and captured Carlisle in November.

The Prince of Wales offered his services to the King, but as he had never done a day's soldiering in his life, he could hardly have expected to be granted a military command. This, rather than a steadfast refusal to let him share his younger brother's glory, was the reason behind the King's rejection. As for the King, he had regular military reports laid before him, ordering special reconnaissances where necessary, and viewing alarmist

reports with scepticism. He was well informed on the true state of Scotland, especially the loyalty of the Presbyterians and the Lowlands in general, excepting Edinburgh, which had not benefited from the Union. Cynical of the value of the Pretender's newly raised Highland regiments, he had ultimate confidence in the Duke of Cumberland and his Fontenoy veterans on their way from Europe, and resisted the temptation to peer over his son's shoulder and interfere in military operations. While his ministers were inclined to overestimate the emergency, he set an example of cool commonsense, keeping his head while others were ready to lose theirs.

He was soon proved right, for the Pretender was already in trouble. As he moved further from the Highlands, his army lost more in deserters than it gained in recruits, returning to Scotland rather than continue their march further into 'inhospitable England'. The rebel army reached Manchester on 28 November, and Derby on 4 December. Two days later, on 'Black Friday', it was learnt that the Jacobite force was within one hundred and fifty miles of the capital. Rumour spread that the royal yacht was waiting to take the King and his family out of the country, that the Duke of Cumberland's army had joined that of Charles Edward Stuart, and that Newcastle and the ministers were planning to make their peace with him. Unknown to the fearful Londoners, the Pretender was on the point of retreat, as it was evident that neither the expected reinforcements of Jacobites south of the border nor promises of French aid were going to materialize.

Cumberland, his staff and men marched by slow stages on the tail of the retreating Jacobites, who were losing morale and eager to return home. With the surrender of the rebel garrison in Carlisle the Stuart cause died in England. At a brief skirmish in December at Clifton, near Penrith, the rebel forces checked the loyalist advance but otherwise did little to change the situation. Prince Charles was briefly encouraged by news from his old tutor and lifelong friend Sir Thomas Sheridan, a son born out of wedlock to King James II and Anne Hyde. According to Daniel O'Brian, a Jacobite agent in Paris, King Louis XV of France was in communication with King Charles Emmanuel of Sardinia, who was dissatisfied with the terms of a recent alliance with King George II and Maria Theresa. King Louis was deciding what terms a victorious France could demand from King George II under a future peace settlement. If he had the cooperation of King Charles Emmanuel and of King Philip V of Spain, it would strengthen his proposal that King George could remain King of England while Scotland reverted to the Stuarts. A Bourbon–Stuart alliance against a weakened England would serve the French interest very well in the European conflict.

Meanwhile the Duke of Cumberland was recalled briefly to London to take charge of preparations for meeting the threat of a French invasion, and Wade, the elderly Commander-in-Chief of the northern forces, was retired on grounds of ill health. He was succeeded by Lieutenant-General

Henry Hawley, reputed to be an illegitimate son of King George I. He had played a prominent part in recent continental campaigns, but his skills as a commander were less notable than his reputation as a fierce disciplinarian. Another Jacobite victory followed at the battle of Falkirk in January, and a few days later it was announced that Cumberland would take over the Scottish command.

At the end of February he went into quarters at Aberdeen to await new supplies, and severe weather kept his troops there during March. In April they set out to recapture Inverness. Cumberland granted his men a day's rest on 15 April to celebrate his twenty-fourth birthday, and the nearby Jacobite forces decided that the time was opportune to make a surprise attack on their enemies. Their plan miscarried, and early next morning both armies faced each other at Culloden Moor. The Jacobite army was inferior in numbers, hungry and exhausted by fruitless marching and countermarching the previous night. Cumberland's superior tactics, artillery and musketry won the day.

News of the victory was brought to King George II at St James's Palace nine days later by Lord Bury, an officer on the Duke of Cumberland's staff, as bells rang out and guns fired salutes throughout the city of London in celebration. 'What's become of my son?' were the King's first words. On being assured that he was well he answered, 'Then, all's well with me.' For a moment he was 'unable to speak with joy'.[1] Recovering his composure, he directed Newcastle to pay Bury a thousand guineas, then retired to read the contents of Charles's despatch case which had been captured and delivered to him.

The Duke of Cumberland was prepared to pardon the rebels if they would give themselves up; in the aftermath of the battle, more than a thousand prisoners joined the British army. But little groups of Highlanders, expecting no quarter, offered resistance and exhausted his patience. Even so, it is only fair to lay the blame for much of the cruelty that followed on Hawley. The rebel wounded and prisoners were bayoneted and hanged without mercy while English and Lowland troops, with little interference from the higher command, burnt, raped and looted for some months in the rebel clans' country. In the face of what amounted to a reign of terror in the Highlands King George II was inclined to show mercy, telling Horace Walpole that he 'felt William had been rough with them', and it was left for the latter to point out that the Duke 'had not gone there to please them.' His Majesty's second son and his officers were doing no more than carrying out government policy in Scotland, namely to 'starve the whole country, put a price on the heads of the chiefs and let the Duke put all to fire and sword'. In mitigation it has frequently been glossed over that the Highlanders themselves had showed 'more than Turkish inhumanity' towards their defeated enemy after the battle of Prestonpans,

slaughtering the wounded in cold blood. As a result Chesterfield had declared that the Commander-in-Chief, at that time Field-Marshal Wade, should be ordered to give no quarter, but pursue the rebels wherever he found them.

As the Duke of Cumberland was primarily responsible for thwarting the most severe challenge to his family and the dynasty since the accession of his grandfather to the throne, the ferocity with which he and his subordinates put down the Highland rebellion is understandable. For a military commander in his circumstances to show clemency might have been the Christian thing to do, but at the same time it could have been construed as foolhardy weakness.

Prince Charles Edward Stuart escaped to France, but his followers were less fortunate. Some eighty were taken to Edinburgh and London to be tried for treason, their verdicts a foregone conclusion. In fact many lesser rebels received the royal pardon. Lord Balmerino, who had deserted to the rebels and been pardoned in 1715, was executed, responding on the scaffold to the prayer 'God bless King George' with a defiant 'God bless King James'. Lord Kilmarnock, who shared his fate, was less reluctant to confess his treason. The following year Lord Lovat, another double-dyed traitor, was also executed, but two months later the King granted a general pardon to all rebels who were prepared to give their allegiance to the crown.

After the rebellion the royal family were far from united in their sympathies or lack of them. Flora MacDonald, who had helped Prince Charles escape to safety disguised as her maid and allowed him to stay in her own home, refusing to follow the advice of friends who begged her to hide, was arrested and taken as a prisoner to London. The Prince of Wales visited her and was so impressed by her gentle yet dignified personality that he secured her a pardon. Though the Princess of Wales rarely disagreed with her husband on anything she criticized Flora savagely, whereupon he turned to her saying that if he himself had been in Prince Charles's plight, he hoped that she would have behaved as Flora MacDonald had done. He led the opposition to much harsh anti-Highlands legislation submitted by the government to Parliament, irritating his father and siblings in the process.

Although Princess Amelia might describe him in a letter to the Princess Royal as 'the hatred and despair of everyone' for doing so, she confessed to some sympathy for the aged Lord Lovat. When part of the wooden platform around the scaffold collapsed and several spectators were fatally injured or maimed, she remarked coldly that they had 'suffered finely for their nonsensical curiosity'.[2]

The Jacobite threat was extinguished, but in Europe the conflict was far from over. King George II was keen to continue the war, and approved a

raid on the French coast. While the French army were successful in the Netherlands, at sea Britain was gaining the upper hand, and Lord Anson routed the French fleet off Cape Finisterre in May 1747. A few weeks later, the Prince of Wales chose his moment to return to political opposition by issuing a manifesto promising 'to abolish all distinctions of party'. Regarding his gesture as a challenge, the King agreed to a request for the dissolution of Parliament and a general election a year early in order to minimize any mischief on the part of his son and heir.

During the election that summer the Prince of Wales took a prominent part against the government. He believed that he could rally disaffected Jacobites round the crown and government, and capitalize on the prevailing view that the Pelhams were bungling the war abroad and neglecting domestic affairs. To one anti-Pelhamite candidate he wrote of his attitude and why he was supporting the opposition: 'My upright intentions are known to you; my duty towards my father calls for it. One must redeem him out of those hands that have sullied the crown and are very near to ruin all.'[3] Nevertheless as astute campaigners and election managers, Pelham and Newcastle managed to ensure that the government was returned with a handsome majority.

As the blockade at sea intensified, so did pressure on France and Spain to make peace. In May 1748 the preliminaries of a treaty were signed at Aix-la-Chapelle, and the King then left for Hanover, followed reluctantly by Newcastle, who dreaded travelling abroad as he was terrified of the sea. Soon after they arrived at Hanover the King was fortunate to escape serious injury in an accident when his chaise overturned. Fortunately he landed on his feet otherwise, Newcastle reported to Pelham, 'his legs, at best, must [would] have been broke to pieces'. Grateful for his narrow escape, His Majesty was 'in a very good humour'.

A more definitive settlement was reached in the autumn. The King was prepared to make peace without Maria Theresa, who had expected Europe to remain at war until Silesia had been restored to the empire. Britain and France virtually wrote the terms of peace between themselves; they and Spain reverted to the territorial status quo which had existed before the war in Europe and beyond, with Anglo-French colonial rivalry unresolved. Nevertheless the French government refused to allow Prince Charles Edward Stuart asylum any longer, and he was ordered to leave France. Holland, which had hoped for military victories but failed to cover herself with any glory, commanded no consideration at the conference table. William of Orange was aware how much his position had been undermined, and while Anne tried to offer encouragement, mocking 'the fat generalissimo', her brother the Duke of Cumberland, it was to no avail. She identified herself thoroughly with the interests of her husband and his nation, and increasing personal animosity against her father and brother

made her blame everything on England, which her husband now called 'the great enemy'.

Though the war of the Austrian succession was now over, the Treaty of Aix-la-Chapelle had merely postponed a lasting solution to national rivalries, particularly as regards European imperial interests beyond the continent. With his wide-ranging knowledge of the European situation, King George II was aware of the need to maintain British support for Austria in the face of French ambition, and looked uneasily on the ever-growing military threat – to Hanover as well as England – from Prussia. His views were shared by Granville but few others. Newcastle and his political allies the Old Whigs had regarded the war as a renewal of the Grand Alliance's struggle against King Louis XIV at the turn of the century. Only Pitt, at the time Paymaster General, had the vision to realize that the real issue was maritime supremacy and control of the New World, and his time had not yet come.

By the end of the war King George II was aged sixty-four, suffering from recurrent agues as well as piles. It was widely assumed that he would not live for much longer. The Prince of Wales confidently expected that he would soon be King, as did many of the ministers and opposition politicians. Accordingly he formed his own 'shadow cabinet', sometimes known mockingly as the Leicester House Party, which gathered regularly at Carlton House to meet contingencies and formulate policies which he would undertake when his time came. The 'manager' was Dodington, who had come out into the open against the Pelhams and had resigned his post as treasurer of the navy to serve the Prince. When King, the Prince would accept for his Civil List no more than £800,000 a year. Other schemes included plans for the detachment of Hanover, the raising of a large militia – more popular than an expensive standing army – and important political reforms, including what they saw as the Whigs' manipulation of the parliamentary system to be ended. There was much talk of 'abuses in offices', although credibility was somewhat strained by reading of the arrangements that were made to ensure the winning of the election that would follow the King's death.

Pelham, First Lord of the Treasury, looked askance on 'the increasing strength of the Prince's Opposition' and his list of supporters whom he had virtually promised senior offices in the government on his accession. But the Prince's interest in the 'party' was probably motivated by a desire to act as a counterweight against his brother's influence with the Pelhams. At the back of the heir's mind was always a suspicion that his father would try to force the Duke of Cumberland onto the nation as his successor. Though there was no evidence to suggest as much, if the Pelhams could be persuaded to support such a scheme, his fears might become grim reality.

All the same, it would be doing King George II a grave injustice to reproach him with trying to alter the succession out of personal spite. The Prince of Wales's fears were largely a figment of his imagination, doubtless encouraged by supporters eager to play on his insecurity and reap their full reward during the reign of King Frederick.

The King was still anxious to restrict his son's influence wherever possible. In 1749 the death of the Duke of Somerset left the Chancellorship of the University of Cambridge vacant. The Prince of Wales allowed his name to be put forward for election, but the King vetoed his move, writing to the University that the application had been made without his consent, and though he did not 'intend to interfere in their election, y[e]t he is persuaded, from the regard & affection, which he had always show'd for the University, & from their duty to him, that they will not chuse any one of the family without his approbation.'[4] The Duke of Newcastle was accordingly elected instead.

In January 1751 the House of Lords was asked to give its close attention to 'a certain scandalous and seditious' pamphlet, *Constitutional Queries Earnestly Recommended to the Serious Consideration of Every True Briton*, published and widely distributed around the City of London and Westminster, and circulated among peers and Members of Parliament. It compared the Duke of Cumberland to King Richard III, and suggested that the Duke would not scruple to use the nation's armed forces to usurp the throne. Both houses joined in ordering its destruction by the hangman, and enquiries were made to discover the author. Though his identity was never established, he was believed to have close connections with or belong to the Leicester House Party. Suspicion was heightened later in the parliamentary session when opposition members, debating the pay of staff officers, made pointed references to Cumberland's wide military powers.

Not long after the furore died down, the Prince of Wales fell ill. Working in his garden at Kew one wet spring day, he was soaked to the skin and caught a cold which turned to pleurisy. Once blistered and bled by the doctors, he seemed to be recovering. On 15 March Dodington reported him out of danger, but later that week he had a relapse. His physicians were with him on the evening of 20 March when he had a severe fit of coughing. Suddenly he laid his hand on his chest, cried out, '*Je sens la mort*', and shivered violently. His German *valet-de-chambre* cried out in alarm, 'Good God, the Prince is going!' The Princess of Wales, watching at the foot of the bed, picked up a candle but before she could hold it to his lips, he had breathed his last.

Because of the suddenness of his death after an apparent recovery, a post-mortem was carried out. The cause of death was given as an abscess or 'imposthume in his breast', that broke and suffocated him.[5] A second abscess 'supposed to have been of long standing and imputed to a blow' was

blamed on a cricket ball that hit him when he was playing at Cliveden about three years before. Medical opinion, however, suggested that the main cause of death was pneumonia.

According to another, rather less convincing, theory he was poisoned by his wife, either because she was having an affair with John Stuart, Earl of Bute, his Lord of the Bedchamber, or because she was ambitious to become Regent in the event of their eldest son succeeding to the throne before he came of age, such motives being somehow intensified as a result of pregnancy. She was several months *enceinte* when she became widowed, and gave birth in June to a daughter named Caroline Matilda, destined to become the tragic, shortlived consort of Christian VII, King of Denmark; but there is no evidence for the poison theory.

The Prince of Wales apparently believed his life might be short, though this could simply be attributed to ill health. He had made a political will in 1749, and transferred his most private papers to safe keeping with the trusted Lord Egmont the following year. As events surrounding the birth of his first daughter showed, he had a tendency to suspect the motives of even his closest relations. In conversation with his sister Princess Amelia not long after his death, the Dowager Princess of Wales spoke of her husband 'with tenderness and sensibility but without any violent emotions of grief. She said that the Prince seemed not apprehensive of death during his illness but had not expected to live long.'[6]

How did King George II receive the news of his hated son's death? The only fact on which contemporaries can agree is that he was playing cards with Lady Yarmouth, the former Baroness von Walmoden, when a messenger brought the news. One version says that he merely muttered, 'Why, they told me he was better,' continued with his game, and some time later remarked how glad he was. According to another, he was visibly upset. Although he rarely gave way to emotion, the latter is the more credible.

He seemed anxious to try and make amends with his widowed daughter-in-law, though some thought he rather overacted the part of a sorrowing father. On the day after her husband's death, she wrote him a touching letter affirming that 'the sorrow which overwhelms me does not make me the less sensible of the great goodness of Your Majesty', and commending her children and herself to his 'paternal love and royal protection'.[7] In reply he sent messages worded 'in the tenderest terms'. He paid her a personal visit, embraced her, and sat with her on a sofa as they both wept. As they dabbed at their eyes with handkerchiefs, he called his grandsons and told them that they must always be brave boys, obedient to their mother, and 'deserve the fortune to which they were born'. On twelve-year old Prince George, who was destined to succeed his grandfather on the throne, the loss of his father had a profound effect. When told the news, he said nothing and nearly fainted. Recovering his composure, he placed his

hand on his heart, saying, 'I feel here as I did when I saw the workman fall from the scaffold at Kew.'

According to Dodington, after examination by the physicians and surgeons the King ordered the bowels to be put in a box covered with red velvet, and buried in King Henry VII's Chapel. The remains were buried unceremoniously at the funeral on 13 April, 'without anthem or organ', and with only the Duke of Somerset as chief mourner. None of the royal family attended. Due to bungling, invitations were only sent out a few hours before the ceremony though it was to be expected that persons of rank, such as members of the House of Lords, would attend. Apart from pall-bearers and others with ceremonial functions, no English lords, no bishops, only one Irish lord, two sons of dukes and two Privy Councillors attended, one of them the faithful Dodington. He deplored the absence of so many people of note, and that so few should bother 'to make a show of duty to a prince, so great in rank and expectation'.

Henry Pelham could not but welcome the heir's death. It put an end to the opposition groups which he suspected of intriguing against him; he even feared that William Pitt, a former Groom of the Bedchamber to the Prince, was planning to join the 'Leicester House party'.

Prince Frederick Louis's reputation has never stood high. Unlike the Duke of Cumberland he was never an object of hatred, but he was rarely respected either. During his lifetime he was moderately popular, if only by default at times when his father was particularly disliked. Generous, amiable, with pronounced artistic tastes, he was however a lightweight in personality who never really matured. While he expressed enlightened and liberal views, it was easy for him to do so while he was in effect in opposition. How much he expressed them from conviction and how much as a result of persuasion by those who were ready to manipulate him can only be guessed at.

It is tempting to suggest that his irresponsible behaviour at the birth of his first child indicated that he would have been a foolish, unsuccessful monarch, although it is hardly fair to damn him for one stupid action; the responsibility of kingship might have been the making of him. Moreover the events of that night in the summer of 1737 did not prevent him from becoming a far more devoted husband and father than his forebears. At the time of his wedding, few thought that the marriage would be a success. He proved his detractors wrong by remaining faithful to his wife; he had sown his wild oats, and was more than eager to settle down, never happier than when he was with his family. Whether his harmonious relationship with his eldest son and heir would have survived his accession to the throne is another of history's imponderables.

It was the misfortune of Prince Frederick Lewis to live in the shadow of parents who disliked him and refused to trust him with a suitable role in

life. Like three future Princes of Wales of the royal line during the next two centuries, he was driven back on to his own resources to find his own way while waiting for the throne – and in each instance, the sovereign found much to be displeased about. Yet to one section of the community, at least, his death was to be regretted. The painter Joshua Reynolds, destined to be the first president of the Royal Academy of Arts within ten years of the Prince's son ascending the throne, lamented the loss of one 'who would certainly have been a great patron'.

Perhaps the last words on the Prince should go to a contemporary versifier:

> Here lies Fred,
> Who was alive and is dead.
> Had it been his father,
> I had much rather;
> Had it been his brother,
> Still better than another;
> Had it been his sister,
> No one would have missed her.
> Had it been the whole generation,
> Still better for the nation.
> But since 'tis only Fred,
> Who was alive and is dead –
> There's no more to be said.

'Now I shall have no more peace'

At the time of the Prince of Wales's death the Duke of Cumberland's reputation was at its nadir. Beside the unmilitary, well-mannered, arts-loving brother with a wife and children, he had cut an unprepossessing picture. As Captain General, after the declaration of peace in 1748 he had begun to initiate several long-overdue military reforms, with particular emphasis on the improvement of discipline and its general standing as a professional force. The gentry resented his attempt to abolish promotion by purchase, while the people grumbled at his increasing the powers of courts martial and at his treatment of English soldiers as if they were Hessian mercenaries. Above all, a strong army in Britain was seen as a potential danger to constitutional liberty; in peacetime, it was believed, there was no need for a large force. The ministers disliked the Duke, while the opposition resented him for being the King's favourite son. His brief honeymoon period after Culloden as the man who vanquished the Scots was over, and exaggerated tales of his cruelty against the Highlanders rebounded on him. Yet in England this much could be forgiven him; the real cause of his unpopularity was his Germanic thoroughness and quest for efficiency. Similar English resentment, although less marked, would await the Coburg-born Prince Albert a century later.

Cumberland was thus an easy target to blacken. The widow and adolescent heir at Leicester House, and several leading ministers all believed, or affected to believe, that in the event of his father's sudden death he was ready to take advantage of his military authority and stage a *coup d'état* by usurping the throne from his nephew, particularly if he was appointed sole Regent.

There was nothing to justify such suspicions, and the King resented this persistent calumny against his son. 'It was the lies they told against my son for the service he did this country, which had raised this clamour against him,'[1] he declared. Peevishly he blamed his unpopularity on 'the Scotch, the Jacobites and the English that don't love discipline'. Even so, the national mood had to be taken into account when considering the possibility of a regency which would be needed if his grandson George should ascend the throne during his minority. At the time of his elder son's death the King was aged sixty-seven, an age surpassed by only two sovereigns

since the Norman conquest (Edward I and Elizabeth), and whatever his state of health he could not be expected to last for much longer.

The Duke of Cumberland, the King notified Henry Pelham, First Lord of the Treasury and Chancellor of the Exchequer, was the proper person to be designated Regent. Nevertheless Pelham and Newcastle opposed the proposal; the general public, they argued, would not tolerate Prince George being placed in the care of his uncle. In the debate on the Regency Bill the Paymaster, William Pitt, warned that if the Princess of Wales died suddenly the Duke would become sole Regent, 'when ambition might excite him to think less of protecting than of bearing the Crown.' Chesterfield's portrayal of the Duke as King Richard III reincarnate, a wicked uncle to a young heir, had evidently taken root. They forced on the King a compromise by which the Princess should be Regent, assisted by a council of twelve, with Cumberland as President. Her powers, however, would be restricted; she would not be able to change any of the ministers left by her father-in-law, save on the advice of a majority in the Council, or an address by both Houses of Parliament.

The Duke yielded to this stipulation with good grace. Though his friends offered to raise the matter in Parliament in an effort to overturn the position he dissuaded them, saying he had no desire to advertise the resentment which he felt at the slight deliberately put on him by the Pelhams and Pitt. Understandably he bore a grudge against them ever after.

The King admitted to Henry Fox, Secretary of State for War, that he accepted the Princess as a Regent, as he had 'a good opinion' of her, but 'I don't quite know her'. In cases of treason, women tended to issue pardons: 'I myself am always inclined to mercy; it is better to have somebody to refuse for her.' While honest enough to admit that he was glad his son was dead, he treated his daughter-in-law and grandchildren with fairness, even with kindness. Waldegrave declared that he behaved to Princess Augusta 'not only with politeness but with the appearance of affection'.

This affection did not extend to the new heir, formally created Prince of Wales in April 1751, a month after his father's death. Prince George was required to go to Hampton Court and live under the King's eye for a time. His heir, the King was soon grumbling, 'lacked the desire to please'. Once he lost his temper with the boy and boxed his ears. Many years later one of King George III's sons, the Duke of Sussex, said that the blow 'so disgusted him that he could never after think of [Hampton Court] as a residence'.

Princess Augusta never trusted her brother-in-law, seeing him as an intriguer against her son and his succession. The King, she told Dodington in October 1751, was 'very respectful' to her, but Cumberland had never paid her a visit, or even enquired after her, all summer; 'she could not help wondering what views were at the bottom of it'. It was partly this aversion to him that persuaded her 'to keep well with the King and consequently countenance those ministers he employed'.[2]

A year later the Princess was complaining to Dodington about the King's refusal to pay her late husband's debts, especially as the Prince's death had left him better off by £30,000 a year. 'She wished he were less civil, and put less of their money into his pocket.' Was it becoming for 'so great a King to leave his son's debts unpaid?'[3] The Duke of Cumberland and Princess Amelia, she was convinced, were causing 'all imaginable mischief' against her.

The Duke was the only one of his surviving children for whom the King really cared. None of his daughters meant much to him any longer. Anne, Princess Royal, wife of the Prince of Orange, had inherited his obstinacy and pomposity in full measure, and attempted to nag her father so much that on his visits to Hanover he refused to play the doting father and see her again. Princess Amelia had become prematurely deaf and peevish; after refusing various offers of marriage from German princes, and having affairs with the Dukes of Newcastle and Grafton, she had settled down to a life of spinsterhood divided between horses, cards and gossip – the more scandalous the better. Normally insensitive to the feelings of others, and aggressive at the card table, she was always particularly drawn to the Duke of Cumberland. She followed all his military campaigns with intense interest, and was wracked with anxiety when he was at the front. When he was in England she lived with him, acting as his hostess at St James's, and later at Cumberland Lodge. It soon went without saying that when noblemen sent out invitations for parties at their country houses, brother and sister should be invited together.

Like her, the Duke had never considered marriage seriously. When the King had suggested in 1743 that he ought to take a deformed princess of Denmark for his wife, he appealed to the Earl of Orford for advice. The wily statesman, who had died not long afterwards, suggested that he ought to accept on condition that he was given 'an immediate and most ample establishment'. The match, he assured the Duke, would 'not then be pressed'.

Princess Amelia evidently throve on her spinsterhood, for she outlived the rest of her generation.* Freedom and self-indulgence certainly gave her something to live for, unlike the other old maid, the pathetic Princess Caroline who had retired into seclusion since the death of Lord Hervey, the

*Her father and the Duke of Cumberland both died in the month of October (1760 and 1765 respectively), and she had a premonition thereafter that she and King Frederick II of Prussia, to whom she had once been almost betrothed, would also die in October, within a few days of each other. In fact Frederick died in August 1786, and she died six weeks later – in October that same year. When she was being prepared for her funeral she was found to be wearing a miniature of him.

only man for whom she had ever really cared, in 1743. Rarely stepping outside St James's Palace, she seldom saw anyone from day to day apart from her father, sister, brother and a few favoured courtiers, and gave most of her money to charities, particularly those connected with the welfare of prisoners.

Any attempts that the Princess Royal had dared to make to find either of them a husband were savagely rebuffed. 'I sometimes believe you think that unmarried women have no places in heaven,' Amelia wrote to her elder sister, 'for you think nobody can have the least happiness without being tied from morning to night to a creature which may tire one's life out and plague one incessantly with their good advice or commands while one is as full as wise as they and only difference of dress and fashion allowing them all lots of things which women must not do because its not discreet . . . we poor women have great disadvantages without making them still worse and putting one self in a Jackanapes power.' She had evidently taken the example of her late mother to heart too much to run the risk of marrying a man who might turn out to be like her father. 'Make no match for Caro or for me Royaux,' she ended her letter; 'if you do I shall get you divorced and make Pépin [Prince William of Orange] marry someone else.'[4]

The two youngest Princesses had escaped spinsterhood, but on balance might have been happier if they had stayed single at home. Mary, said to have 'the softest, mildest temper in the world', had married the brutal Prince Frederick of Hesse-Cassel, who treated her badly. Louisa, the youngest, pretty and vivacious, had inherited much of her mother's strength of personality. Married to Crown Prince Frederick of Denmark, who ascended the throne as King Frederick V in 1746, she made the best of an unsatisfactory husband and would never admit to her family how unhappy she was. They had seemed perfectly suited at first. One lady at court was touched to see them, soon after their marriage, eating a bowl of cherries together, one holding the stalk between the lips while the other bit the fruit off. Such mutual devotion, however, did not last; nor did the Princess's health. Like her mother she suffered agonies for years as the result of a strangulated hernia, since the seventh month of her first pregnancy. Even so she gave birth to five more children, and was carrying a sixth when she became seriously ill and died, aged twenty-seven, in December 1751. Though he had not been the most attentive of husbands, King Frederick was grief-stricken, and a second marriage did not keep him from the bottle to drown his sorrows. He succumbed to cancer of the liver in 1766 at the age of forty-two.

Only a few weeks earlier the Princess Royal had been widowed. The Prince of Orange died in October 1751 at the age of forty, shortly after several weeks of failing health which culminated in a massive stroke. A post-mortem revealed that his twisted backbone, the cause of his deformity, had

gradually narrowed the gap between collarbone and breastbone so that the jugular vein was pressed, and the increasing curvature had finally blocked the blood supply to his lungs and heart.[5] Though he was not by nature the most paternal of men, the King was moved to tears at this catalogue of mortality:

> This has been a fatal year for my family. I lost my eldest son – but I am glad of it. The Prince of Orange died, and left everything in confusion. Poor little Edward [his grandson, the Duke of York] has been cut open (for an imposthume in his side). Now the Queen of Denmark is gone. I know I did not love my children when they were young. I hated to have them running into my room; but now I love them as well as most fathers.[6]

To his daughter he wrote with sympathy and more affection than he had expressed to her for a long time; 'Never doubt my dear daughter the very sincere share I have in your great affliction . . . be sure you will find always in me a father who will cherish you tenderly.'[7] Yet Anne was not one to accept an olive branch lightly. As head of government in succession to her husband, she could not forgive or forget how humiliated they had been by British government policy, and she assumed that her father thought he could dictate his own terms to her. His envoy, the Earl of Holderness, was granted a chilly reception.

Anne, the King readily admitted, had more dedication and talent for business than her husband, but she was 'arrogant, imperious, false and foolish.' He returned to Hanover again late in 1752, but still declined to visit her. Instead he asked William Bentinck, a member of the Dutch court since Anne's marriage, to send him a personal report on her. Bentinck was a son of Lord and Lady Portland, the latter having been Anne's governess, and knew her from childhood. He told the King that she did more work in a day than her husband had done in fourteen, but her application to industry was not appreciated; her arrogance made her her own worst enemy, and 'day by day her personal credit and the love of the people is lost'.[8]

To this catalogue of family woe was added the breakdown of Princess Mary's marriage some three years later. Prince Frederick of Hesse-Cassel had bullied her mercilessly, and while she could submit to this meekly, he put himself beyond the pale by becoming a Roman Catholic. For his wife and her family, who had grown up in the shadow of the Catholic and Jacobite threat, this was too much. She left him, settling with their three sons at Hanau on the River Main where she rebuilt the Schloss Rumpenheim. Her health, it was said, improved since 'the release from her tyrant'.

Though King George II had generally enjoyed good health, he too was feeling the weight of his years. In 1753 he attained the age of seventy. In

one scene of a play he saw soon afterwards, a young woman said to her elderly admirer, 'You are villainously old; you are sixty-six; you can't have the impudence to think of living above two years.' He turned about in a passion, exclaiming crossly, 'This is damned stuff!' To his ladies at court, he would lament that he 'was once a very strong man, though now grown old and useless.'

By now he had merited and attained a certain amount of respect, albeit occasionally grudging. That he had reached such an age was ascribed to his strong constitution and temperance. For all his faults, ministers readily gave him credit for his insight into people and situations. If they sometimes found him 'hasty and passionate when any measure is proposed which he does not approve of', they still recognized that once his temper had cooled, few people of high rank could put up with contradiction better, provided the arguments were sound. To his servants he was unfailingly gracious and affable, as long as they were careful not to ask after his piles. From the early years of his reign, he had always been diligent as a sovereign in attending to business; now it was one of the few diversions left to him.

With her dread of Cumberland, the Dowager Princess of Wales feared what he might do if the King died while her son was too young to rule. One day Prince George was visiting his uncle at Cumberland Lodge, where the walls were decorated with souvenirs of his campaigns. Trying to arouse his interest, the Duke took one of his favourite swords down from the wall to show him properly. He was about to draw it when the timorous Prince turned pale and began to tremble. The Duke was horrified that his avuncular hospitality should be misinterpreted in this manner, and complained afterwards to his mother, whom he blamed for the boy's suspicious state of mind.

Since her husband's death she had come to rely increasingly on the Earl of Bute, who was now the young Prince of Wales's tutor, and it was rumoured that he and the Princess were lovers. In addition there were difficulties with the household of the Prince of Wales when the King had to intervene in an internal quarrel. Two of the boy's tutors alleged that other male members of the household were endeavouring to turn the heir to the throne into a Jacobite. The King said the charges were frivolous, and replaced them with Earl Waldegrave and John Thomas, Bishop of Peterborough. These appointments were the subject of some parliamentary disapproval, for Waldegrave was distrusted on account of his left-handed connection with King James II, his grandmother having been an illegitimate daughter of the King, and Bishop Thomas was regarded as 'a High Tory churchman'.

In March 1753 the matter was debated in the House of Lords, but the Duke of Bedford's demands for an enquiry to be instituted into the appointments was defeated. For once the Dowager Princess of Wales was full

of praise for her father-in-law, telling Dodington that she admired his 'steadiness and resolution' in dealing with the affair, and much appreciated his 'good sense and proper firmness'; otherwise she was sure the Lords of the cabinet would not have behaved so well. It was the first time Dodington recalled her speaking favourably of the King. Lord Waldegrave observed that the young Prince was bored and thoroughly disliked his work, though he was not unintelligent.

While he had nothing of his late wife's or son's cultural interests, it was King George II's good fortune to preside over, or at least put his signature to, the formation of the British Museum. The private natural history collection formed by Sir Hans Sloane, Sir Robert Cotton's priceless medieval manuscripts, and the library and manuscripts of Robert Harley, Earl of Oxford, were united to form a national museum worthy of the name. In June 1753 the King gave his assent to the Act of Parliament which formally created the Museum, and four years later he added to it by presenting the Old Royal Library, built up by successive Kings since the fifteenth century. Perhaps it was ironic that the reign of the King who so despised learning would be associated with the country's greatest monument to scholarship and learning.

Hatred of 'bainters' and his contempt for Hogarth did not prevent the latter from being appointed Serjeant Painter to the King. In June 1757 the *enfant terrible* of English painting was chosen to succeed John Thornhill by the Lord Chamberlain, the Duke of Devonshire, who had sat to him in 1740. The office carried a salary of £10 per annum, and gave the holder a monopoly of painting and gilding all royal palaces and conveyances, all banners and tents of royal troops and ships.

In March 1754 the King lost the man who, like Walpole, had been his prime minister for some years in all but name. Henry Pelham, First Lord of the Treasury and Chancellor of the Exchequer, died after a short illness. Despite their differences, notably on foreign affairs, King and minister had come to respect each other. 'Now I shall have no more peace,' the King exclaimed despairingly. In his place his elder brother, the Duke of Newcastle, became First Lord of the Treasury and effectively leader of the government. Under him there was indeed to be little peace. The Treaty of Aix-la-Chapelle had left many issues undecided. France was becoming more of a threat and a rival to England with every year that passed, particularly in overseas possessions such as North America and India. In her turn France felt threatened by British colonial expansion. Yet neither country wanted war, especially as the King feared that a renewal of conflict in Europe would lead to a French attack on Hanover, German princes would require the payment of vast subsidies for their support, England would be dependent

on Austrian help and, as Lord Holderness established when he accompanied the King on a *Hanoverreise* in the spring of 1755, the Dutch would probably remain neutral.

Newcastle's dilemma was the protection of British settlers' interests in North America and Canada while doing nothing to precipitate war closer to home. Yet he was determined not to abandon them to their fate. For the last few years the French had been constructing a chain of forts along the rivers St Lawrence, Ohio and Mississippi, which served also as depots for trading with the Indian tribes, and the British colonists appealed for regular troops to defend them. Unlike his ministers, the military-minded King saw that for fighting the French and their Indian allies in the depths of the American forests, regular troops trained for war in the Low Countries would not do. He wanted munitions, officers and instructors to train and strengthen the colonial militia, and let them do the job. But he allowed himself to be persuaded by Cumberland, who strongly believed in the ability of regular troops, to send two regiments under the command of Major-General James Braddock, a sound conventional officer who had distinguished himself at Dettingen. The King's fears that even the best troops in Europe would be no use in such hostile terrain were soon realized, and in July 1755 Braddock, moving on Fort Duquesne, marched straight into a French-Indian ambush. Firing valiantly in the general direction of an invisible foe, they never had a chance, and the entire force was massacred. Braddock, the King insisted crossly, should never have been sent.

The King and Newcastle favoured the time-honoured system of an Anglo-Austrian-Dutch alliance against France and perhaps Prussia. Hanover was always vulnerable to the threat of Prussian invasion. An alternative policy existed, a Prussian alliance against France and perhaps Austria, But the King did not propose to ally himself against Prussia as this would surely mean the loss of other allies. Instead he opened negotiations with King Frederick for a promise not to attack Hanover. At the same time, he considered, a marriage alliance might also play its part and help to safeguard the position of his electorate against his unpredictable nephew.

It was time, the King thought, that his grandson should choose a bride or have one chosen for him. While in Hanover during the summer and early autumn of 1755 he had met the Duchess of Brunswick-Wolfenbüttel and her two unmarried daughters. A matrimonial alliance between the second, the attractive seventeen-year-old Princess Sophie, and his heir, was the answer. On political and personal grounds, the case was incontestable. As Brunswick was a close ally of Prussia, such a betrothal would facilitate a *rapprochement* with King Frederick II, thus relieving the constant threat of a Prussian attack on the ancestral home. Moreover the King had taken a particular liking to the Princess. As he was too old to make her his wife, wrote Waldegrave, he wished to make her his granddaughter instead; had he been

only twenty years younger, he declared, 'she should never have been refused by a Prince of Wales but should at once been Queen of England'.[9]

The Dowager Princess suspected that this young girl had sufficient strength of character to dominate her easily led son if they should become betrothed, and would destroy her influence with him in no time. To her son, she was adamant that he was being made a sacrifice, merely to gratify the King's private interests in the electorate of Hanover. As for the princess in question, she 'was most cruelly misrepresented', until the young credulous prince took his own deep-seated aversion to her. To the King, his mother insisted that it was too soon to consider marriage for her 'shy and backward boy'. That she should openly speak of him in such terms seemed almost tantamount to an admission of failure on her part and that of Bute to prepare him for his station in life. From then, on the Prince's side, all duty and obedience to his grandfather apparently ceased. The King had done his best to show the utmost fairness, if not affection as well, towards his prematurely bereaved daughter-in-law and her family. But on his return from Hanover to St James's, he summoned the Prince for a royal reprimand. Waldegrave thought that it would have been more politic for the King to tackle the trouble at source, by speaking to his mother instead and asking her to keep her son in order.

The Prince's eighteenth birthday in June 1756 seemed an appropriate time for removing him from his mother's overpowering influence and from Bute, for whom the King had the utmost contempt. The Princess and her son were informed that he should thenceforth have a separate establishment, his own apartments at Kensington Palace and St James's, and an allowance of £40,000 a year. But the Prince instructed Lord Waldegrave to thank His Majesty and express his earnest wish that he might continue to live with his mother. He also desired that Lord Bute might be placed in some principal position about him. Old and tired, the King agreed to his grandson's demands, only requesting in return an assurance of dutiful obedience. Bute was made Groom of the Stole to the Prince, but the King firmly refused to receive him.

'In perfect tranquillity at home'

To the end of his days King George II retained a keen interest in foreign and military affairs. While he confessed that he still preferred the Hanoverian system, 'where the government is military, as here it is legal', he conceded that his family came to England 'to preserve the laws, and were therefore [obliged] to retain them'. For his last four years, matters foreign and military would engage his attention and concentrate the minds of his ministers to a considerable degree once more.

Although a virtual state of open war had existed between Britain and France in America for several months, hostilities were not officially declared until May 1756. Newcastle was still reluctant to provoke the French in Europe, and France had no intention of being forced into action before her fleet was ready. When Admiral Byng and his small, inadequately manned fleet was sent to meet the French threat to the British Mediterranean garrison of Minorca, he attacked the enemy fleet in an indecisive battle and sailed back to Gibraltar, leaving France in control. It was the signal for war, to be followed by reverses in North America and the spread of fighting to mainland Europe when King Frederick of Prussia invaded Saxony, much to King George's fury.

Newcastle's administration inevitably suffered much of the blame, and the country called for Pitt to be given greater office in the Commons. Whether he would serve with Fox and Newcastle, and whether the King would accept him in the ministry, was another matter. 'Mr Pitt won't do my German business' was the main royal objection, but Newcastle assured him gravely that: 'If he comes into your service, Sir, he must be told he must do Your Majesty's business.' After several days of heated negotiations between the King and his ministers Newcastle offered his resignation, and a new administration was formed under the leadership of the Duke of Devonshire. Having named his conditions, which included the formation of an efficient militia which, with the navy, could defend the kingdom, freeing the regular troops, Hanoverian and Hessian, for service abroad, and an inquiry into the discipline and legal position of the Hanoverian soldiers, Pitt accepted the seals of the Southern Department. These policies were outlined in the King's speech from the throne at the opening of the session. The militia, which His Majesty had always ridiculed, was now warmly praised;

Hanoverian and Hessian soldiers would be sent back to Germany; and the success and preservation of the American colonies would be the main object of the royal attention and solicitude. Privately the King thought that the words he uttered were 'stuff and nonsense', complaining that Pitt 'made him long speeches, which possibly might be very fine, but were greatly beyond his comprehension; and that his letters were affected, formal and pedantic'.[1] Even so his relations with Pitt were better than expected, if only because the minister suffered from gout so badly that winter that he was only able to attend the King in his closet six times during his first spell in office.

One of the ministry's first problems was the fate of Byng, held responsible for the loss of Minorca. Pitt wished clemency to be shown, out of common humanity and political expediency. For him to be acquitted or pardoned would point the finger of blame at his political masters, Pitt's rivals in government. But Byng had been burnt in effigy in every town in England, and public opinion demanded his head. While the ministers wanted him to be spared, they were equally anxious to be spared the odium of protecting him.

On 27 January 1757 the Court Martial exonerated him on charges of 'cowardice and disaffection', but found him guilty of 'neglect of duty in the face of the enemy' and sentenced him to death. Only a royal pardon could annul the death sentence, and Pitt said he was satisfied that mercy 'was more likely to flow from His Majesty if he was left entirely free.' Though the King thought Byng guilty of cowardice, he was inclined to spare him. Yet as Parliament had made this very harsh law, he considered it his duty to abide by it and not reprieve the first prominent offender, or as some suggested, allow Byng to escape from prison. To gain time and in the hope that he would be relieved of this dreadful burden, he referred the sentence to the judges for a legal review of the case; they pronounced it legal in accordance with the findings of the court. When Pitt told him that the general opinion of Parliament was for pardoning the Admiral, the King replied coldly, 'Sir, you have taught me to look for the sense of my subjects in another place than in the House of Commons.'[2] After a stay of execution called for by the King, on the grounds that there may have been technicalities which rendered the Court Martial unjust, the law took its course and on 14 March Byng bravely faced the firing squad.

As Secretary of State, Pitt at last appreciated the wisdom of English support for Prussia and Hanover. An army of observation which would defend Hanover and cover Frederick of Prussia's right flank was of value, as the more deeply engaged France was in Europe, the better chance there was of English military victory in America. The obvious commander for such an army was Cumberland, but he refused to accept command so long as Pitt,

whom he distrusted as a 'Leicester House Secretary of State', was more or less in control of government policy. Pitt was therefore dismissed in April 1757, but Newcastle soon found him impossible to replace in government, and he was reappointed to his post in June. Putting personal prejudices to one side, King George managed to get on better with him than ever before. The Lord Chancellor, the Earl of Hardwicke, commented that it came partly from the King putting Pitt into a good humour rather than vexing him, and from the man who had baited the King for most of his political career now exerting all his charm to gain the royal confidence. Above all, Pitt put paid to the King's reservations by showing he was prepared to 'do his German business'. For all his radicalism the politician was, in the words of Edmund Burke, 'intoxicated by the least peep into the royal Closet'.

The 'German business' was not destined for success, certainly not as far as the Duke of Cumberland was concerned. Still a comparatively young man of thirty-six, he was in poor health, suffering from his old wound and from obesity, compounded by chronic asthma. As an English general in command of English troops fighting for their country he would have been in his element, particularly if he was fit and well; but his heart was not in commanding a largely Hanoverian army under orders from his father to defend Hanover, and only to attack enemy forces 'if you think it can be effected with any moral certainty of success, and without waiving the main point which is covering my German dominions'.[3] Far from satisfied with some of the senior officers and the troops under his command, the King commiserated with him on 'the negligence of those old fools', and promised him that anybody who disobeyed his orders through cowardice or otherwise would be strictly tried by Court Martial.

In July his force was intercepted by a superior French army and defeated at Hastenbeck. The losses were small and he disengaged successfully, making the best of a difficult situation. However he was unable to prevent the French from invading Hesse-Cassel and much of Hanover. The King took the bad news well, saying calmly that his son 'must get out of it as well as he could'. Yet he was anxious that the French might push demands too far, insisting on disarming his troops and making them prisoners of war. While he would try to help the Landgrave of Hesse-Cassel and the Dukes of Wolfenbüttel and Gotha, he could do no more for King Frederick of Prussia. In his electoral capacity he was obliged to make a separate peace for Hanover, a move which his English ministers deplored but could not prevent. He wrote secretly to the Duke of Cumberland, giving him discretionary powers to make terms with the French, as long as he could save his father's army 'in the best manner possible', and not submit to terms which included the disarming of troops.

The Convention of Klosterzeven was signed on 8 September, its terms providing for the disbanding of the army of observation, immobilization of

the Hanoverian troops, and the disbanding of those of Hesse-Cassel and Brunswick. French forces were permitted to occupy Bremen and Verden, thus putting Hanover and the allied states at the mercy of their enemies. Defeated and unwell, the Duke was in no position to press for anything better. The treaty was greeted with dismay by ministers and public alike in London. In a rare political intervention Lady Yarmouth, a Hanoverian herself, mischievously suggested to the King that making a separate peace for the electorate would be contrary to his honour and taint his memory for ever after. Having second thoughts, the King sent off a message to his son rescinding his decision, but too late; the Convention had been signed.*

Bitterly regretting his delegation to the Duke, the King was beside himself with rage. A furious letter referring to 'a convention shameful and pernicious' had been signed without writing for his ratification: 'come back at once by a warship and explain.' To those around him he inveighed against his 'rascally son' whose blood was tainted, while blaming himself at the same time for entrusting such a difficult negotiation to an inexperienced negotiator to undertake.

Cumberland returned early in October, aware of his father's anxiety but confident in the knowledge that he had carried out His Majesty's written orders to the best of his ability. He had no idea of his father's true state of mind. Calling upon his old ministerial ally Henry Fox, the Paymaster, who expressed surprise at the Duke's calmness and confidence that all would be well, the latter assured him that he was 'perfectly easy' with respect to His Majesty. He had the King's orders in writing for everything he had done, 'and I have done better for him than I thought the exigency would have allowed of'.

However, on presenting himself at court the next day he was coldly received. The King was at his card-table, and on his appearance he exclaimed angrily that here was his son 'who has ruined me and disgraced himself'. When Cumberland defended himself by referring to the orders upon which he had acted, the King lost his temper, shouting at his son that 'he had ruined his Country and his Army, had spoiled everything and lost his own Reputation'. Horace Walpole maintained that the King had been jealous of the Duke of Cumberland ever since the death of the Prince of Wales; if so, perhaps this explosion of fury against the son of whom he had previously been so proud was the culmination of years of pent-up envy.

When the King withdrew, Cumberland asked Lady Yarmouth 'in the most respectful and most submissive manner, to let the King know that he had it

*In fact the cabinet and the King, acting as Elector of Hanover, managed to repudiate the Convention of Klosterzeven in November, because the French had already infringed its terms by attempting to disarm the Hessian soldiers on their way home.

not in his power to serve HM any longer, and that he had no favour left to ask, but leave to quit.' Perhaps stricken with remorse at her part in the crisis, she asked him 'to take no resolution', but he said he had had time to reflect on his own unimpeachable conduct, 'and on the impossibility of his showing due regard to his own honour by any other method than what he now pursued.'[4] He would resign his regiment, his post as Captain General, and all his offices, even his Colonelcy of the Foot Guards. Bitterly hurt by his father's shabby treatment, he was too good a German soldier, too loyal a son and subject to attempt to clear his name by the military channels open to him.

Ironically in view of past events, the Duke had a ready defender in Pitt. When the King sent Gerlach Munchhausen, the minister for Hanover in London, to inform the cabinet that Cumberland had acted against orders, Pitt announced that he must, 'as a man of honour and a gentleman, allow everywhere that HRH had full powers to do what he has done.' 'I gave him no orders to conclude this treaty,' the King insisted. 'But very full powers, sir, very full powers,' Pitt pointed out, infuriated at the King's duplicity.

A couple of days later the King reproached himself bitterly for having acted so hastily, and begged the Duke to reconsider his decision. Would he not at least retain his Colonelcy of the Regiment of Guards, so as to avoid severing his connection with the army, so that in case of invasion he might take his place at the head of the forces once more? The cabinet council went to St James's to try and persuade the Duke, but he was obdurate; he had made his decision and would abide by it. Shortly afterwards when there were rumours of a French invasion, the Duchess of Bedford told Cumberland that everyone expected him to be given the army command once more. He said he did not believe it would be offered to him, 'but when no wise man would accept it, and no honest man would refuse it'.

Ill-merited as his disgrace had been, the Duke behaved with dignity. He retired into private life, devoting himself to the largely honorary position of Ranger of Windsor Forest. While his health permitted, he also consoled himself with a succession of mistresses and a passion for horse racing.

William Pitt, whom King George II had so reluctantly allowed to hold the seals of office, was confident of victory and above all of his part in it: 'I know that I can save this country and that I alone can.' To him the war was a worldwide struggle to be fought in Europe, North America, the West Indies, the West Coast of Africa and the East Indies. None of these fronts engaged his enthusiasm more than North America, where his objective was the removal of the French threat and subsequent opening of the continent for the settlement by Britons. In the other territories his intention was to eliminate imperial competition, secure the acquisition of the French trading posts, and much of the slave trade. By 1758 he had devised a three-

pronged attack on the French in North America. One army was to attack and seize Louisburg, the key to the St Lawrence River and Quebec; a second was to invade Canada and take Ticonderoga, Crown Point and eventually Montreal or Quebec; and the third would attack French forts in the Ohio valley, retake Fort Duquesne and re-establish British power there.

Pitt and the King still had their differences, particularly over the appointment of commanders. A product of the old military school, and as head of his kingdom's armed forces, the King rated experience and seniority above everything else in a leader, whereas Pitt favoured younger commanders with flair. Two men whom Pitt chose for the North American campaign, Jeffrey Amherst (second in command to the new Commander-in-Chief, James Abercromby), and George Howe (Abercromby's Chief of Staff), met with the King's disapproval on the grounds of youth and inexperience respectively, but Pitt threatened to abandon his whole strategy rather than concede, and the King reluctantly accepted his appointments. Louisburg was captured in July, though it was too late in the year to continue campaigning to take Quebec. The British forces however suffered a serious reverse with the death of Howe in a skirmish with the French forces, and with defeat soon afterwards at Ticonderoga. Although another army arrived at Fort Duquesne in November to find it abandoned, the campaign was going Britain's way and the Indian tribes, sensing who would probably win the war, began to transfer their allegiance to the British. The war proved a severe strain on British finances, but Pitt and the King knew that they had the expulsion of the French from North America firmly within their sights; and they intended the British to be undisputed masters of the sub-continent by the end of the year.

Though King George II could hardly be described as a family man, and had little affection for his children, the fact that he survived most of them inevitably added to the loneliness of his old age. The reclusive Princess Caroline had become old before her time. She was a persistent hypochondriac, and Princess Amelia had on occasion written to their eldest sister in Holland that Caroline was better, 'though pray don't mention it to her, for she only allows of her not being worse'.[5] Now as she lay dying in her bed at St James's Palace, she gently but firmly declined to see any of her family. When the pain ceased and the 'mortification' began, she said resignedly, 'I feared I should not have died of this!'[6] Aged forty-four, she passed away on 28 December 1757.

'Her goodness was constant and uniform, her generosity immense, her charities most extensive,' Horace Walpole observed. 'In short I, no royalist, could be lavish in her praise.'[7] Death for her was undoubtedly a release; perhaps her father, growing old and infirm, envied her. She was laid to rest in Henry VII's Chapel, Westminster Abbey, on 5 January the following year.

The King had always loved fresh air, the colder the better. Newcastle liked his rooms well heated, and after an audience with the King he would return complaining bitterly that His Majesty kept all window sashes up, so there was no avoiding the draught. None of the ministers were surprised when he caught a severe cold in November 1758 while driving from Kensington to London with his coach windows open. Although already suffering agonies from an attack of gout, he made light of his troubles. Within a few days he was so ill that the doctors ordered him to bed, and for a while they despaired of his life, but his iron constitution pulled him through. When told that rumours about his poor health were harming the government he struggled out of bed, and on the coldest day of the winter he put in an appearance at court. Still far from well, his spirits were raised by the undisguised expressions of loyalty, and he was touched when Pitt praised him for his courage in coming to the government's rescue. Taken by surprise, the doctors said that he would probably last until the following summer at least.

He was certainly made of stronger stuff than most of his children. The new year of 1759 had barely begun before news came of the widowed Princess of Orange's death. Anne, Princess Royal, had once been her father's favourite daughter, but since her much-delayed departure from England in 1734 there was little love lost between them. They were too similar in nature, their strong characters tended to clash, and he held her responsible for not checking anti-British feeling in Holland. After her husband's death in 1751 her own health had declined. Her temper, contemporaries asserted, was 'neither ingratiating nor bending'. Adding to her anxieties were arguments between Britain and Holland over commercial treaties. Dutch ships were repeatedly boarded, searched and harassed by British government officials and illegal privateers, their cargoes seized, and Dutch merchants were so incensed that the likelihood of war between both nations loomed. The Princess felt harassed and unable to cope with pressures from the English government, especially as she was evidently a sick woman by the summer of 1758. She died on 12 January 1759, dropsy being given as the cause of death.

Meanwhile the war was fulfilling the previous year's promise. 1759 was the *annus mirabilis* of King George II's reign when, Horace Walpole could note cynically, the bells were worn threadbare with ringing for victories. By common consent, writes a recent authority, the year of 1759 stands with 1588, 1704, 1815, and 1940, 'as one of the greatest in our modern annals'; for despite months of disappointments and moments of alarm, 'the overall achievement was none the less most impressive and irresistible to the pride of the nation'.[8] Abercromby was recalled and the advance in Canada was to be pressed under Amherst and Major-General James Wolfe. When

politicians questioned Wolfe's sanity, King George retorted that if he was mad, 'I wish he would bite some of my other generals.' He completed his mission to seize Quebec, only to be mortally wounded just as victory was assured.

Meanwhile the West Indies expedition had been crowned with success by the capture of Guadeloupe. Closer to home there was another threat of a French invasion, launched from the Austrian Netherlands. In July the King reviewed the Norfolk militia which marched past through London to the south-eastern shires and expressed his satisfaction with the regiment's discipline, turnout and bearing, and exhorting them 'to play their part like men'. The French plan, so rumour had it, was for the Toulon fleet to evade the blockading squadron, join the Brest fleet and between them gain full naval control of the English Channel, thus enabling forces to be landed in south-east England, Ireland and the Clyde. Friends and courtiers were astonished at the youthful enthusiasm of the elderly monarch, who suddenly seemed rejuvenated. In his excitement the years had evidently fallen away from him; his tents and equipage were ordered to be ready at an hour's notice, in case he was needed to lead his men to another victory, another Oudenarde or Dettingen, only this time on English territory. Had it come to pass, and had he died in the moment of victory like Wolfe, he would have surely desired no other fate.

Equally carried away by the fervour of war and victory, the Prince of Wales wrote to his grandfather offering his services. Begging leave to lay himself at His Majesty's feet, he wrote: 'While the country remained in tranquillity I thought my time best employed in acquiring a thorough knowledge of all matters peculiarly suited to my situation; but now that every part of the Nation is arming for its defence, I cannot bear the thoughts of continuing in this inactive state.' More than anything else, he wanted 'an opportunity of convincing the world that I am neither unworthy of my high situation nor of the blood that fills my veins.'[9]

The King understood him to be asking indirectly for a post such as command of the home forces. Remembering a similar application by the young Prince's father in 1745, he did not take it seriously, seeing it as an ill-judged attempt to embarrass the Ministry. Lady Yarmouth thought it masked the Prince's fear of Cumberland regaining supreme command. While the King expressed the 'highest satisfaction of his grandson's spirit and zeal', he tactfully let it be known that 'on the proper occasion' he would give the young man a chance to prove himself. Always ready to maintain his influence over the heir at the King's expense, Bute tried to convince the former and his mother that it was part of a sinister move to put Cumberland on the throne as his father's successor. It all helped to foster the sad picture of a fatherless boy victimized and conspired against by his cruel grandfather. According to Lady Yarmouth, if the French landed, it was

the King's intention to place himself at the head of the army, taking the Prince of Wales with him, as he had taken Cumberland to Dettingen.

The naval menace was shortly to be dealt with. During the summer Admiral Boscawen and his squadron were blockading the French ships in their home ports, but at one stage had to return to Gibraltar, the nearest naval base, for refitting and supplies. The French fleet took their opportunity to get through the Straits by night, but within hours Boscawen pursued them into Portuguese waters and routed them in a swift battle at Lagos Bay. In November Lord Hawke inflicted a similar crushing defeat on the Brest fleet at Quiberon Bay. Six days later the guns roared out their triumphant salvo in Hyde Park and the Tower of London, and a service of thanksgiving was held at St Paul's. The danger of French invasion was over, and with it the Prince of Wales's last chance of exercising such untapped reserves of military talent as he might have possessed.

The future King was not the only person to disturb the ageing monarch's equilibrium by making a nuisance of himself. Lord Temple, a particular *bête noire* of the King who had had the effrontery during the Byng controversy to compare the hapless Admiral's conduct at Minorca with that of His Majesty at the battle of Dettingen, resigned from his post of Lord Privy Seal in November 1759. It was the culmination of a year of complaints that 'His Majesty continued to slight and ill-use him before all the world', and in compensation he demanded 'some public token of esteem to wipe out that reproach'. Nothing less than the Order of the Garter would do. This was an honour very much in the King's personal gift, and one which could only be held by a specific number of people. Newcastle pointed out tactfully that there were only two vacancies, and these were certain to be filled by personages who had a prior claim. Temple asked Pitt, who had recently become his brother-in-law, to intercede for him. Reluctantly Pitt approached Lady Yarmouth with a threat to resign if the King refused to yield to what virtually amounted to blackmail.

His Majesty lost his temper and asked why they had been tormenting Lady Yarmouth about it. He thought Pitt was bluffing and did not believe he would resign, saying that he 'will not oppose his own measures'. If Temple was rewarded for his insolence with the Garter, the King insisted, 'the world shall see how I am used'. Pitt firmly denied any intention of forcing the King by threats of resignation. Yet Newcastle did not give up, the King still declaring he would not be bullied. If Temple was not honoured, Pitt said, he would boycott the Court and make no secret of his disapprobation. At length the King conceded defeat: 'If I am confined and bound, I will do it.'

In the meantime a few vacancies had occurred in the Order, and in February 1760 Temple received the Garter, bestowed with the worst possible grace. Instead of placing the ribbon decorously over the new Knight's shoulder the King averted his head, muttering crossly to himself, threw it

across the room at him, and promptly rumped him. However Temple was more than satisfied, and proudly wore the ribbon on every possible occasion.

He was also magnanimous in his admittedly petty victory. The close of His Majesty's reign, he wrote to Pitt, was strikingly distinguished by lustre of every sort; 'may he feel it as he ought.' His Lordship evidently sensed that King George II's reserves of vitality were running out. He was becoming blind; the sight of one eye had gone completely, and a cataract was forming on the other, while deafness allowed him to hear scarcely a word that officials and foreign ambassadors uttered. These handicaps notwithstanding, his health was good for a man in his mid-seventies, in an age when life expectancy was considerably less. For relaxation he could still enjoy a game of hazard in the evenings, or drone away to his mistresses and courtiers, not too bothered if he could not hear their replies. Like many an elderly widow or widower he was lonely, and any company was better than none at all.

He knew that his days were numbered. One day he asked the Duchess of Hamilton what she most wanted to see. Rather tactlessly she answered, 'A coronation.' In that case, he said, she would not have long to wait. After all, nobody was immortal. The Duke of Cumberland was old before his time. Only thirty-nine, he had never fully recovered from the wound to his leg at Dettingen, and at between eighteen and twenty stone he was grossly overweight. In August he suffered the first of a series of paralytic strokes, and some wondered whether he would predecease his father.

On 5 October an issue of the *Extraordinary Gazette* announced that Montreal had fallen to General Amherst and his army. The North American campaign had begun on a sombre note that year, when a severe winter prevented Amherst from sending reinforcements to General Murray, commanding a small garrison at Quebec. By the spring the 7,000-strong force was badly stricken with scurvy and frostbite, and the fitter were suffering from cold and lack of suitable clothing. In April the French army appeared within sight of Quebec, and eight days later a pitched battle was fought at St Foy, resulting in British defeat and over a thousand casualties. However British reinforcements soon arrived and the French had to withdraw to Montreal, the last French stronghold in Canada. A carefully planned attack by three different British armies converged on the French forces at Montreal early in September, demanding complete surrender not only of the town but of the whole province of Canada, and the sending of the French regulars back to France.

Four months earlier, the news reaching Britain from North America had been gloomy. The situation was now transformed, and the war in Canada was over. People came out of their houses in London, cheering and calling out 'God bless the good news!' Full of patriotic fervour, a crowd marched cheerfully to Kensington Palace, shouting for their King. The aged

monarch, who could hardly see or hear the crowds still welcomed the glad tidings and the unrestrained joy of his subjects. Time after time he happily acknowledged the salutes. It was an appropriate note on which to end the reign, for it was probably the last occasion on which he was seen in public. Within three weeks he would have gone to eternal rest.

In 1727 King George II had received the news of his accession in circumstances which lacked the full measure of regal dignity. Some thirty-three years later his reign closed in an even less dignified manner, though it was mercifully sudden.

On 25 October 1760 at Kensington Palace he rose at his normal hour of 6 a.m. to call for his customary morning cup of chocolate. He asked his German *valet de chambre* about the weather and direction of the wind, and when told that both were fair, he said he would take his regular walk in the palace gardens. While dressing he retired to the lavatory. The valet was suddenly roused by a loud noise and a groan; he found his master on the floor, having cut his face on the corner of a bureau in falling. He was laid on his bed and blooded, but not a drop flowed: 'the ventricle of his heart had burst.' Lady Yarmouth was woken by the commotion, and on being told that the King was dying, she ordered the valet to fetch Princess Amelia and the court physicians. The Princess, 'very purblind and more than a little deaf', did not seem to understand. When she bent over her father's face, she insisted, he spoke to her. The others gently took her aside and explained what had happened.

He had died three weeks short of his seventy-seventh birthday. No previous monarch of England had attained the age of seventy.

The Prince of Wales had been aware for some time that his grandfather would not live for much longer, and the news came as no surprise. He was riding at Kew when the message came from Kensington Palace. If he felt any emotion at the King's death he kept his feelings well hidden as he turned back to Kew House, pretending that his horse had become lame and pledging the rest of the company to silence. From Kew he set out for London, meeting Pitt en route, coming to give His Majesty official confirmation of the news. The long reign of King George III was just beginning.

As several historians and biographers have observed, few men came to the throne at a moment of greater exaltation than George III. It was little wonder that in his first speech from the Throne he told the assembled Lords and Commons that he 'gloried in the name of Briton' or, as some sources would insist, 'Britain'.

King George II's miserly habits had long since been legendary, and he was said to have been the most frugal King since Henry VII.[10] Yet it was

discovered at his death that he had left only £36,000. £6,000 went to Lady Yarmouth, supplemented by a further grant of £2,000 from the new King's pocket, while the remaining £30,000 was divided equally between the King's three surviving children, the Duke of Cumberland and Princesses Amelia and Mary.*[11] The Duke magnanimously handed over to his sisters his share of the bequest. Horace Walpole noted that the Duke had indeed been forgiven for his transgressions; the King 'owns that [Cumberland] was the best son that ever lived, and had never offended him; a pretty strong comment on the affair of Klosterzeven!'[12]

The funeral took place on 11 November in Henry VII's Chapel at Westminster Abbey. It was a striking scene, with the coffin under a canopy of purple velvet illuminated by silver lamps, and six vast chandeliers of silver on high stands. Mourners and guests walked in procession through a line of foot guards, every seventh man carrying a torch, horse guards lining the outside, their officers with drawn sabres and crepe sashes on horseback, to the beat of muffled drums and the sound of fifes, bells tolling, and minute-guns.

It was an imposing and dignified scene until they entered the Chapel, at which point 'all solemnity and decorum ceased; no order was observed, people sat or stood where they could or would'. In the midst of this disorganization, the Yeomen of the Guard complaining because the coffin was too heavy for them, and the Bishop blundering in the prayers, the Duke of Cumberland was the most dignified and pitiful figure of all. His face was bloated and distorted from the effects of the stroke, one eye was giving him trouble, and with his weak leg he found standing for two hours painful, yet 'he bore it all with a firm and unaffected countenance'.[13]

The same could not be said for the First Lord of the Treasury, the Duke of Newcastle. The moment he came into the chapel he began sobbing, and retired to a stall while the Archbishop hovered over him with a smelling bottle. It evidently took effect almost at once, for within a couple of minutes he was on his feet again, running about the chapel with his eyeglass in one hand to see who was there, mopping his eyes with the other. When the Duke of Cumberland tried to move he felt himself weighed down. Newcastle, as afraid as ever of catching cold from standing on the cold floor, was warming his feet on the long train of His Royal Highness's black cloak.

The press of the day did not shrink from reporting that His Majesty had expired on the lavatory, a fact discreetly omitted from accounts of his life published in the more decorous nineteenth century. Little was paid in the

*The *Dictionary of National Biography* states that according to one unsubstantiated account the King left £50,000, according to another £35,000; but all are agreed that apart from a legacy of between £8,000-£10,000 to Lady Yarmouth, the rest was divided equally between his children.

way of tributes, apart from the *Gentleman's Magazine* publishing in its issue of November 1762, with questionable taste, a coloured diagram of the King's dissected heart.[14]

Those who had known him were more generous, even when allowing for the fact that civility generally prevents one from speaking ill of the recently departed. Horace Walpole, neither royalist nor sycophant, called his passing 'an enviable death', especially as it came 'in the greatest period of the glory of this country and of his reign, in perfect tranquillity at home, at seventy-seven [sic], growing blind and deaf, to die without a pang, before any reverse of fortune, or any distasted peace, nay, but two days before a ship-load of bad news: could he have chosen another such moment?'[15]

Newcastle lamented at losing the best King, the best Master 'and the best Friend that ever subject had'. Hardwicke was even more generous, writing that he had died at the height of his glory, 'loved, honoured and respected by all Europe'.[16] His subjects found him an honest King, who according to Lord Charlemont, was renowned for his straightforwardness: 'he might offend, but he never deceived.' Five years earlier John Wesley had seen the King in the robing-chamber at the House of Lords, and commented with derision on an insignificant-looking little man being dressed up in a 'blanket of ermine' and a 'huge heap of borrowed hair'. 'Is this all the world can give, even to a King?' he muttered. Now, he asked sadly, 'When will England have a better prince?'

Was King George II a good man and a good sovereign? His main personal faults were meanness, vanity and an explosive temper, by no means uncommon faults of monarchs. Spendthrift princes without personal pride and with placid temperaments do not necessarily – and in fact very rarely – make successful Kings. As a husband he was selfish, in an age where any wife (even a Queen Consort) who did not submit meekly and gracefully to her husband's every wish was derided as a heretic, and his infidelities were mild by the standards of the day. As a father he could be cruel and unforgiving, but no more than most other monarchs of the house of Hanover, and certainly less cruel than his own father had been towards him and his mother. His most obvious fault as King of England was his devotion to Hanover, although, as he was born and spent his first thirty years in the electorate, such devotion is perfectly understandable, even excusable.

As Lord Waldegrave had observed with perspicacity in 1758, the King had been born, bred and schooled in the benevolent despotism of Hanover, and as there was something alien to him in 'the violence of party, the injustice of popular clamour, the corruption of parliaments, and the selfish motives of pretended patriots, it is not surprising that he would have contracted some prejudices in favour of those governments where the royal authority is under less restraint.'[17]

On the other side of the balance sheet, in general he was shrewd rather than clever. Most eighteenth-century Kings in Europe were either obstinate or weak-willed; despite verging occasionally on obstinacy, on the whole his commonsense saved him from both. Unlike his father who was first and foremost Elector of Hanover and only grudgingly King of England as well, King George II would be remembered as the first crowned head of his nation who really understood the limitations to which a constitutional monarch was subject. He might resent them, but accepted them nonetheless, and made no effort to extend the prerogative of the crown beyond its proper limits. He was never ruled by favourites; the only women who ever influenced him were Queen Caroline and, after her death, Lady Yarmouth. Such political power or initiatives as they exercised were generally for the good. Initially reluctant to dismiss favourite ministers like Carteret or to appoint talented popular mavericks like Pitt, he could be persuaded that to do so would ultimately benefit government and country.

If his reign had been one of one failure after another, it would have boded ill for his reputation. Yet during his thirty-three years on the throne his subjects benefited from improvements in health, wealth and political stability, the Union with Scotland was consolidated, and liberty under the law and religious tolerance were established. The European predominance of over-mighty France was ended, and colonial territories of vast potential were acquired. Granted, he had the good fortune to be served by a succession of talented statesmen. To quote Reginald Lucas, 'He was neither excellent nor contemptible, but his mediocrity was redeemed by the fact that he was served by the greatest peace minister [Walpole] and the greatest war minister [Pitt] that ever lived in England.'[18] As Clive Bigham later observed, the former built up England's industry and finance, the latter her patriotism and Empire; 'A King under whose auspices such events can occur has some claim on the praise of posterity.'[19] It is only fair to grant him some of the reflected glory for their triumphs. The transition period of Kings of England from despotic gods of war to constitutional heads of state was just beginning, and he was fortunate to be the only one able to lay a claim to being both at the same time.

THE PROTESTANT SUCCESSION AND THE HOUSE OF HANOVER

JAMES I m. Anne of Denmark
(1566–1625) (1574–1619)

Elizabeth
(1596–1662)
m.
Frederick,
Elector Palatine,
King of Bohemia
(1596–1632)

CHARLES I
(1600–49)
m.
Henrietta Maria
of France
(1609–69)

Sophie
(1630–1714)
m.
Ernest Augustus,
Elector of
Hanover
(1622–98)

CHARLES II
(1630–85)
m.
Catherine of
Braganza
(1638–1705)

Mary
(1631–60)
m.
William,
Prince of
Orange
(1626–50)

JAMES II m. (1) Anne m. (2) Mary of
(1633–1701) Hyde Modena
(1637–71) (1658–1718)

GEORGE I
(1660–1727)
m.
Sophie Dorothea
of Celle
(1666–1726)

WILLIAM III m. MARY ANNE
(1650–1702) (1662–94) (1665–1714)
m.
George of
Denmark
(1653–1708)

GEORGE II
(1683–1760)
m.
**Caroline of
Ansbach**
(1683–1737)

James Francis Edward
('The Old Pretender')
(1688–1766)
m.
Clemetine Sobieski
(1702–35)

Frederick,
Prince of Wales
(1707–51)
m.
Augusta of
Saxe-Gotha
(1719–72)

Charles Edward
('The Young Pretender')
(1720–88)
m.
Louise of Stolberg
(1752–1824)

GEORGE III
(1738–1820)
m.
Charlotte of
Mecklenburg-Strelitz
(1744–1818)

Characters of no importance to the lines of descent
have been omitted from both these tables

THE HOUSE OF HANOVER

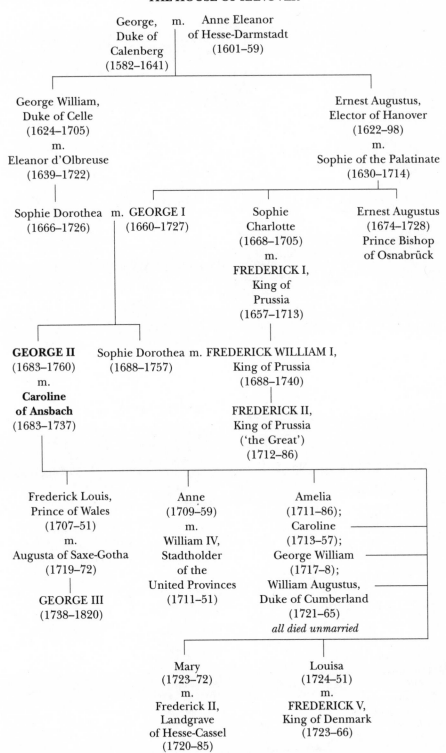

George, m. Anne Eleanor
Duke of of Hesse-Darmstadt
Calenberg (1601–59)
(1582–1641)

George William, Ernest Augustus,
Duke of Celle Elector of Hanover
(1624–1705) (1622–98)
m. m.
Eleanor d'Olbreuse Sophie of the Palatinate
(1639–1722) (1630–1714)

Sophie Dorothea m. GEORGE I Sophie Ernest Augustus
(1666–1726) (1660–1727) Charlotte (1674–1728)
 (1668–1705) Prince Bishop
 m. of Osnabrück
 FREDERICK I,
 King of
 Prussia
 (1657–1713)

GEORGE II Sophie Dorothea m. FREDERICK WILLIAM I,
(1683–1760) (1688–1757) King of Prussia
m. (1688–1740)
Caroline
of Ansbach FREDERICK II,
(1683–1737) King of Prussia
 ('the Great')
 (1712–86)

Frederick Louis, Anne Amelia
Prince of Wales (1709–59) (1711–86);
(1707–51) m. Caroline
m. William IV, (1713–57);
Augusta of Saxe-Gotha Stadtholder George William
(1719–72) of the (1717–8);
 United Provinces William Augustus,
GEORGE III (1711–51) Duke of Cumberland
(1738–1820) (1721–65)
 all died unmarried

Mary Louisa
(1723–72) (1724–51)
m. m.
Frederick II, FREDERICK V,
Landgrave King of Denmark
of Hesse-Cassel (1723–66)
(1720–85)

219

Notes

CHAPTER ONE (pp. 3–10)

1 Hatton 63
2 Jordan 236
3 Lucas 10
4 Davies 6
5 Bigham 425

CHAPTER TWO (pp. 11–17)

1 Arkell 7
2 Wilkins I 30 (all Wilkins references herewith are to *Caroline the Illustrious*)
3 ibid I 34
4 ibid I 38
5 Arkell 19
6 Wilkins I 44
7 ibid I 49
8 ibid I 56
9 Arkell 23

CHAPTER THREE (pp. 18–26)

1 Wilkins I 88–9
2 Arkell 24
3 Wilkins I 92
4 Arkell 43
5 Churchill II 413
6 Arkell 46

CHAPTER FOUR (pp. 27–32)

1 Wilkins I 103–4
2 Young 19
3 Arkell 54
4 Wilkins I 115–16
5 Green 310
6 Hatton 108
7 Green 310
8 Davies 32

CHAPTER FIVE (pp. 35–43)

1 Hatton 109–10
2 Wilkins I 138
3 Montagu I 126
4 ibid I 133

CHAPTER SIX (pp. 44–52)

1 Cowper 99–100
2 Wilkins I 151
3 Melville II 6
4 Colley 199
5 Cowper 102
6 Wilkins I 168

CHAPTER SEVEN (pp. 53–61)

1 Hatton 197
2 Young 21–2
3 Plumb, *Walpole: making of a statesman* 228–9
4 Cowper 117
5 ibid 126–7

CHAPTER EIGHT (pp. 62–75)

1 Lucas 4
2 Wilkins I 280
3 ibid I 284
4 ibid I 313–14
5 ibid I 290–1
6 Cowper 132
7 Wilkins I 337
8 ibid II 6
9 Cowper 135
10 ibid 137
11 Arkell 122
12 Cowper 152

CHAPTER NINE (pp. 76–88)

1 Chevenix Trench 124
2 Gwynn 226
3 Montagu I 103
4 Cowper 38
5 Wilkins II 86

CHAPTER TEN (pp. 91–99)

1 Wilkins II 20
2 ibid II 15
3 ibid II 17

CHAPTER ELEVEN (pp. 100–108)

1 *Dictionary of National Biography* XXI 170
2 Victoria II 44
3 Wilkins II 44
4 Montagu I 133–4
5 Wilkins II 61–2
6 Hervey II 212–3
7 Wilkins II 222
8 Egmont II 34
9 Williams 46

CHAPTER TWELVE (pp. 109–120)

1 Arkell 158
2 Lucas 38
3 Egmont I 208
4 Millar 105
5 Wilkins II 131

CHAPTER THIRTEEN (pp. 121–128)

1 Thackeray 50
2 Gaunt 39–40
3 Young 58
4 Flower 176
5 Hervey I 281
6 Baker-Smith 24
7 Lucas 118

CHAPTER FOURTEEN (pp. 129–136)

1 Hervey, *Some materials . . .* 275
2 Wilkins II 94

3 Baker-Smith 36
4 Arkell 212
5 Baker-Smith 59

CHAPTER FIFTEEN (pp. 137–145)

1 Chevenix Trench 173
2 Hervey II 206
3 ibid II 201–2
4 Wilkins II 286
5 Hervey II 217
6 Wilkins II 292

CHAPTER SIXTEEN (pp. 146–154)

1 Wilkins II 296
2 ibid II 311
3 Chevenix Trench 182
4 Arkell 262
5 Hervey *Some materials . . .* 626
6 ibid 628–9

CHAPTER SEVENTEEN (pp. 155–167)

1 Davies 157
2 Hervey, *Some materials . . .* 813
3 ibid 843–4
4 Wilkins II 351
5 ibid II 355
6 Ewald 318
7 Baker-Smith 73
8 Wilkins II 368
9 Arkell vii
10 Wilkins I x
11 Davies 169
12 Sedgwick 355

CHAPTER EIGHTEEN (pp. 171–183)

1 Davies 205
2 ibid 205
3 Pemberton 209
4 Davies 200 quoting
Gentleman's Magazine
5 Egmont II 276
6 Tunstall 67
7 Davies 225

Chapter Nineteen (pp. 184–193)

1 Maclean 224
2 Baker-Smith 100
3 Davies 261
4 Edwards 155
5 Ayling 31
6 Young 219
7 Brooke 26

Chapter Twenty (pp. 194–202)

1 Chevenix Trench 249
2 Ayling 35
3 Brooke 33
4 Baker-Smith 81
5 ibid 136
6 Walpole *Memoirs* I 227–8
7 Baker-Smith 137–8
8 ibid 142–3
9 Brooke 49

Chapter Twenty-One (pp. 203–216)

1 Tunstall 179
2 ibid 178
3 Chevenix Trench 282
4 Charteris *William Augustus . . . seven years war* 312–3
5 Baker-Smith 98
6 Walpole *Memoirs* III 83
7 Walpole *Letters* III 121
8 Brown 201–2
9 Brooke 67
10 Lucas 28
11 Davies 356
12 Lucas 43
13 Walpole *Letters* III 361–2
14 Colley 229
15 Walpole *Letters* III 354
16 Yorke III 156
17 Waldegrave 5
18 Lucas 95
19 Bigham 435

Bibliography

BIOGRAPHY, MEMOIRS AND LETTERS

Andrup, Otto, *Bonds of kinship between the royal houses of Great Britain and Denmark.* Gylendalske Boghandel Nordisk Forlag, 1948

Arkell, R.L., *Caroline of Ansbach, George the Second's Queen.* Oxford University Press, 1939

Ayling, Stanley, *George the Third.* Collins, 1972

Baker-Smith, Veronica P.M., *A life of Anne of Hanover, Princess Royal.* E.J. Brill/Leiden University Press, 1995

Bigham, Clive, *The Kings of England 1066–1901.* John Murray, 1929

Brooke, John, *King George III.* Constable, 1972

Brown, Peter Douglas, *William Pitt, Earl of Chatham: the Great Commoner.* Allen & Unwin, 1978

Charteris, Evan, *William Augustus, Duke of Cumberland, his early life and times (1721–1748).* Edward Arnold, 1913

— *William Augustus, Duke of Cumberland, and the seven years war.* Hutchinson, 1925

Chevenix Trench, Charles, *George II.* Allen Lane, 1973

Churchill, Winston, *Marlborough, his life and times,* 2 vols. Harrap, 1947

Cowper, Mary, Countess, *The diary of Mary, Countess Cowper, 1714–20.* John Murray, 1864

Curtis, Gila, *The life and times of Queen Anne.* Weidenfeld & Nicolson, 1972

Davies, J.D. Griffith, *A King in Toils* [George II]. Lindsay Drummond, 1938

Dictionary of National Biography

Edwards, Averyl, *Frederick Louis, Prince of Wales, 1707–1751.* Staples, 1947

Egmont, Earl of, *Manuscripts of the Earl of Egmont,* 3 vols. Historical Manuscripts Commission, 1920

Ewald, Alex Charles, *Sir Robert Walpole: a political biography.* Chapman & Hall, 1878

Green, David, *Queen Anne.* Collins, 1970

Gwynn, Stephen, *Life and friendships of Dean Swift.* Butterworth, 1933

Hatton, Ragnhild, *George I, Elector and King.* Thames & Hudson, 1978

Hervey, John, Lord, *Memoirs of the reign of George the Second: from his accession to the death of Queen Caroline,* 3 vols. Bickers, 1884

— *Some materials towards memoirs of the reign of George II* (ed. Romney Sedgwick), 3 vols. Eyre & Spottiswoode, 1931

Hill, B.W., *Sir Robert Walpole.* Hamish Hamilton, 1989

Jordan, Ruth, *Sophie Dorothea.* Constable, 1971

Kroll, Maria (ed.), *Letters from Liselotte, Elizabeth Charlotte, Princess Palatine and Duchess of Orléans, 'Madame', 1652–1722.* Victor Gollancz, 1970

— *Sophie, Electress of Hanover: a personal portrait.* Victor Gollancz, 1973

Kybett, Susan Maclean, *Bonnie Prince Charlie: a biography.* Unwin Hyman, 1988

Lucas, Reginald, *George II and his ministers.* Arthur L. Humphreys, 1910

Maclean, Fitzroy, *Bonnie Prince Charlie.* Weidenfeld & Nicolson, 1988

Marlow, Joyce, *The life and times of George I.* Weidenfeld & Nicolson, 1973

Marples, Morris, *Poor Fred and the Butcher: sons of George II.* Michael Joseph, 1970

Melville, Lewis, *The first George, in Hanover and England,* 2 vols. Pitman, 1908

Montagu, Lady Mary Wortley, *The letters and works of Lady Mary Wortley Montagu;* ed. Lord Wharncliffe, 2 vols. Swan Sonnenschein, 1893

Pemberton, W. Baring, *Carteret: the brilliant failure of the eighteenth century.* Longmans, Green, 1936

Plumb, J.H., *The first four Georges.* Batsford, 1956

— *Sir Robert Walpole: the making of a statesman.* Cresset, 1956

— *Sir Robert Walpole: the King's Minister.* Cresset, 1960

Quennell, Peter, *Caroline of England.* Collins, 1939

Redman, Alvin, *The house of Hanover.* Alvin Redman, 1960

Sedgwick, Romney (ed.), *Lord Hervey's memoirs.* William Kimber, 1952

Sinclair-Stevenson, Christopher, *Blood royal: the illustrious house of Hanover.* Jonathan Cape, 1979

Stuart, Dorothy Margaret, *Molly Lepel, Lady Hervey.* Harrap, 1936

Thackeray, W.M., *The Four Georges* and *The English Humourists.* Sutton, 1995 [first published 1855 and 1852]

Victoria, Queen, *The girlhood of Queen Victoria: a selection from Her Majesty's diaries between the years 1832 and 1840*; ed. Viscount Esher, 2 vols. John Murray, 1912

Vulliamy, C.E., *Royal George: a study of George III.* Jonathan Cape, 1937

Wakeford, Geoffrey, *The Princesses Royal.* Robert Hale, 1973

Waldegrave, Lord, *Lord Waldegrave's memoirs from 1754 to 1758.* London, 1821

Wallace, Ann, & Taylor, Gabrielle, *Royal mothers.* Guild, 1986

Walpole, Horace, *Memoirs of the reign of King George the Second*, 3 vols. Colburn, 1847

— *The letters of Horace Walpole, Earl of Orford*; ed. Peter Cunningham, 9 vols. Bickers, 1877

Walters, John, *The royal griffin: Frederick, Prince of Wales, 1707–51.* Jarrolds, 1972

Whitworth, Rex, *William Augustus, Duke of Cumberland: a life.* Leo Cooper, 1992

Wilkins, W.H., *Caroline the Illustrious: Queen-Consort of George II and sometime Queen-Regent: a study of her life and times*, 2 vols. Longmans Green, 1901

— *The love of an uncrowned Queen: Sophie Dorothea, Consort of George I*, 2 vols. Hutchinson, 1900

— *A Queen of tears: Caroline Matilda, Queen of Denmark and Norway and Princess of Great Britain and Ireland*, 2 vols. Longmans Green, 1904

Yorke, P.C., *The life and correspondence of Philip Yorke, Lord Chancellor Hardwicke*, 2 vols. Cambridge University Press, 1913

Young, Sir George, *Poor Fred, the people's prince.* Oxford University Press, 1937

GENERAL HISTORY AND THE ARTS

Black, Jeremy, *Culloden and the '45.* Alan Sutton, 1990

Burford, E.J., *Royal St James's: being a story of kings, clubmen and courtesans.* Robert Hale, 1988

Colley, Linda, *Britons: forging the nation 1707–1837.* Yale University Press, 1992

Flower, Newman, *George Frideric Handel, his personality and his times.* Cassell, 1959

Gaunt, William, *The world of William Hogarth.* Jonathan Cape, 1978

Haynes, John, *Kensington Palace.* Historic Royal Palaces Agency, 1995

Hedley, Olwen, *Hampton Court Palace.* Pitkin, 1971

Marshall, Dorothy, *Eighteenth century England.* Longman, 1974

Millar, Oliver, *The Queen's pictures.* Weidenfeld & Nicolson/BBC, 1977

Plumb, J.H., *The growth of political stability in England 1675–1725.* Macmillan, 1967

Plumb, J.H., & Wheldon, Huw, *Royal heritage: the story of Britain's royal builders and collectors.* BBC, 1977

Roberts, Jane, *Royal artists: from Mary Queen of Scots to the present day.* Grafton, 1987

Seymour, William, *Battles in Britain and their political background, 1066–1746.* Sidgwick & Jackson, 1979

Turberville, A.S.., *English men and manners in the eighteenth century: an illustrated narrative*, 2nd ed. Clarendon, 1929

Williams, E.N., *Life in Georgian England.* Batsford, 1962

Index

Kings, Queens. Princes and Princesses are of Great Britain (England, pre-union) unless stated otherwise. Abbreviations: C – Queen Caroline; F – Frederick, Prince of Wales; G I – King George I; G II – King George II; W – William, Duke of Cumberland

Abercromby, General James (1706–81) 208, 209
Addison, Joseph (1672–1719) 45
Alberoni, Guilio, Cardinal (1664–1752) 71
Albert of Saxe-Coburg Gotha, later Prince Consort (1819–61) 194
Aldworth, Colonel 38
Alfred the Great, King (c. 849–99) 124
Amelia, Princess ('Emily') (1711–86) 38, 78, 82, 83, 97, 98, 161, 166, 187, 191, 208, 214; birth 24; engagement to Frederick of Prussia discussed 86, 118n; love of hunting 107; character 129–30, 196–7; at Anne's wedding 133; and Mrs Howard's departure 137; and C's last illness and death 162–3; and G II's death 213
Amherst, Jeffrey, Baron Amherst (1717–97) 208, 209, 212
Amigomi, Jacopo (1682–1752) 114
Anne, Queen (1665–1714) 4, 9, 10, 21, 23, 24, 41, 45, 50, 53, 55, 94, 97, 101, 102, 119; last months and death 27–32, 36
Anne, Princess Royal and Princess of Orange (1709–59) 38, 61, 73, 82, 97, 126, 164, 182, 187, 188, 196; birth 24; character and arrogance 78, 84, 196; betrothal to Louis XV, discussed 84; musical and intellectual interests 84, 129; and Anne Brett 96–7; F's letter to 109; and Handel 128; betrothal and marriage 130–6; C's letters to 134, 136, 150; and Mrs Howard's departure 137; widowed 197; death 209
Anson, George, Lord (1697–1762) 188
Arbuthnot, Dr 82
Argyll, Colonel John Campbell, 2nd Duke of (1678–1743) 56, 69, 82, 148
Arkell, R.L. 165
Arne, Thomas (1710–78) 173
Ashburnham, Lord 178
Atterbury, Francis, Bishop of Rochester (1662–1732) 35
Augusta, Princess of Saxe-Gotha, later Princess of Wales (1719–72) 139, 147, 180, 199; wedding 144–5; first pregnancy and birth of Augusta 155–7; and F's punishment, 158–9; and F's death 190–1; Regency issue and distrust of W 195–6
Augusta of Wales, Princess (1737–1813) 156–8

Augustus II, King of Poland and Elector of Saxony (1670–1733) 108
Augustus III, King of Poland and Elector of Saxony (1696–1763) 182
Augustus Frederick, Duke of Sussex (1773–1843) 195

Bacon, Francis (1561–1626) 124
Balmerino, Arthur Elphinstone, 6th Baron (1688–1746) 187
Bar, Count Christian (1684–1765) 86
Bathurst, Henry, 2nd Earl (1714–94) 106
Bedford, John, 4th Duke of (1710–71) 199
Bedford, Gertrude, Duchess of (d. 1794) 207
Bellenden, Mary 52, 81
Bentinck, William, later 3rd Duke of Portland (1738–1809) 198
Berkeley, George (c. 1693–1746) 138
Berkeley, Admiral James, 3rd Earl of (1680–1736) 63, 95
Bernstorff, Andreas Gottlieb, Baron von (1649–1726) 42, 50, 75
Betterton, Thomas (c. 1635–1710) 50
Bielefeld, Baron von 79
Bigham, Clive 216
Bolingbroke, Henry St John, Viscount (1678–1751) 30, 35, 53, 115–16, 122, 137
Borgman, Baron 164
Boscawen, Admiral Sir Edward (1711–61) 211
Bothmer, Hans von (1656–1732) 27, 29, 32, 35, 36, 42, 50, 56–7
Boyle, Henry 124
Braddock, General Edward (1695–1755) 201
Brandshagen, Miss 26
Brett, Anne 87, 96–7
Bridgeman, Charles (d. 1738) 101–2, 164
Bristol, Elizabeth, Countess of (1677–1741) 111, 112
Buckenburgh, Joanne Sophie, Countess of (1673–1743) 50, 60, 64, 67
Buononcini, Giovanni Battista (1672–1750) 125, 144
Burke, Edmund (1729–97) 205
Burnet, Bishop 51
Bury, Lord 186

Bute, John Stuart, 3rd Earl of (1713–92) 191, 199, 202, 210

Byng, Admiral John (1704–57) 203–4, 211

Cadogan, William, 1st Earl (1675–1720) 56

CAROLINE, Queen, formerly Princess Caroline of Ansbach (1683–1737) as Princess – birth 11; early life 12–14; betrothal and marriage 15–17; inability to manage G I 18; and birth of F 19; and G II's English titles 21; stricken with smallpox 21–2; pride in G II 23; and children's health and upbringing 24, 82–5; and Mrs Howard 25, 90; cultural and intellectual interests and friendships 26, 45–6, 49, 82; letters to and from Leibniz 27–8, 31; and plans to send G II to England 31; journey to and arrival in England 36, 38, 41; wants F in England 39; at G I's Coronation and birthday celebrations 42; praises the English 44; and court life 45; relations with G I, and distrust of his entourage 47, 50, 62; religious views and churchgoing 49–50; patronage of theatre 50; and maids of honour 51; intercedes on behalf of Jacobite rebels 54; at Hampton Court 57–9; and stillborn prince 60; and birth and christening of George William 62–3; and G II's quarrel with Newcastle 64; separated from children 65–7, 72, 75; at Leicester House 65; at Richmond 68–9; and Walpole 70, 79, 81; and G II's reconcilliation with G I 71–2, 74; and birth of younger children 78; household 78–9; gardening 80; and 'wild boy' 82; and plan to nominate W as G II's successor 86; and mother-in-law's death 87; as Queen – becomes Queen 91; and Walpole 92–4, 112–13; and G I's will 96; Coronation 97–9; court routine 100–1; at Kensington Palace 101–2; at Richmond 102, 123; 'manages' G II 102–3; Lady Mary Wortley Montagu on 104; and Mrs Howard 107, 137; churchgoing, languages, and hunting 107; health 108, 136; relations with F 109–12; and Lord Hervey 112, 115; and G II's visit to Hanover, and Regency (1729) 116, 118–29; literary, artistic and musical tastes and patronage 122–5; and F's allowance 126; Regency (1732) and prison reform 118–20; and Excise Bill 127; and Amelia's flirtations 129; and Anne's betrothal and marriage 131, 133; and Hogarth 133–4; and Anne's departure and return 134–6; and war of Polish succession 138; Regency (1735) 138–9; and Walmoden 141; King complains at her spending 143; and wedding of F and Augusta 144; Regency (1736) 146–9; and anxiety at G II's sea crossing 150–2; and Augusta's first pregnancy and confinement 155–7; and F's punishment 158–9; final illness and death 159–63; funeral, 164; assessment 165; also mentioned 171, 175, 177, 216

Caroline, Princess (1713–59) 38, 78, 81, 83, 97, 98; birth 24; character and interests 130; at Anne's wedding 133; hatred of F 151, 154, 157; and C's

last illness and death 160–3, 165; last years and death 196, 208

Caroline Matilda, Princess, later Queen of Denmark (1751–75) 191

Carteret, Lord John, 1st Earl Granville (1690–1763) 127, 157, 159, 175–81, 189

Charbonnier, Martin (d. 1720) 3

Charlemont, James Caulfield, 1st Earl of (1728–99) 215

Charles I, King (1600–49) 4, 10, 102, 114, 130, 142

Charles II, King (1630–85) 4, 10, 35, 41, 46, 59, 102, 142

Charles II, King of Spain (1665–1700) 22

Charles XII, King of Sweden (1682–1718) 71

Charles VI, Holy Roman Emperor, formerly Archduke of Austria (1685–1740), 13, 15, 22, 117, 138, 174

Charles VII, Holy Roman Emperor, Elector Charles Albert of Bavaria (1697–1745) 174

Charles Emmanuel I, King of Sardinia (1701–73) 185

Charlotte Amelia of Denmark, Princess 139

Chesterfield, Philip Dormer Stanhope, 4th Earl of (1694–1773) 45, 69, 96, 125, 131, 177, 180, 187, 195

Chesterfield, Duchess of, *see* Schulenburg, Petronella

Chetwynd, John, Lord 48

Christian VII, King of Denmark (1749–1808) 191

Chudleigh, Colonel 38

Clarendon, Henry Hyde, 4th Earl of 45

Clarke, Dr Samuel 46

Clayton, Charlotte, *see* Sundon, Viscountess

Compton, Sir Spencer, Earl of Wilmington (1673–1743) 69, 79, 91–5

Congreve, William (1670–1729) 44

Cooper, Samuel (1609–72) 123

Cope, Sir John (d. 1760) 184

Cotton, Sir Robert (1570–1631) 200

Cowper, Lady Mary, Countess of (1685–1723) 41, 44, 45, 50, 56, 57, 70, 72–5

Cromwell, Oliver (1599–1658) 4, 35; and Richard (1626–1712) 4

Crowe, Dr 165

Defoe, Daniel (1660–1731) 82

Delaware, Lord 139, 144

Deloraine, Lady 50, 154, 161, 166

Derwentwater, James, 3rd Earl of (1689–1715) 54

Devonshire, William Cavendish, 2nd Duke of (1672–1730) 79

Devonshire, William Cavendish, 4th Duke of (1720–64) 200

Dickens, Charles (1812–70) 64

Dodington, George Bubb, Lord Melcombe (1691–1762) 115, 189, 190, 192, 196, 199

Dolci, Carlo (1616–86) 123

Dorchester, Catherine Sedley, Countess of (1657–1717) 41

Dorset, Lionel, 10th Earl of (1688–1765) 35

Duck, Stephen (1705–56) 122

Edward I, King (1239–1307) 195
Edward, Duke of York (1739–67) 198
Egmont, John, 2nd Earl of (1711–72) 108, 191
Eleanor of Saxe-Eisenach, Princess, later Margravine of Ansbach (d. 1696) 11
Eleanor d'Olbreuse, Duchess of Celle (1639–1722) 4, 8, 24
Elitz, Madame d' 147
Elizabeth I, Queen (1533–1603) 27–8, 104, 195
Elizabeth, Electress Palatine, 'Winter Queen' of Bohemia (1596–1662) 7, 65
Elizabeth of Brunswick and Bevern, Princess (1715–97) 118n
Elizabeth Charlotte, Duchess of Orléans ('Liselotte') (1652–1722) 17, 29, 67
Eltz, Philip Adam, Baron von (1665–1728) 15–16
Ernest Augustus, Elector of Hanover (1629–98) 5, 8
Ernest Augustus, Prince-Bishop of Osnabrück, Duke of York and Albany (1674–1728) 38, 56, 62, 85, 88, 96, 97, 117
Eugene, Prince of Savoy (1663–1736) 22, 29

Flower, Newman 125n
Fox, Henry, 1st Lord Holland (1705–74) 195, 206
Fox, Stephen 112
Francis of Lorraine, Duke of Tuscany (1708–65) 174, 182, 183
Frederick III, Elector of Brandenburg, later Frederick I, King in Prussia (1657–1713) 12–14, 16, 19
Frederick II, King of Prussia ('the Great') (1712–86) 86, 118n, 129, 174, 176, 183, 196n, 201, 203–5
Frederick V, King of Denmark (1723–66) 180, 197
Frederick of Hesse-Cassel, Prince (1720–85) 197, 198
Frederick Louis, Prince of Wales (1707–51) 58, 70, 78, 83, 95, 118, 133,, 184, 187; birth 19–20; childhood 24, 38–9; relations with G I 85; plans for early marriage 85–6, 109; and G I's will 96; mourning for G I 109–10; arrival in England 110; relations with G II and C 110–13, 147; artistic interests 111, 113–14; created Prince of Wales 112; sporting interests 113; and Lord Hervey 114–15; and Bolingbroke 115–16; and Buononcini 125; finance and allowances 125–6; disliked by sisters 130; wants to join Hanoverian forces 138; wedding 144; and Gin Act 147; popularity 149; during G II's sea crossing 151–2; and Augusta's first pregnancy and confinement 155–7; punished by G II 158–9; and C's last illness 161; and birth of George 171–2; and war with Spain 173; reconciliation with G II 176; and 1747 election 188; political initiatives 189; fatal illness, death and funeral 190–2; reputation and assessment 192–3
Frederick William I, King of Prussia (1688–1740) 9, 12, 16, 19, 63, 78, 86, 117–18, 174

Gay, John (1685–1732) 45, 121
Gemmingen, Baroness von 68

George I, King (1660–1727) 12, 24, 45, 61, 78, 91, 94, 101, 103, 109, 158, 186; early life, marriage and divorce 5–7; relations with G II 8, 46–7, 62, 80; and G II's betrothal and marriage 15–16; and son's titles 20–21; sends Bothmer to England 27; and proposal to send G II to England 29–30; accession 32, 35; arrival in England 36–7; creates G II Prince of Wales 38; Coronation and Lord Mayor's Day (1714) 41–2; and G II's resemblance to 46; relations with C 47; and government 48; language problems 48–50; churchgoing 52; and 1715 Jacobite rebellion 53–4; visits to Hanover (1716) 54–6, (1719) 71, (1720) 76–7; and G II's quarrel with Newcastle 63–4; separates G II and C from children 65–6; controls G II's household and income 66; proposes to separate crowns of England and Hanover 70; reconciliation with G II 71–5; and 'wild boy' 82; relations with F 85; and idea of Anglo-Prussian engagement 86; and death of Sophie Dorothea 86–7; last return to Hanover and death 88; papers and will examined by G II 95
GEORGE II, King (1683–1760) as Prince – birth 5; childhood 7–9; early problems with G I 8; betrothal and marriage 14–17; restless for battlefield 18–19; and English titles 20–21; stricken with smallpox 21–2; and war of Spanish succession 22–3; and birth of Anne 24; and Mrs Howard 25–6, 51; possibility of being sent to England 29–30; arrival in England, and Lady Mary Wortley Montagu on 36–7; created Prince of Wales 38; reception with C and children 39; at Lord Mayor's Day (1714) 42; and lack of privacy 43; praises the English 44; and court life 45; character and increasing resemblance to G I 46, 79, 82; at cabinet meetings 47–8, 55; speaking English and churchgoing 49; theatre patronage 50; distrust of G II's entourage 50; G I's jealousy of 54, 61; made Guardian of the Realm 55–7, 60; at Hampton Court 58–9; and stillborn son 60; increasing differences with G I 62; and birth of George William 62; and quarrel with Newcastle 63–4; separated from children 65–6; at Leicester House 65; household and income controlled by G I 66; at Richmond 68–9; and G I's proposal to separate crowns of England and Hanover 70; and reconciliation with G I 71–5; and Welsh Copper Company 77; household 78; political influence 79; improving relations with G I 79–80; parsimony 80; and mother's death 87; as King – accession and Walpole's retention of office 91–5; and father's will 95–6; Coronation and Lord Mayor's Show 97–9; Court routine 100–1; at Windsor 101; at Kensington Palace 101; character and military interests 102–6; and Mrs Howard 105–7, 137; churchgoing, languages, and hunting 107; Egmont on 108; relations with F 109–13, 116; and plans for F's marriage 110, 112, 118; and Lord Hervey 115–16; creates F Prince of Wales 112; at Hanover (1729) 116–17; and disputes

with Frederick William of Prussia 117–18; despises learning 121; and painters 124; and Handel 125; parsimony 126, 144; at Hanover (1732) 126; and Excise Bill 127; criticized by Anne 129; and Anne's betrothal and marriage 130–4; anger with Anne 136; and war of Polish succession 138; and F's marriage 139; at Hanover (1735) 139–40; and Walmoden 140; return from Hanover 141–2; finds fault with everything English 142; Walpole on 'political cowardice' of 144; at F's wedding 145; at Hanover (1736) 146–9; almost lost at sea 150–2; ill-health 152–3, 208–9; and F's demand for new allowance 153–4; and Augusta's first pregnancy and confinement 155–7; punishes F 157–9; and C's illness, death and funeral 160–5; grief for C 165–6; and birth of George (later G III) 171–2; and war in Europe 172–4, 176–7, 181, 188–9; and army 173; and Walpole's resignation 175; and Carteret 175, 180–1; and reconciliation with F 176; angered by parliamentary attacks 177; at battle of Dettingen 178–9 and Pelham's ministry 181; at Convention of Hanover 183; and 1745–6 rebellion 184–6; and F's death 189–91; and calumny against W 194; and George Prince of Wales 195; and family deaths of 1751 197–8; in Hanover (1753) 198; more respected in old age 199; and artistic and cultural achievements of reign 200; and death of Pelham 200; and war in North America 201, 208; and Pitt 203, 205, 207; and Byng 204; and Klosterzeven and W's disgrace 205–7; on Wolfe 209; and George, Prince of Wales' offer of service 210; and Temple 211–12; death 213; funeral 214; assessment 215–16

George, Prince of Wales, later King George III (1738–1820) 194, 199; birth 171–2; and F's death 191; created Prince of Wales 195; wife proposed for 201–2; offers to fight 210–11; and G II's death 213

George IV, King (1762–1830) 158

George, Prince of Denmark (1653–1708) 9

George Frederick, Margrave of Ansbach 11

George William, Duke of Celle (1624–1705) 4, 14, 17, 42, 96

George William, Prince (1717–18) 62, 67, 78

Grafton, Charles Fitzroy, 2nd Duke of (1683–1757) 107, 129, 196

Grantham, Lord 65, 143

Guelfi, Giovanni Batista 133

Gyllenborg, Karl, Count (1679–1746) 61

Halifax, Charles Montagu, 1st Earl of (1661–1715) 45

Halley, Edmond (1656–1742) 46

Hamilton, Lady Archibald 139, 156

Hamilton, Sir David (1663–1721) 32, 59

Hamilton, Duchess of 212

Handel, George Frideric (1685–1759) 25, 40, 50, 85, 98–9, 125, 133, 135, 144, 159, 164, 179

Harcourt, Simon, 1st Viscount (1661–1727) 29

Hardwicke, Philip Yorke, Earl of (1690–1764) 181, 205, 215

Harley, Robert, 1st Earl of Oxford (1661–1724) 29–30, 76, 200

Harrington, William Stanhope, 1st Earl of (1690–1756) 115, 140, 146, 157

Hatton, Ragnhild 7

Hawke, Sir Edward, 1st Baron (1705–81) 211

Hawley, General Henry 186

Henrietta Maria, Queen (1609–69) 142

Henry VII, King (1457–1509) 213

Henry VIII, King (1491–1547) 123

Hervey, John, Lord (1699–1743) 81, 104, 111, 112, 114–15, 117, 126, 129–31, 133–4, 140–3, 147, 150–1, 156, 158–9, 161, 163, 196

Hervey, Molly, see Lepel

Highmore, Joseph, 124

Hobart, Sir Henry 25

Hogarth, William (1697–1764), 124, 133–4, 200

Holbein, Hans (1497–1543) 123

Holderness, Robert d'Arcy, 4th Earl of (1718–78) 198, 200

Hollar, Wenceslaus (1607–77) 123

Howard, Henrietta, later Countess of Suffolk (c. 1681–1767) 24–6, 36, 49–50, 60, 64, 69, 81, 83, 105–6, 137

Howard, Henry, later Earl of Suffolk (d. 1733) 24, 81, 106, 137

Howe, Emanuel Scrope (d. 1709) 19, 20

Howe, George, 3rd Viscount Howe, (c. 1725–58) 208

Howe, Sophia 51

Hume, Sir Gustavus 65

Humphries, John 68

Hyde, Anne (1637–71) 185

Irwin, Lady 111

James I, King (1566–1625) 7, 9, 10

James II, King, formerly Duke of York (1633–1701) 4, 7, 9, 20, 28, 41, 102, 185, 199

Jenkins, Robert 172

Jervas, Charles (c. 1675–1739) 125

John, Frederick, Margave of Ansbach (d. 1686) 11

John, George IV, Elector of Saxony (d. 1694) 11

Kendal, Duchess of, see Schulenberg, Countess of

Kenmure, William, 6th Viscount (d, 1715) 54

Kent, William (c. 1684–1748) 101–2, 123–5, 133–4, 160

Ker, Lord Mark 184

Kielmansegge, Johann von (1668–1717) 43

Kielmansegge, Sophie Charlotte (1675–1725) 6, 43, 50, 69, 82, 97

Kilmarnock, William Boyd, 4th Earl of (1704–46) 187

Knapton, George 114

Kneller, Sir Godfrey (1646–1723) 124

Königsegg, Marshal 182

Königsmarck, Count Philip von (1665–94) 6–7, 116

Launay, Colonel de 110

Leibniz, Gottfried Wilhelm von (1646–1716) 13–15, 19, 25, 27, 29, 30, 31
Leopold, Holy Roman Emperor (1640–1705) 5
Lepel, Molly, later Lady Hervey (1700–86) 81, 112
Locke, John 124
Lotti, Antonio 125
Louis XIV, King of France (1638–1715) 3, 10, 22, 53, 189
Louis XV, King of France (1710–74) 53, 84, 178, 181, 185
Luoisa, Princess, later Queen of Denmark (1724–51) 121, 136, 180; birth 78; marriage and death 197–8
Lovat, Simon Fraser, Lord (c. 1667–1746) 187
Lucas, Reginald 216

Macaulay, Thomas Babington, 1st Baron (1800–59) 64
Macclesfield, Countess of 87
MacDonald, Flora (1722–90) 187
Maitland, Dr Charles 83
Maria Theresa, Empress (1717–80) 174–6, 182–3, 185, 188
Marlborough, John Churchill, 1st Duke of (1650–1722) 22–3, 27, 32, 36, 47, 56, 127, 138, 178
Marlborough, Sarah, Duchess of (1660–1744) 56, 83, 121, 132, 153
Mary II, Queen (1660–94) 9, 41, 45, 83, 123
Mary, Princess, later Landgravine of Hesse-Cassel (1723–72) 197, 198, 214; birth 78
Maximilian of Brunswick-Lüneberg, Prince (1666–1726) 20
Mehemet 43
Melbourne, William Lamb, Viscount (1779–1848) 102
Mercier, Philippe (1689–1760) 113
Milton, John (1608–74) 113, 122
Montagu, Lord Edward Wortley 83
Montagu, Lady Mary Wortley (1689–1762) 37, 42, 83, 104
Munchausen, Gerlach, Baron von 207
Mustapha 43

Newcastle, Thomas Pelham-Holles, 1st Duke of (1693–1768) 95, 108, 119, 129, 173, 180, 181, 186, 188, 190, 195, 196, 200–1, 203, 205, 211, 214; and quarrel of 1717 63–4, 66
Newton, Sir Isaac (1642–1727) 46, 124
Northumberland, George, Duke of 46

O'Brian, Daniel 185
Oliver, Peter 123
Orkney, Earl and Countess 119
Ormonde, James, 2nd Duke of (1665–1745) 68
Osterwyck, Maria van 123

Pan, Barthélemy du 123
Pelham, Henry (1696–1754) 181, 188, 189, 192, 195, 200
Peter the Great, Tsar of Russia (1672–1725) 63
Peterborough, Lord 69

Philip V, King of Spain (1683–1746) 22, 185
Philips, Charles 114
Pitt, William, 1st Earl of Chatham (1708–78) 177, 179–80, 189, 192, 195, 203–5, 207–9, 211–13, 216
Platen, Clara Elizabeth von (1648–1700) 5, 43
Platen, Francis Ernest, Count von (1631–1709) 15
Pomfret, Lady 130
Pope, Alexander (1688–1764) 45, 69, 122–3, 137
Porteous, John (d. 1736) 148–9
Portland, Jane Martha, Countess of (1672–1751) 66–7, 81, 83
Portland, William Bentwick, 2nd Duke of (d. 1762) 198
Portsmouth, Duchess of 59
Potter, Dr John 98, 162–4
Pulteney, William, 1st Earl of Bath (1684–1764) 73, 112, 137, 157, 159, 175

Queensberry, Charles Dougles, 3rd Duke of (1698–1778), and Catherine, Duchess of (c. 1700–77) 121–2

Ranby, Dr John (1703–73) 161–2, 179
Reynolds, Sir Joshua (1723–92) 193
Richard III, King (1452–85) 190, 195
Richmond, Charles Lennox, 1st Duke of (1672–1723) 59
Robethon, Jean de (c. 1660–1722) 42, 50, 57
Robinson, Sir Thomas, later Lord Grantham (1695–1770) 176
Röohlitz, Magdalen Sybil von (d. 1694) 11
Roucy, Lady Charlotte de 83
Rupert of the Rhine, Prince (1619–82) 51
Rysbrack, John Michael (1693–1770) 123

St Albans, Duchess of 51
Savage, Richard 122
Saxe, Marshal Maurice (Comte de) (1696–1750) 182
Scarborough, Richard, 1st Earl of (d. 1721) 59
Scarborough, Richard, 2nd Earl of of (d. 1739) 103, 127
Schulenberg, Ermengarde Melusina von der, later Duchess of Munster, then Duchess of Kendal (1667–1743) 6, 72, 82, 96
Schulenberg, Petronella Melusina von der, later Countess of Walsingham, then Countess of Chesterfield (1693–1778) 7, 43, 50, 97
Schütz, Salentin von 29–30, 112–13
Schütz, Mlle 50
Selwyn, Mrs 141
Shakespeare, William (1564–1616) 99
Shepherd, James 71
Sheridan, Sir Thomas 185
Shippen, William ('Honest') (1673–1743) 94, 165
Skerrett, Maria, later Lady Walpole (1702–38) 166
Sloane, Sir Hans (1660–1753) 200
Somerset, Charles Seymour, 6th Duke of (1662–1749) 190
Somerset, Sir Edward Seymour 8th Duke of (c. 1695–1757) 192
Sophie, Electress of Hanover (1630–1714) 7–9, 13–14, 18–22, 24–7, 29–30, 49, 51, 96, 97, 160;

and G II's betrothal and marriage 15–16; collapse and death 31–2

Sophie Caroline of Brunswick-Wolfenbüttel, Princess 201

Sophie Charlotte, Princess, later Queen of Prussia (1668–1705) 12–14, 105

Sophie Dorothea, Princess of Celle, later Countess of Ahlden (1666–1726) 4–8, 17; death 86

Sophie Dorothea, later Queen of Prussia (1687–1757) 5, 19, 74, 86, 110, 116–17

Stair, Field-Marshal Sir John, 2nd Earl of (1673–1747) 178

Stanhope, Charles (1673–1760) 95

Stanhope, James, 1st Earl (1672–1721) 56–7, 60, 63, 76

Strafford, Thomas Wentworth, Earl of (1672–1739) 92

Stuart, Prince Charles Edward ('The Young Pretender') (1720–88) 184–5, 187, 196

Stuart, Prince James Edward ('The [Old] Pretender') (1688–1766) 7, 23, 27, 28, 35, 53–4, 71; proclaimed James III by Bishop of Rochester 35

Suffolk, Countess of, *see* Howard, Henrietta

Sunderland, Charles, 3rd Earl of (1674–1722) 56, 76

Sundon, Viscountess, formerly Charlotte Clayton 67, 160

Swift, Jonathan (1667–1745) 82, 122–3

Temple, Richard, Earl (1711–79) 211–12

Thomas, John, Bishop of Peterborough 199

Thomson, James (1700–48) 173

Thornhill, Sir James (1675–1734) 58

Thornhill, John 200

Titchburne, Mrs 156

Toland, John (*c.* 1670–1722) 4, 9

Townshend, Charles, 2nd Viscount (1674–1738) 47, 48, 55–6, 60, 61, 66, 69, 74–5, 80, 88, 91, 95, 116, 118–19

Tron, Madame 45

Van Dyck, Sir Anthony (1599–1641) 142

Vane, Anne ('Vanella') 114–15, 139, 155

Van Loo, Jean-Baptiste (1684–1745) 114

Vasari, Giorgio (1511–74) 142

Vendôme, Louis Joseph, Duc de (1654–1712) 22–3

Vernon, Admiral Edward (1684–1757) 172, 173

Vertue, George (1684–1756) 114, 123, 124

Victoria, Queen (1819–1901) 102, 165n

Vinci, Leonardo da (1452–1519) 123

Wade, Field-Marshal George 181, 185, 187

Wager, Admiral Sir Charles 155

Wake, William, Archbishop of Canterbury (1657–1737) 95, 98

Waldegrave, James, 2nd Earl of (1715–63) 195, 199, 201–2, 215

Walmoden, Amerlia Sophia, Baroness von, later Countess of Yarmouth (1704–65) 140, 143, 146–7, 149, 150, 153, 160, 166, 171, 191, 206, 210, 213, 214, 216

Walpole, Catherine, Lady (d. 1737) 93, 160

Walpole, Horace, 4th Earl of Orford (1717–97) 116, 160, 179–80, 186, 206, 208, 209, 224, 225

Walpole, Horatio, 1st Baron Walpole of Wolterton (1678–1757) 93, 113, 114, 135

Walpole, Sir Robert, later 1st Earl of Orford (1676–1745) 47, 56, 57, 59, 60, 61, 66, 69, 102, 107, 109, 111, 115, 116, 120, 122, 126, 129, 140, 141, 143, 146, 147, 149, 152, 171, 177, 180, 181, 196, 200, 216; and C 70–2, 79, 82; and reconciliation between G I and G II 72–5; appointed to high office 77–8; and G I 80; and G II's accession, and reappointed to office 91–4; and C 104–5; and F 112, 150; satirized by Gay 121; and Excise Bill 127; anxiety at C's health 136; dislike of Mrs Howard 137; and war of Polish succession 138; and F's allowance 153–4; and D's illness and death 160–2; gloom at war fever, and resignation 172–5

Watteau, Antoine (1684–1721) 113

Wentworth, Peter (d. 1739) 44–5

Wesley, John (1703–91) 215

Wilhelmina of Prussia, Princess, later Margravine of Bayreuth (1709–58) 86, 110, 118

Wilkins, W.H. 165

William III, King (1650–1702) 9, 10, 41, 42, 45, 58, 83, 102, 123, 124, 138

William IV, Prince of Orange (1711–51) 130–6, 164, 188, 197–8

William, Duke of Cumberland (1721–65) 20, 46, 83, 109, 111, 121, 134, 150, 158, 189; birth 78; gambling 108; preferred to F by parents 111, 155, 157; petted by sisters 130; at Anne's wedding 133; at mother's deathbed and funeral 162, 164; at Dettingen 178–9; at Fontenoy 182; and Culloden campaign 184–7; and Regency issue 194–6; distrusted by Princess of Wales 199; and war in North America 201; and seven years' war 204–5; in disgrace with G II 206–7; ill-health 212; at G II's funeral 214

William, Duke of Gloucester (1689–1700) 9

William Frederick, Margrave of Ansbach 11, 15, 38

William Henry, Prince, later Duke of Gloucester (1743–1805) 179–80

Wolfe, James (1727–59) 179, 209–10

Wolfenbuttel, Augustus William, Duke of 95

Wootton, John 114

Wren, Sir Christopher (1632–1723) 58

Zincke, Frederick (*c.* 1683–1767) 124